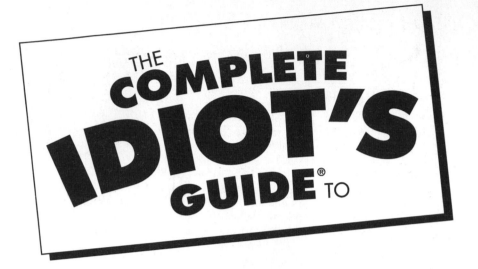

THE

COMPLETE **IDIOT'S** GUIDE® TO

Personal Financial Documents

by Ken Little

ALPHA

A member of Penguin Group (USA) Inc.

This book is dedicated to everyone who has looked at a form, document, or financial report of some kind and wondered what language it was written in.

ALPHA BOOKS

Published by the Penguin Group

Penguin Group (USA) Inc., 375 Hudson Street, New York, New York 10014, U.S.A.

Penguin Group (Canada), 10 Alcorn Avenue, Toronto, Ontario, Canada M4V 3B2 (a division of Pearson Penguin Canada Inc.)

Penguin Books Ltd, 80 Strand, London WC2R 0RL, England

Penguin Ireland, 25 St Stephen's Green, Dublin 2, Ireland (a division of Penguin Books Ltd)

Penguin Group (Australia), 250 Camberwell Road, Camberwell, Victoria 3124, Australia (a division of Pearson Australia Group Pty Ltd)

Penguin Books India Pvt Ltd, 11 Community Centre, Panchsheel Park, New Delhi—110 017, India

Penguin Group (NZ), cnr Airborne and Rosedale Roads, Albany, Auckland 1310, New Zealand (a division of Pearson New Zealand Ltd)

Penguin Books (South Africa) (Pty) Ltd, 24 Sturdee Avenue, Rosebank, Johannesburg 2196, South Africa

Penguin Books Ltd, Registered Offices: 80 Strand, London WC2R 0RL, England

Copyright © 2005 by Kenneth E. Little

International Standard Book Number: 1-59257-446-7
Library of Congress Catalog Card Number: 2005933825

08 07 06 05   8 7 6 5 4 3 2 1

Interpretation of the printing code: The rightmost number of the first series of numbers is the year of the book's printing; the rightmost number of the second series of numbers is the number of the book's printing. For example, a printing code of 05-1 shows that the first printing occurred in 2005.

Printed in the United States of America

Note: This publication contains the opinions and ideas of its author. It is intended to provide helpful and informative material on the subject matter covered. It is sold with the understanding that the author and publisher are not engaged in rendering professional services in the book. If the reader requires personal assistance or advice, a competent professional should be consulted.

The author and publisher specifically disclaim any responsibility for any liability, loss, or risk, personal or otherwise, which is incurred as a consequence, directly or indirectly, of the use and application of any of the contents of this book.

Most Alpha books are available at special quantity discounts for bulk purchases for sales promotions, premiums, fund-raising, or educational use. Special books, or book excerpts, can also be created to fit specific needs.

For details, write: Special Markets, Alpha Books, 375 Hudson Street, New York, NY 10014.

Publisher: *Marie Butler-Knight*
Editorial Director: *Mike Sanders*
Senior Managing Editor: *Jennifer Bowles*
Senior Acquisitions Editor: *Paul Dinas*
Development Editor: *Ginny Bess Munroe*
Production Editor: *Janette Lynn*
Copy Editor: *Keith Cline*
Cartoonist: *Jody Schaeffer*
Cover/Book Designer: *Bill Thomas*
Indexer: *Julie Bess*
Layout: *Rebecca Harmon*
Proofreading: *Donna Martin*

Contents at a Glance

Contents

Appendixes

Foreword

How many times have you been approached to buy insurance for yourself or a loved one, but you have never really understood the advantages of the different types available?

When you get your credit card statements or adjustable loan bills, do you find yourself confused about the interest or late fees charged? And what about the taxable income information on those end-of-the-year tax statements from your stock and bond investments? What does it all mean anyway?

Well, Ken Little can help. Ken's book, *The Complete Idiot's Guide to Personal Financial Documents*, has successfully accomplished a nearly impossible goal: explaining in layman's terms the most common financial documents we encounter every day of our lives. As an accountant and tax advisor to many individuals and corporations, I am excited to finally find a book that clearly answers the most frequent questions about money and finances that I hear from all my clients, whether they are sophisticated corporate clients who have been in business for years or my new younger clients who have just joined the work force.

Most people are hesitant to make decisions when money is involved. In part, it is because so much of the information they receive takes the form of statements that are often complicated and difficult to understand. This book takes the mystery out of reading most financial documents. From bank statements to mortgage agreements, from car loans and leases to tax forms and monthly bills and more, Ken Little clearly and concisely explains each one. And even if you decide to seek professional financial advice, this book will give you a basic foundation of financial knowledge so that you understand your advisor's suggestions and gain confidence to make the right decisions about your finances.

Written in easy-to-understand terms, with samples of each document annotated and explained, *The Complete Idiot's Guide to Personal Financial Documents* is a must-read handbook to taking charge of your finances.

—Gerald A. Muroff, EA

Gerald Muroff currently has an accounting and tax practice in the metropolitan New York area. He has been in both the private and public sectors of accounting for the past 35 years and has represented clients before the Internal Revenue Service. He is also a director of Paying Agent Services at the Geller Group Ltd., an actuarial company headquartered in New York City.

Introduction

Managing your financial life is very much like running a business—you can't just focus on one part, you have to see the whole picture. This means understanding and managing the financial documents that are part of everyday life.

Financial documents come from many different sources—some that you probably wouldn't immediately consider "financial." However, if you think about it, anything that involves your money is worthy of your time to understand.

When you take the time to understand a financial document, you gain more control over your life because you can make better decisions about the products and services you use. When you stick it in a drawer because it doesn't make any sense, the document has control over you.

This book is about helping you understand the financial documents that you have to face every day. Sample documents with keys to important points help you figure out just what you need to know. Armed with that knowledge, you'll be a smarter consumer.

The *Complete Idiot's Guide to Personal Financial Documents* has six sections. Each section groups like documents for easier reference.

Part 1, "You Are a Business," looks at the monthly bills that keep your household afloat. You may want to race through these bills and be done with them, but you could be overlooking some important points—not the least of which is that you may be spending much more for some of your monthly services than needed.

From bank accounts to credit cards, all of your money flows through this section in one way or another. This part covers the "basics," but don't drop your guard, there's money to be saved and lost without a thorough understanding of these documents.

Part 2, "On Borrowed Time," covers the interesting (pun intended) topic of debt. It's almost impossible to get through modern life without going into some level of debt. Using debt effectively can be a smart financial move—but let it get out of hand and you are in real trouble.

If you don't understand the financial documents associated with your loan, how are you going to know if you got a good deal and how are you going to know if mistakes are made? When your home is on the line, you don't want to be in the dark. Even if your home is not at risk, your credit rating is. This section will guide you through home and home equity loans, as well as auto loans and leasing, along with student loans and consumer debt. Borrower beware!

Part 3, "Got You Covered," looks at insurance documents top to bottom from auto to health to life to long-term care and disability. Is there anything more annoying than paying insurance premiums for years and never filing a claim? Yes, having a claim and no insurance.

The language of insurance is all its own, and that is especially true for health-care insurance. This section looks at the financial documents from insurance companies that can overwhelm you and helps you understand what they are trying to tell you.

Part 4, "Taking It Easy," looks at those retirement plans that are going to support us in our golden years. Given the crisis looming in Social Security, everyone should be saving extra for retirement. Yet, many people with access to a company-sponsored retirement plan don't participate because they don't understand it.

This section looks at a variety of retirement plans and helps you understand the documents and reports that are part and parcel of that industry. You'll also get a look at Social Security and some tips on figuring out what you can expect based on the agency's personalized report.

Part 5, "Market Mogul," helps you with the flood of documents that follows the investment business. Thanks to regulators who want to make sure they protect your rights, you have tons of information on your investments, but may not know how to digest it.

This section covers the major investment documents from statements to annual reports. You'll get insight into what is really important and what is window dressing.

Part 6, "Taxes, My Taxes," looks at some of the common tax forms and how they can affect your taxes. It focuses on forms and documents rather than on actually filing your taxes at the federal, state, and local levels. Taxes take a big chunk out of your paycheck—don't let that happen without knowing all you can.

Document Aids

There are four types of sidebars in this book. They are little extras to point out special information or send up a red flag for a danger.

Paper Clips

Little known tips and hints. These give you additional information and tips on understanding and managing financial documents.

Form Alarm

Cautions. Yes, you should read the fine print, but not all of the sneaky language is buried there. This sidebar points out particular concerns or areas that you may overlook or misunderstand.

Fill In the Blank

Answers and information. These point you to additional sources of information or help in understanding financial documents or forms.

Financial Speak

Glossary terms. These highlight key words to help you translate the sometimes-baffling jargon of the financial world.

Acknowledgments

Thanks to Paul Dinas, senior acquisitions editor with Alpha Books, for the opportunity to work on this challenging project. Paul's attention to this book made it a reality, and I thank him for that. This is not the first time I have worked with Paul, and I'll count myself lucky if it's not the last.

A big part of what makes this book work are the graphics that guide the reader through the sample forms and documents. The challenge to make sense of my samples fell to Bill Thomas. His efforts are literally clear to see. Our goal for this book was to help people understand the financial documents in their lives. We couldn't have come close without the top-notch contributions of the design department.

As always, I thank my family for putting up with my mental absence while writing this book. My wife, Cyndy, in particular shouldered most of my share of the household chores during a period when she was hard-pressed for time as she began serving a church as their new pastor. Special thanks to my writing buddy Andy, whose 85 pounds of unconditional need for attention never failed to break my concentration with his wagging tail thumping against the back of my chair.

Trademarks

All terms mentioned in this book that are known to be or are suspected of being trademarks or service marks have been appropriately capitalized. Alpha Books and Penguin Group (USA) Inc. cannot attest to the accuracy of this information. Use of a term in this book should not be regarded as affecting the validity of any trademark or service mark.

Part 1

You Are a Business

Your financial life is no different from running a business. There are countless details to attend to when what you really want to do is enjoy the fruits of your labor. This part of the book examines those financial documents that fill up your mailbox every month. Bills, statements, and forms require your attention, and this part will help you cut through the clutter to find the important points to verify and understand.

Devil in the Details

In This Chapter

- Financial documents touch all parts of our lives
- What you don't know can hurt you
- Discovering hidden bombs
- Taming the paper tiger
- The online alternative

Does it seem like there is no end to the pieces of paper that require your attention?

Paying bills, reviewing insurance forms, and checking those seemingly endless financial documents we have to handle is about as much fun as clipping your toenails. However, bungle either job and you'll be hurting. This chapter focuses on the importance of staying on top of your increasingly complicated financial world.

Financial Documents—They're Everywhere!

Financial documents turn up everywhere in your life, maybe in places you haven't considered. You may picture financial documents as only dealing with heavy numbers and accounting-looking columns. However, the truth is that anything in our lives that involves spending or receiving money is financial and generates financial documents. Just like a business, we can categorize our lives by income, expenses, assets, and liabilities.

Ignorance Is Not Bliss

You open your mailbox and there it is ... the letter from your bank. You know the kind. It's not a statement and it's too thin to be another marketing brochure; besides, it's one of those window envelopes where your name and address printed on the letter inside shows through.

Form Alarm

Banks charge heavy fees if you bounce a check. You also will likely face a fee from the company to which you sent a bad check. You can get overdraft protection through your bank, but you don't need it if you are in control of the financial documents in your life.

This is not good news. The terse letter informs you that your account did not have sufficient funds to cover two checks you wrote last week and the bank did not honor them. You also owe the bank a bad check fee of $35 for each. How could this happen, you wonder? You were sure you deposited your paycheck before these checks could have hit the bank.

If you automatically assume you are wrong and the bank is right, you may be in for a shock—banks (and many others) make mistakes.

Don't Ask, Don't Complain

Our society places a great value on wisdom, as long as it fits on a bumper sticker. Years ago, a popular bumper sticker read: "Question Authority."

That's good advice when it comes to dealing with the financial documents in your life. Don't automatically assume they are right and you are wrong. In addition, don't assume you can't get a wrong corrected. In almost every case, the law is on your side if you can prove your case. If you understand the financial documents in your life, it will be much easier to spot errors and have the data to back up your claim if needed.

Most vendors are happy to correct mistakes, especially when you have the facts to back up your claim. However, even if you just have concerns about items on a bill or document, don't hesitate to ask questions.

If you don't get the answers to your questions because you didn't ask, you don't have any right to complain if you find out later that you have been overpaying. Most vendors are honest and correct mistakes brought to their attention. However, you have a responsibility to review your bills, statements, and other financial documents for completeness and accuracy.

Little Type, Big Bombs

Yes, you really do need to read the fine print. The major points of agreements should be in regular-size type, but don't be surprised to find some bombs buried in the footnotes.

Because I am writing this on a computer, it brings to mind a classic example of the consequences of not reading agreements. If you have installed new software on a computer before or downloaded some program from the Internet, you know that at some point you come to a "User Agreement."

It might be called something else, but it is usually several screens of legalese type. At the end, the program gives you the choice to accept or decline the agreement. Of course, if you decline, the software does not install. Most people skip right over the text and click the Accept button as fast as they can to get on with the installation. What you might not know is that some "agreements" give companies the right to install additional software on your computer, unrelated to what you bought (software that directs certain Internet ads to your browser every time you want to surf the Web). This is not true of all software agreements, and reputable companies will disclose their intentions.

Making Sense Makes Cents

Does it really matter whether you save a few dollars here or there? Is it worth the trouble to go over bills, statements, and other financial documents?

Let's take one example. Many bank accounts offer different checking accounts based on your average account balance and the number of transactions you post each month. Suppose you keep an eye on your checking usage and notice you can switch to a different type of account and save a $15 fee every month. What is that worth?

You can't buy much for $15—three fancy coffees, maybe, or one movie ticket and a small soda. What if you invest that money instead in a mutual fund that earns 8% and keep investing that $15 you save each month for 20 years? At the end of that period, you would have $8,800 (ignoring taxes and fees), which would buy you a pretty nice vacation.

That's not bad for just knowing what's going on with one financial document in your life. Imagine the possibilities if you could do the same with a couple of the other financial obligations in your life.

Beyond Bean Counting

Few of us, unless we are accountants by choice, enjoy poring over statements, numbers, and balancing accounts. So how do we keep up with the financial documents in our lives and still have any time for a life?

Two things come to mind. First, you need to know how to read the documents so you can process them efficiently. That's where this book can help. In this book, we go over the major financial documents you are likely to process on a regular basis and the keys to deciphering the important information.

Second, you need a system. Whether it's a shoebox or a computer-based program or something in between, you must find a system that works for you. Your system will let you process the financial documents in a timely and efficient manner.

Getting Control of the Paper

Sometimes it's the sheer volume of paper that overwhelms you when you are trying to organize your finances. Bills, reports, statements, forms—it never seems to end.

Some people find it easier to collect everything and process it on one day each week. Other folks want to deal with it the day it arrives in the mail. Unfortunately, too many people are inclined to put aside anything that isn't an obvious bill and look at it whenever, if ever.

Consider the bank account example again. The person who can't be bothered with anything that doesn't require a check is throwing away good money each month by not paying attention. Even if he doesn't invest the savings, he is cheating himself out of a couple of good cups of coffee.

Form Alarm

Look for items marked with an asterisk (*) when reviewing financial documents. A footnote will explain the marked item; pay attention to the explanation. It often qualifies an offer or guarantee or in some way limits your rights.

Paper Clips

Here's a tip for handling financial documents: Set up a special place—whether it's an inbox or one of those stiff, multi-pocketed folders or just a plastic container—for all the financial documents that arrive in the mail so that you don't mix them up with other mail.

For people into computers, several software packages can help you keep track of your personal finances and some of the financial documents in your life. They don't cover everything, because the primary focus is on checking, credit, and investing accounts.

Paper Clips

Check out your favorite office supply store for a variety of filing systems to see whether one makes sense for you. It doesn't matter what system you use as long as you use it.

Microsoft Money and Intuit Quicken are the two leading personal-finance software packages. Both serve as electronic checkbooks and much more. They help you record your income and expenses, and include bill-paying capabilities. Both are relatively inexpensive and easy to learn. You can start with the basic checkbook function and work into the more sophisticated parts such as budgeting, bill paying, and tracking investments.

You can transfer information from these programs into tax-preparation software when that time comes. Other people find simple files work just fine. In the end, whatever you will use consistently is the best system for you.

Turning to the Internet

One of the ways more people are finding they can gain some control over the paper in their lives is to get rid of the paper and transfer functions to online (Internet-based) services. Internet, or Net, banks offer all or most of the services of traditional banks without the physical locations. One of the advantages is the bank goes wherever you go—no more looking for a new bank each time you move.

Traditional banks have responded with many online services of their own, including checking and access to cash through nationwide ATMs (automatic teller machines). Online bill-paying services put an end to check writing for many of your monthly bills. Automatic debit of regular bills has been around for a long time and is still popular.

The online alternative is clearly attractive to many people—fewer checks, less paper. The transition is still incomplete, however, because many vendors still send paper bills even if you pay online.

Direct deposit of payroll checks means your money gets in the bank earlier than if you deposit a paper check. Some employers pay all employees this way. However, they still provide a payroll stub, so they don't eliminate that piece of paper. What you eliminate is a trip to the bank.

Chapter 2

Checking Out Checking

In This Chapter

- Figuring out no frills
- Reviewing a variety of transactions
- Understanding transaction descriptions
- Taking advantage of online technology

Checking accounts used to be simple before deregulation turned banks into marketing machines. This chapter looks at bank statements, from the plain vanilla accounts to the more-sophisticated money market accounts that pay interest.

Handling paper checks is expensive, and banks are eliminating steps wherever possible. One of the big innovations is the debit card or check card that customers use rather than a check. Transactions driven by bankcards figure prominently in most bank statements these days and can create havoc if not accounted for correctly.

Your Father's Checking

Back in the good old days, when Fred Flintstone opened his account, about the only choice you had was the style and color of your checks. Each month you got a fat envelope from the bank with all your canceled checks, deposit slips, your statement, and any other communications. Then, depending on your record-keeping skills, you spent from 30 minutes to 3 hours balancing your bank statement.

Times have changed, and so has the basic checking account. What hasn't changed is the need to understand and balance your monthly statement. I spend most of this chapter on the basic bank statement because all the other statements are enhancements of it. When you understand the basic statement, the more complicated account statements come easy.

Ⓐ Your balance on this date

Ⓑ Total of all deposits you made during this statement period

Ⓒ Withdrawals made by bankcard, used either as debit or credit card

Ⓓ Withdrawals by automatic debits, transfers, and fees

Ⓔ Checks that have cleared your account this statement period

Ⓕ Your balance on this date

Ⓖ Direct deposit of payroll checks

Ⓗ Telephone transfer from one of your other accounts

Ⓘ Indicates a check missing from the sequence

Account Summary

Ⓐ	Beginning Balance of 01/15/06	$5,354.59
Ⓑ	Deposits/Credits	$10,337.86
Ⓒ	Card Withdrawals	$2,041.55
Ⓓ	Other Withdrawals	$936.38
Ⓔ	Checks Paid	$6,838.11
Ⓕ	Ending Balance on 02/15/06	$5,876.41

Deposit/Credits

	Date	Description	Ref. Number	Amount
	01/20/06	Deposit	084888843	1,304.34
Ⓖ	01/23/06	Electronic Deposit- From Acme Ind. Payroll	REF=29000443343	2,342.34
	01/23/06	Electronic Deposit – From Apple Orchids PAYROLL	REF=39490403033	1,974.42
Ⓗ	01/25/06	Telephone transfer	From Account 9300038	400.00
	02/07/06	Electronic Deposit – From Acme Ind. PAYROLL	REF=29475543343	2,342.34
	02/07/06	Electronic Deposit – From Apple Orchids PAYROLL	REF=39490495033	1,974.42
		Total Deposits/Credits:		10,337.86

Checks

	Number	Date	Ref. Number	Amount
	1123	01/23/06	9948948948	65.26
	1124	01/23/06	9498938984	231.43
	1125	01/23/06	9040490904	132.34
	1126	01/25/06	9494898484	45.00
	1127	01/25/06	9848948888	1,354.87
	1128	01/25/06	9898494888	54.69
		[items skipped]		
	1145	02/12/06	9849848444	349.56
Ⓘ	1147*	02/12/06	9485774443	142.34
	1148	02/12/06	9849448844	65.00
	1149	02/12/06	9484848333	126.90
		Total Checks Paid:		6,838.11

J *Card Withdrawals*

Date	Description	Ref. Number	Amount
K 01/20/06	Purchase (Non-PIN) Gas Stop 123 Street Anytown 2354556765	REF #84080580840	19.03
L 01/20/06	Purchase With PIN Bob's Bakery 234 Road Anytown 9000800809	REF #97497497948	23.88
01/20/06	ATM Withdrawal 694 5th Anytown 9000800809	Serial No. 894895479793879	60.00
01/21/06	Purchase (Non-PIN) Greasy Garage 1453 Blvd Anytown 2346334675	REF #82453380840	245.43
01/21/06	Purchase (Non-PIN) Sue's Shoes 706 Road Anytown 2354446732	REF #84033380840	33.43
01/21/06	Purchase (Non-PIN) Bill's Drug Store 749 Nowhere Anytown 2354446760	REF #84088980840	48.09
01/23/06	Purchase (Non-PIN) Bookstore 134 Street Anytown 2355666743	REF #8423380840	76.60
01/23/06	Purchase With PIN Mary's Store 234 Road Anytown 9004353809	REF #9457497948	125.44
01/20/06	ATM Withdrawal 694 5th Anytown	Serial No. 894895479793879	60.00

J Withdrawals using bankcard

K Card used as a credit card

L Card used as a debit card

(M) Insurance bill paid by automatic debit

(N) Money transferred to another account

(O) Utility bill paid by automatic debit

(P) Mutual fund direct debit

(Q) Bank fee debited

Card Withdrawals   (continued)

Date	Description	Ref. Number	Amount
	[items skipped]		
02/14/06	Purchase (Non-PIN) Lola's Laundry 233 10th Anytown 23789346758	REF #82445680840	56.03
02/14/06	Purchase (Non-PIN) Larry's Liquor 456 Road Anytown 23547947657	REF #84348480840	42.09
02/14/06	Purchase (Non-PIN) Harry's Hardware 459 8th Anytown 23544523689	REF #84088980840	48.09
	Total Card Withdrawals:		2,041.55

Other Withdrawals

	Date	Description	Ref. Number	Amount
(M)	01/20/06	Electronic Withdrawal From Acme Insurance	REF #940905904980	124.89
(N)	01/20/06	Telephone Transfer	To Account 09094404099	500.00
(O)	01/21/06	Electronic Withdrawal From Giant Utility Co.	REF #904858049090	249.49
(P)	02/01/06	Electronic Withdrawal From Mega Mutual Fund	REF #040580480303	50.00
(Q)	02/01/06	Electronic Withdrawal From Big Bank Activity Fee	REF #508408048058	12.00
		Total Other Withdrawals:		936.38

Ⓡ *Balance Summary*

Date	Balance	Date	Balance	Date	Balance
01/15	5,346.76	01/26	3,457.76	02/06	5,590.59
01/16	5,134.56	01/27	2,467.87	02/07	4,809.90
01/17	4,590.78	01/28	5,689.43	02/08	4,393.43
01/18	4,139.09	01/29	5,439.87	02/09	4,123.67
01/19	3,576.58	01/30	4,983.98	02/10	3,894.89
01/20	3,450.23	01/31	4,503.40	02/11	3,504.04
01/21	3,684.09	02/01	4,120.40	02/12	4,393.03
01/22	3,904.54	02/02	3,894.59	02/13	4,895.83
01/23	3,293.21	02/03	3,503.02	02/14	4,984.59
01/24	3,582.12	02/04	3,984.92	02/15	5,876.41
01/25	3,489.30	02/05	4,592.60		

Ⓡ Daily balance for statement period

Statement Detail

There is no standard format for bank statements, so the example I constructed may or may not look like the one you get every month. It should contain all the same information—maybe just in a different place or in a different configuration. Your statement tracks the activity in your checking account for the month indicated. The month may or may not start on the first day of the calendar month.

Account Summary	
Ⓐ Beginning Balance of 01/15/06	$5,354.59
Ⓑ Deposits/Credits	$10,337.86
Ⓒ Card Withdrawals	$2,041.55
Ⓓ Other Withdrawals	$936.38
Ⓔ Checks Paid	$6,838.11
Ⓕ Ending Balance on 02/15/06	$5,876.41

Ⓐ Your balance on this date

Ⓑ Total of all deposits you made during this statement period

Ⓒ Withdrawals made by bankcard, used either as debit or credit card

Ⓓ Withdrawals by automatic debits, transfers, and fees

Ⓔ Checks that have cleared your account this statement period

Ⓕ Your balance on this date

The top portion of most bank statements summarizes your activity for the month and gives you the key information concerning your account.

◆ Beginning and Ending Balances

Your bank calculates the beginning and ending balances on the dates indicated by simply "freezing" your account for a moment in time to take a snapshot of its position. Which checks have cleared? What deposits are accounted for? Are there other charges or credits? The bank applies all charges and deposits to the balance as they are recorded.

Paper Clips

A bank may hold a deposit for five business days or more before crediting it to your account.

Form Alarm

Banks charge heavy fees if you bounce a check. You also will likely face a fee from the company to which you sent a bad check. You can get overdraft protection through your bank, but you don't need it if you are in control of the financial documents in your life.

At the end of your statement month, the bank determines your ending balance, which becomes the beginning balance for the next month, and the process begins again. It never hurts to make sure these two numbers are the same. Check last month's statement for the ending balance and that number should be the beginning balance for the current month. For most active accounts, there is seldom a day that some piece of business isn't processed through the account.

◆ Deposits/Credits

This item captures all of your deposits, such as payroll, transfers from other accounts, and any credits you may receive, either from the bank or through your debit/credit card. This last item might include a return of merchandise to a store that credits your card for the original purchase. Any credits to your account, whether from merchants or the bank itself, appear here.

◆ Card Withdrawals

If you use your debit card, either with or without a PIN (personal identification number), the charge will show up in this total. Typically, if you use the card as a debit card with a PIN at a terminal, the money comes out of your account almost immediately. If you use the card as a credit card—that is, you sign a slip instead of using a PIN—it may take up to two to three days before the money comes out of your account.

The third way you can use your card is to access an ATM (automatic teller machine) to obtain cash or use the other services offered. ATMs offer account services such as balance lookups, transfers, loan payments, and many other features. You can use your ATM card at many nonbank locations including other ATMs and many retail stores to get cash, but beware of high fees that go along with these transactions.

◆ Other Withdrawals

Other withdrawals can cover items such as bills that automatically debit your account every month, transfers to other accounts, or fees paid to the bank. Keep an eye on the detail of this item for extra bank charges and fees. This area is also one that identity thieves hit if they have access to your account information.

◆ Checks Paid

This item totals all the checks that have cleared your account this statement month. Make sure this number agrees with the item farther down in the report. If you write a lot of checks, you will have outstanding checks that have not cleared your account.

Deposit/Credits

Date	Description	Ref. Number	Amount
01/20/06	Deposit	084888843	1,304.34
01/23/06	Electronic Deposit- From Acme Ind. Payroll	REF=29000443343	2,342.34
01/23/06	Electronic Deposit – From Apple Orchids PAYROLL	REF=39490403033	1,974.42
01/25/06	Telephone transfer	From Account 9300038	400.00
02/07/06	Electronic Deposit – From Acme Ind. PAYROLL	REF=29475543343	2,342.34
02/07/06	Electronic Deposit – From Apple Orchids PAYROLL	REF=39490495033	1,974.42
	Total Deposits/Credits:		10,337.86

G Direct deposit of payroll checks

H Telephone transfer from one of your other accounts

Deposits/Credits

The detail on this statement reveals direct deposits from two employers (Acme Ind. and Apple Orchids). It is always a good idea to check your account on the day your payroll direct deposit was to have been made. If something is amiss, you want to know before you start writing checks on a nonexistent deposit. The system is not perfect, and it may be impossible to notify every person affected if a problem exists.

This detail also reveals a telephone transfer from another account for $400. This technology is older than dirt, but it still works just fine if you need to move some money around. Most banks offer this feature, and all you need is your account numbers and a telephone, plus a security code.

Checks

Number	Date	Ref. Number	Amount
1123	01/23/06	9948948948	65.26
1124	01/23/06	9498938984	231.43
1125	01/23/06	9040490904	132.34
1126	01/25/06	9494898484	45.00
1127	01/25/06	9848948888	1,354.87
1128	01/25/06	9898494888	54.69
	[items skipped]		
1145	02/12/06	9849848444	349.56
1147*	02/12/06	9485774443	142.34
1148	02/12/06	9849448844	65.00
1149	02/12/06	9484848333	126.94
	Total Checks Paid:		6,838.11

I Indicates a check missing from the sequence

Checks

Long gone are the days when your bank statement recorded the payee, and going fast are the days when you will get your canceled checks returned with your statement. Now the bank provides you with a reference number. If you need a canceled check to prove payment, this number will help locate it. Electronic substitute checks are now legal representations to settle disputes.

The asterisk (*) indicates a check has not cleared, is out of sequence, or may have cleared in a previous month. In a real-world checking account, there would undoubtedly be many more of these at the end of this item detail.

J Withdrawals using bankcard

K Card used as a credit card

L Card used as a debit card

Card Withdrawals

Date	Description	Ref. Number	Amount
01/20/06	Purchase (Non-PIN) Gas Stop 123 Street Anytown 2354556765	REF #84080580840	19.03
01/20/06	Purchase With PIN Bob's Bakery 234 Road Anytown 9000800809	REF #97497497948	23.88
01/20/06	ATM Withdrawal 694 5th Anytown 9000800809	Serial No. 894895479793879	60.00
01/21/06	Purchase (Non-PIN) Greasy Garage 1453 Blvd Anytown 2346334675	REF #82453380840	245.43
01/21/06	Purchase (Non-PIN) Sue's Shoes 706 Road Anytown 2354446732	REF #84033380840	33.43
01/21/06	Purchase (Non-PIN) Bill's Drug Store 749 Nowhere Anytown 2354446760	REF #84088980840	48.09
01/23/06	Purchase (Non-PIN) Bookstore 134 Street Anytown 2355666743	REF #8423380840	76.60

Card Withdrawals (continued)			
Date	**Description**	**Ref. Number**	**Amount**
01/23/06	Purchase With PIN Mary's Store 234 Road Anytown 9004353809	REF #9457497948	125.44
01/20/06	ATM Withdrawal 694 5th Anytown	Serial No. 894895479793879	60.00
	[items skipped]		
02/14/06	Purchase (Non-PIN) Lola's Laundry 233 10th Anytown 23789346758	REF #82445680840	56.03
02/14/06	Purchase (Non-PIN) Larry's Liquor 456 Road Anytown 23547947657	REF #84348480840	42.09
02/14/06	Purchase (Non-PIN) Harry's Hardware 459 8th Anytown 23544523689	REF #84088980840	48.09
	Total Card Withdrawals:		2,041.55

Card Withdrawals

You can use your debit card as either a pure debit card or a "credit card." When you use it as a debit card, you swipe it through a small terminal at a checkout or a gas pump and enter your PIN. In many cases, you can also get extra cash back with your purchase, but watch out for hefty fees associated with getting cash this way. Always check with your bank for fees associated with debit card use, as some banks may charge you a fee even if you don't get money back. If that's the case, find another bank that doesn't charge such a fee.

Other times, you can use your card like a credit card, at least that's the way banks promote them. The truth is they are still going to debit your account; no credit is extended. It may take up to two or three days, but the money will come out.

The other usage of bankcards is as an ATM card to access the machines for cash or other services. If you get cash from a machine that is not from your bank, you may be hit with a fat fee for the privilege. Banks use terms like "bankcards" and "checkcards" to describe their products, but in most cases it is still a debit card. If money is debited from your account at the time of purchase or within a few days if you sign a charge slip, you are using a debit card regardless of what the bank calls it.

CAUTION   Form Alarm

When you use your debit or bankcard as a credit card (you sign a charge slip instead of using your PIN), the money still comes out of your bank account, so it's not really a credit charge.

(M) Insurance bill paid by automatic debit

(N) Money transferred to another account

(O) Utility bill paid by automatic debit

(P) Mutual fund direct debit

(Q) Bank fee debited

The detail of these items is extensive compared to checks. You get the date and name and address of the merchant. The reference numbers will help you resolve any questionable charges.

Other Withdrawals

	Date	Description	Ref. Number	Amount
(M)	01/20/06	Electronic Withdrawal From Acme Insurance	REF #940905904980	124.89
(N)	01/20/06	Telephone Transfer	To Account 09094404099	500.00
(O)	01/21/06	Electronic Withdrawal From Giant Utility Co.	REF #904858049090	249.49
(P)	02/01/06	Electronic Withdrawal From Mega Mutual Fund	REF #040580480303	50.00
(Q)	02/01/06	Electronic Withdrawal From Big Bank Activity Fee	REF #508408048058	12.00
		Total Other Withdrawals:		936.38

Other Withdrawals

This catchall category covers everything from bills that debit your account to fees charged by the bank. In the example, I have an insurance bill and a utility bill that debit the account. The assumption is that you can count on these fixed amounts each month.

You should watch this category carefully for several reasons. If one of your creditors changes the amount of the debit or files an incorrect debit, it can play havoc with your finances. You also want to make sure no unauthorized persons or businesses are debiting your account.

The bank charged this account an activity fee of $12 for the month, and that charge shows up here. An activity fee is usually charged to accounts that do not maintain a certain balance or have too many transactions per month. Other items include a debit from a mutual fund, which is a recurring charge each month, and a transfer to another account you own.

Ⓡ *Balance Summary*

Date	Balance	Date	Balance	Date	Balance
01/15	5,346.76	01/26	3,457.76	02/06	5,590.59
01/16	5,134.56	01/27	2,467.87	02/07	4,809.90
01/17	4,590.78	01/28	5,689.43	02/08	4,393.43
01/18	4,139.09	01/29	5,439.87	02/09	4,123.67
01/19	3,576.58	01/30	4,983.98	02/10	3,894.89
01/20	3,450.23	01/31	4,503.40	02/11	3,504.04
01/21	3,684.09	02/01	4,120.40	02/12	4,393.03
01/22	3,904.54	02/02	3,894.59	02/13	4,895.83
01/23	3,293.21	02/03	3,503.02	02/14	4,984.59
01/24	3,582.12	02/04	3,984.92	02/15	5,876.41
01/25	3,489.30	02/05	4,592.60		

Ⓡ Daily balance for statement period

Balance Summary

The balance summary gives you the ending balance on the days indicated. Many banks include only days when activity occurred in the account. The value of this portion of the report is minimal. However, if you notice that your account balance is dipping perilously low about the same time each month, you may want to examine the sequence of your automatic debits. For example, you may have several automatic debits occurring just when you have paid a major share of the bills for the month.

If this is the case, ask the merchant involved whether you can have your account debited on a different day of the month. Most will be happy to accommodate you.

Online Version

Most banks offer some form of online statement for you to examine. The formats are all over the map, so I don't go over them here. The important point is that everything found on your paper statement should be available online and more. In many cases, the bank will format the information to look like your paper statement, so the headings will be the same.

The big advantage of online statements is that some banks let you look at your historical statements, which can prove handy if you want to look for a payment, but don't remember exactly when you made it. It also is more convenient than shuffling through stacks of old statements and makes it easier to compare certain expenses over time.

Not Your Father's Checking

One of the big revolutions in banking deregulation came when banks began offering interest-bearing checking accounts. This innovation opened the door to fierce competition among all types of financial institutions, but credit unions and banks in particular.

How does an interest-bearing checking account differ from the basic account described at the beginning of this chapter? The answer is: not much. The bank may require a minimum balance ($1,000 is typical), but some do not. They may want direct deposit of your paycheck, and so on.

Ⓐ Your balance on this date

Ⓑ Total of all deposits you made during this statement period

Ⓒ Interest paid on your account for statement month

Ⓓ Withdrawals made by a bankcard, used either as a debit or credit card

Ⓔ Withdrawal by automatic debits, transfers, and fees

Ⓕ Checks that have cleared your account this statement period

Ⓖ Your balance on this date

Account Summary	
Ⓐ Beginning Balance of 01/15/06	$5,354.59
Ⓑ Deposits/Credits	$10,337.86
Ⓒ Interest Paid	$5.63
Ⓓ Card Withdrawals	$2,041.55
Ⓔ Other Withdrawals	$936.38
Ⓕ Checks Paid	$6,838.11
Ⓖ Ending Balance on 02/15/06	$5,882.04
Current Interest Rate:	**1.5%**
Date	**Interest Paid**
02/15/06	$5.63

Statement Detail

The statements for interest-bearing bank accounts are almost identical to the basic account at the beginning of this chapter. Rather than repeat the whole statement, I have constructed an example of the top portion of an interest-bearing account to point out the single most important difference.

This statement has two new related data elements. The first is in the Account Summary on the third line. There you see a notation of the interest paid to the account for this statement month. Banks may use different methods to compute this amount, but a common practice is to use the average daily balance. From there, banks can pay interest daily or get an average for the statement month and figure the interest on that number.

The second new element comes after the Account Summary. This section states the current interest rate and the amount of interest paid for the statement period. If you're interested, the bank will tell you how they determine the interest rate.

Fill In the Blank

Banks are very competitive. The interest rate paid on these accounts is one factor in deciding which bank to use. You should consider fees, services, and other factors in addition to the interest paid when choosing a bank.

Online Version

The online version of this statement adds very little that you won't find in the basic statement. Some banks may offer a daily computation of interest earned, but unless you carry a huge balance, the amount reported will still be small.

Money Market Momma

Money market accounts, sometimes called money market demand accounts, are bank checking accounts that pay interest. It is important to make this distinction because they sound very much like money market mutual funds.

These bank accounts are falling out of favor, in part because of the greater benefits of mutual fund accounts. However, they are still around. They are unique bank accounts because you must maintain a high balance and rules limit you to a maximum number of transactions each month, usually no more than six. However, they do pay a higher interest rate than the standard interest-bearing checking account. They pay more than passbook savings accounts at most banks.

Account Summary

Ⓐ Beginning Balance of 01/15/06	$5,354.59	
Ⓑ Deposits/Credits	$10,337.86	
Ⓒ Interest Paid	$45.56	
Ⓓ Checks Paid	$6,838.11	
Ⓔ Ending Balance on 02/15/06	$8,899.63	
Ⓕ **Current Interest Rate:**	**2.75%**	
Ⓖ **Date**	**Interest Paid**	
02/15/06	$45.56	

Deposit/Credits

	Date	Description	Ref. Number	Amount
Ⓗ	01/20/06	Deposit	084888843	$3,337.86
Ⓘ	01/25/06	Telephone transfer	From Account 9300038	$7,000.00
	Total Deposits/Credits:			**$10,337.86**

	Check Number	Date	Ref. Number	Amount
Ⓙ	1124	01/23/06	9498938984	$4,000.00
	1125	02/13/06	9040490904	$2,838.11
		Total Checks Paid:		$6,838.11

Ⓐ Beginning balance this statement month

Ⓑ Total of all deposits

Ⓒ Interest paid to the account for this month

Ⓓ Checks paid to date

Ⓔ Ending balance

Ⓕ Current interest rate paid on this account

Ⓖ Interest paid this statement month

Ⓗ A direct deposit into the account

Ⓘ The transfer by telephone of funds from a related account

Ⓙ Checks processed this statement

Statement Detail

The money market account statement is straightforward. Because of the transaction limitations, you won't find many on the statement. If you exceed the number allowed by your account, the bank will charge you a fee. Likewise, if your balance dips below the minimum, which can range from $1,000 and up, the bank will hit you with a fee.

A Beginning balance this statement month

B Total of all deposits

C Interest paid to the account for this month

D Checks paid to date

E Ending balance

F Current interest rate paid on this account

G Interest paid this statement month

Account Summary	
A Beginning Balance of 01/15/06	$5,354.59
B Deposits/Credits	$10,337.86
C Interest Paid	$45.56
D Checks Paid	$6,838.11
E Ending Balance on 02/15/06	$8,899.63
F **Current Interest Rate:**	**2.75%**
G **Date**	**Interest Paid**
02/15/06	$45.56

Account Summary

The Account Summary and Current Interest sections give you the most important information on the statement. These sections summarize your activity in the account for the month and record the interest you earned. Some accounts may give you a cumulative interest earned figure in addition to the current month's amount.

H A direct deposit into the account

I The transfer by telephone of funds from a related account

J Checks processed this statement

Deposit/Credits			
Date	**Description**	**Ref. Number**	**Amount**
H 01/20/06	Deposit	084888843	$3,337.86
I 01/25/06	Telephone transfer	From Account 9300038	$7,000.00
Total Deposits/Credits:			**$10,337.86**
J **Check Number**	**Date**	**Ref. Number**	**Amount**
1124	01/23/06	9498938984	$4,000.00
1125	02/13/06	9040490904	$2,838.11
	Total Checks Paid:		**$6,838.11**

Checks Paid

Although you may have written only a few checks for a specific month, don't fail to check each statement. Most people use these accounts to pay large bills, such as college tuitions or mortgages or to transfer money to other accounts. The checks tend to be for large amounts, so you don't want any errors slipping past you.

Online Version

Banks that offer online services will undoubtedly let you look at your money market account online, and it will reflect the information available on the paper statement. Like other accounts, the online version may allow you to look at the history of your transactions if you need to spot a particular deposit or check.

Nothing but Net Banking

Up until this point, I've been talking about the online versions of traditional checking accounts. Banks give customers the option to access account information and may add some functionality such as bill paying. However, it's still a basic checking account presented in a slightly updated fashion.

Since the late 1990s, a new type of bank has been struggling to take hold. Some call themselves "Net" banks, whereas others prefer "virtual" banks. Whatever the name, they are banks without walls that exist on the Internet. This is not the book to talk about the benefits and drawbacks of virtual banking; however, it is appropriate to look at a generic statement. Virtual banks offer at least one service that most "brick" banks do not: account aggregation.

Account Aggregation

Account aggregation is the gathering of account information from different vendors and the presentation of it in a consolidated format. Some brick banks offer this service, too, but many of the virtual banks had it first. Because you must provide detailed and personal information, such as account numbers, PINs, and so on, security concerns have slowed the growth of these services.

Because much of what virtual banks offer is identical to regular banks, I have just presented the Account Aggregation portion of what you might see on your account.

Financial Speak

Account aggregation is an online service that permits you to view all of your financial accounts, such as banking, brokerage, credit cards, and so on, on one screen. The service requires you to provide passwords and account information for the information you want aggregated.

A The online bank's accounts

B The main online checking account

C An online money market account

D An account with a traditional bank amalgamated into this statement

E A traditional bank certificate of deposit reported by the online bank

F Brokerage account values

G Account balances from your credit cards (brought in with your permission)

Deposit Accounts

Ⓐ Virtual Bank Accounts

Account Name	Account Number	Account Type	Available Balance	Current Balance	Interest Earned
Ⓑ Main	123456	SuperNet Checking	$5,243.24	$5,790.45	$43.98
Ⓒ Money Market	898763	Money Market	$9,393.23	$8,235.34	$88.74
	Subtotal:		$14,636.47		

Brick Bank Account

Account Name	Account Number	Account Type	Current Balance
Main	123456	Plain Checking	$2,234.24
	Subtotal:		$2,234.24

(Ⓓ)

Savings

Account Name	Account Number	Account Type	Current Balance	Interest Earned	Interest Accrued
Ⓔ CD	123456	24-Month CD	$10,000	$0.00	$46.28
	Subtotal:		$10,000		

Stock Brokerage Account

Account Name	Account Number	Account Type	Current Balance	As of This Date
Ⓕ Brokerage	123456	Discount Brokerage	$9,342.98	02/15/06
	Subtotal:		$9,342.98	

Credit Cards

Account Name	Account Number	Account Type	Current Balance	Monthly Payment	As of This Date
Ⓖ MasterCard	123456	Credit Card	$1,256.78	$35.00	02/15/06
Visa	437822	Credit Card	$2,890.56	$48.00	02/15/06
	Subtotal:		$4,147.34	$83.00	

Account Summary:

Account Assets:	**$36,213.69**
Account Liabilities:	**$4,144.34**

Statement Details

Much of the virtual bank statement is similar to what I've already discussed. The difference is that transaction files look more like web pages; the files don't just duplicate a checkbook register onscreen. If you are comfortable moving around in websites, you will find a well-constructed virtual bank statement easy to learn.

Expect to take some time to set up your account because of the obvious security needs. If the virtual bank offers account aggregation, you will need website information, account names, passwords, and other information. If it all seems a bit overwhelming, many banks will help you set up your online banking in their office.

(A) *Virtual Bank Accounts*

Account Name	Account Number	Account Type	Available Balance	Current Balance	Interest Earned
(B) Main	123456	SuperNet Checking	$5,243.24	$5,790.45	$43.98
(C) Money Market	898763	Money Market	$9,393.23	$8,235.34	$88.74
	Subtotal:		$14,636.47		

(A) The online bank's accounts

(B) The main online checking account

(C) An online money market account

Virtual Bank Accounts

These two accounts are from the virtual bank, so collecting them here is no big whoop. What differs, however, is that you can see not only your Current Balance, but also your Available Balance. Your Available Balance is the one that counts because it is immediately accessible. Your Current Balance reflects transactions that have not cleared yet. This could include a deposit waiting payment from another bank, for example. Making deposits is one of the awkward processes with virtual banks—you have to mail in deposits or use a third-party acceptance arranged by the bank. You can have money transferred from one bank to another, but there will be fees involved.

Brick Bank Account

Account Name	Account Number	Account Type	Current Balance
Main	123456	Plain Checking	$2,234.24
Subtotal:			**$2,234.24**

Savings

Account Name	Account Number	Account Type	Current Balance	Interest Earned	Interest Accrued
CD	123456	24-Month CD	$10,000	$0.00	$46.28
Subtotal:			**$10,000**		

Regular Bank Accounts

These two accounts come from your regular "brick-and-mortar" bank. Some people find it convenient to have a regular bank in addition to a virtual bank so that they can make deposits and get cash from ATMs conveniently. In this case, you have two accounts aggregated within the statement: a checking account and a certificate of deposit.

Stock Brokerage Account

Account Name	Account Number	Account Type	Current Balance	As of This Date
Brokerage	123456	Discount Brokerage	$9,342.98	02/15/06
Subtotal:			**$9,342.98**	

Brokerage Account

This brokerage account report simply takes the value of your account as of the close of business on the date indicated. Your bank may require a relationship with the brokerage before they can aggregate this information within your statement. Of course, they'll be glad to transfer your account if you use another broker.

Credit Cards

Account Name	Account Number	Account Type	Current Balance	Monthly Payment	As of This Date
MasterCard	123456	Credit Card	$1,256.78	$35.00	02/15/06
Visa	437822	Credit Card	$2,890.56	$48.00	02/15/06
	Subtotal:		**$4,147.34**	**$83.00**	
Account Summary:					
Account Assets:			**$36,213.69**		
Account Liabilities:			**$4,144.34**		

G Account balances from your credit cards (brought in with your permission)

Credit Cards

With your permission, the virtual bank can capture your credit card balances on a certain date, especially if they issue the cards.

Account Assets:	$36,213.69
Account Liabilities:	$4,144.34

Account Summary

Some virtual bank statements provide a simple summary either at the end or at the beginning of your statement. It may be more detailed than this, but most are simple compilations of cash and brokerage accounts and credit card balances.

Saving for a Rainy Day

In This Chapter

- ◆ Savings account savvy
- ◆ Interesting CDs
- ◆ Tracking your bonds

Savings accounts, certificates of deposit, and bonds are three varieties of savings instruments. Each has its own documentation that ranges from the simple to the more complex.

Savings Accounts

For such a simple concept, banks, savings and loans, and credit unions offer an amazing variety of saving accounts. Although they may offer different bells and whistles, the basic account remains the same.

Most savings accounts provide a monthly statement, although some may only provide one quarterly. These statements arrive in the mail, just like regular bank account statements for the most part, although you still can find true "passbook" accounts that require you to bring in a passbook to update your account.

Paper Clips

For many years, savings and loan associations offered their main savings account in the form of a passbook. Customers brought this small book in with their deposit and a mechanical calculator would print their deposit and compute their interest earned to date in the passbook.

(A) The beginning balance on the statement month

(B) Deposits credited to the account

(C) Interest paid to the account

(D) Withdrawals from the account

(E) Other debits from the account

(F) Ending balance at end of statement month

(G) A direct deposit to the account

(H) A telephone transfer from another account

(I) Interest rate for this period

(J) Interest paid this period

(K) An ATM withdrawal

(L) A bank fee charged to this account

Account Summary

(A)	Beginning Balance 01/15/06	$485.39
(B)	Deposits	$150.00
(C)	Interest Paid	$0.44
(D)	Withdrawals	$100.00
(E)	Other Debits	$5.00
(F)	Ending Balance 02/15/06	$530.83

Deposits

	Date	Description	Reference	Amount
(G)	01/20/06	Direct Deposit	98479398	50.00
(H)	02/08/06	Telephone Transfer	90409409	100.00
		Total Deposits:		150.00

Interest

(I)	Current Interest Rate:	1%
(J)	Interest Paid:	0.44

Withdrawals

	Date	Description	Reference	Amount
(K)	02/02/06	ATM Withdrawal	49404909	100.00

Other Debits

	Date	Description	Reference	Amount
(L)	02/15/06	Bank Fee	98479398	5.00

Statement Detail

This "generic" savings account statement captures the most important elements you will find on all statements, although they may appear formatted differently on other statements. Most statements are generally straightforward and follow a familiar banking logic of presenting a summary first and detail second.

Account Summary	
(A) Beginning Balance 01/15/06	$485.39
(B) Deposits	$150.00
(C) Interest Paid	$0.44
(D) Withdrawals	$100.00
(E) Other Debits	$5.00
(F) Ending Balance 02/15/06	$530.83

(A) The beginning balance on the statement month

(B) Deposits credited to the account

(C) Interest paid to the account

(D) Withdrawals from the account

(E) Other debits from the account

(F) Ending balance at end of statement month

Account Summary

The account summary captures the important data for your attention in one spot. If you don't have much activity in the account (and savings accounts tend to have low activity), you should be able to spot anything strange immediately. If one of the items seems " wrong," you have the detail for reference. Pay particular attention to the Other Debits section.

Deposits			
Date	Description	Reference	Amount
(G) 01/20/06	Direct Deposit	98479398	50.00
(H) 02/08/06	Telephone Transfer	90409409	100.00
	Total Deposits:		150.00

(G) A direct deposit to the account

(H) A telephone transfer from another account

Deposits

The detail in this transaction category shows two deposits: one a direct deposit, which could be a check presented at a teller, for example; and the other a telephone transfer from another account at the same bank. If there is a problem with a deposit, such as an incorrect amount on your statement, the Reference Number will help you sort things out with the bank.

Interest	
(I) Current Interest Rate:	1%
(J) Interest Paid:	0.44

(I) Interest rate for this period

(J) Interest paid this period

Interest

This section tells you what the interest rate was for the statement period. Most savings accounts offer a variable interest rate that may change from month to month. Some accounts compute interest on a daily basis and credit it monthly, whereas others compute it monthly and credit it quarterly.

Statements usually report the amount of interest paid to the account this period and may include a year-to-date total. Your bank will disclose the method it uses to determine the interest rate and how and when interest is credited to your account.

K An ATM withdrawal

Withdrawals			
Date	**Description**	**Reference**	**Amount**
02/02/06	ATM Withdrawal	49404909	100.00

Withdrawals

Not all savings accounts offer ATM withdrawals, but I include one in this example for those that do. Because savings accounts do not have checks, your methods of withdrawal beyond using an ATM are limited to in-person transactions and telephone or online transfers.

L A bank fee charged to this account

Other Debits			
Date	**Description**	**Reference**	**Amount**
02/15/06	Bank Fee	98479398	5.00

Other Debits

The charges in this category are typically fees charged by the bank, either ongoing account fees or penalty fees. Some accounts charge a fee if your balance falls below a minimum. Others ding you if you use a human teller too often (for example, if you make more than three in-person deposits during the statement period). Watch this item carefully. If your goal is to actually save money, notice the relationship between the Interest Paid and Other Debits to see how you're doing. Your best bet is to read all the fine print when choosing an account so you won't be surprised by fees and charges.

Online Version

The online version of the savings account statement will not offer much new in the way of information you won't find on the paper one. What it probably will give you is an easier way to look at the history of your account if you need to look up a previous transaction.

Paper Clips

Few savings accounts offer an ATM card directly. You usually need a checking account with the bank to get an ATM card. You can then gain access to your savings account.

Bank Certificate of Deposit

Like most bank products, bank certificates of deposit, or CDs, have changed with the times. Gone are the days when you handed over your money for a fixed period and got it back along with some interest at the end of the period. And woe unto you if you wanted out before maturity! The bank rained down fees that meant you took out less than you deposited.

Certificate of deposit statements are as varied as the products they represent. Some come monthly; others only show up quarterly. CDs with very short maturities (90 to 120 days) may only issue a statement at maturity. Whenever they're issued, the statements all contain basic key elements you need to know.

Form Alarm

There are still plenty of CDs with penalties for early withdrawal, so don't buy one until you understand all of the terms and are comfortable tying up your money for the term of the CD.

Certificate Terms

(A)	Account Opened	02/15/06
(B)	Maturity Date:	02/15/09
(C)	Length of Term:	36 months
(D)	Initial Investment	$10,000
(E)	Interest Rate	3.5% APR / 3.66% APY
(F)	Interest Compounded	Daily
(G)	Renewal	Automatic

Account Summary

(H)	Beginning Balance 06/15/06	$10,000.00
(I)	Deposits	$500.00
(J)	Interest Earned	$30.17
(K)	Interest Paid	($30.17)
(L)	Ending Balance 07/15/06	$10,500.00

(A) Date CD was opened
(B) Date CD will mature
(C) Length in months of CD's term
(D) Initial investment in CD
(E) Interest rate (APR is noncompounded rate; APY is the compounded rate.)
(F) How often interest is compounded
(G) How renewal of CD is handled
(H) Beginning balance of the account for this statement month
(I) Deposits to this CD this month
(J) Interest earned this statement month
(K) Interest paid to CD owner
(L) Ending balance this statement

Statement Details

This statement combines the important elements available today from CDs, although the formatting may not look like your statement. Several key elements require your attention and understanding if you are going to take advantage of all the features of modern CDs.

Ⓐ	Date CD was opened	
Ⓑ	Date CD will mature	
Ⓒ	Length in months of CD's term	
Ⓓ	Initial investment in CD	
Ⓔ	Interest rate (APR is noncompounded rate; APY is the compounded rate.)	
Ⓕ	How often interest is compounded	
Ⓖ	How renewal of CD is handled	

Certificate Terms	
Ⓐ Account Opened	02/15/06
Ⓑ Maturity Date:	02/15/09
Ⓒ Length of Term:	36 months
Ⓓ Initial Investment	$10,000
Ⓔ Interest Rate	3.5% APR / 3.66% APY
Ⓕ Interest Compounded	Daily
Ⓖ Renewal	Automatic

Certificate Terms

This portion of the statement duplicates the original CD terms, which spell out the details of the CD. Banks offer a wide variety of CDs with many different options. However, they all address these key elements. Although there are many options, take care to read the marketing material fine print for phrases such as "minimum balance required" or "substantial penalty for early withdrawal."

Length of Term

CDs typically have a beginning and end or maturity date. The length of term is expressed in months or, in the case of very short-term CDs, days. Some banks offer a flexible CD that never matures; it keeps going until you cash it in. Some would argue that these are not CDs, but a different type of savings account.

Initial Investment

The initial investment is how much you deposit to open the account. For some CDs, that is all you can ever put in, whereas other CDs allow additional deposits. Generally speaking, the more money you put in up front, the more options you have regarding additional deposits, interest, and so on.

Interest Rate

Many CDs have an interest rate fixed when you open the account. The rate is determined in part by the size of your investment (the more you invest, the higher the rate) and how long you are willing to commit your money (the longer the term, the higher the rate). Some banks offer variable interest rates based on some key interest rate, such as 2% over the 10-year U.S. Treasury Note rate. The bank may recompute the rate monthly or quarterly, but they must disclose this to you up front.

The bank may compound the interest on a daily, monthly, or quarterly basis. Obviously, daily compounding is better, so watch for that feature when shopping for a CD. Frequently, banks reserve daily compounding for higher-balance accounts.

The two rates quoted represent the difference between the stated rated APR (*annual percent rate*) and the rate that reflects compound interest APY (*annual percent yield*). If you want to receive the higher interest rate, you must reinvest the interest back into the CD.

Financial Speak

Annual percent rate (APR) is the annual interest rate a borrower pays or lender receives. It does not take into account the effect of compounding. Annual percent yield (APY) is the effective rate of return when you consider compounding of interest. Compounding of interest is interest earning interest. For example, you deposit $100 and it earns $1 interest the first compounding period (day, month, year). The next compounding period interest is paid on $101, and so on.

Renewal

Almost all CDs, except those with no maturity, renew automatically. This means the CD in this example will renew to a new 36-month CD automatically on 02/15/09. It will earn the prevailing interest rate and be bound by other conditions or restrictions relevant to CDs issued on that date.

The bank should send you a notice that this is going to happen two to three weeks before the date. If you don't want the CD to renew, but miss the notice, you usually have a grace period of 10 business days to notify the bank. If you notify the bank within that period that you want your money, you can avoid a penalty for early withdrawal.

Account Summary	
H Beginning Balance 06/15/06	$10,000.00
I Deposits	$500.00
J Interest Earned	$30.17
K Interest Paid	($30.17)
L Ending Balance 07/15/06	$10,500.00

H Beginning balance of the account for this statement month

I Deposits to this CD this month

J Interest earned this statement month

K Interest paid to CD owner

L Ending balance this statement

Beginning and Ending Balances

These numbers reflect the balances at the start and end of the statement month. For CDs that do not accept deposits and credit interest only quarterly, these numbers will change only four times a year. Because interest is paid out on this example account, the only time the balance changes is after you make a deposit.

Deposits

This particular CD allows deposits. Depending on the CD, you may be limited to the number of deposits you can make and when you can make them (the first five business days of the month, for example). Other CDs allow unlimited deposits.

Interest Earned

You earned this much interest for the statement month on the CD. This particular CD credits interest monthly, but that is not a requirement. Some CDs only credit interest quarterly. How interest is compounded (daily or monthly) and how it is credited (daily, monthly, or quarterly) directly impacts your earnings. The more frequently interest is compounded and credited, the more you earn.

Interest Paid

You have chosen to withdraw the interest on your CD, so each month it is paid to you. Most CDs allow you to transfer it to another account with the same bank, or you can receive a check. Withdrawing the interest will lower the total return from the CD because you are taking interest out of the compounding equation. Leaving the interest in the CD to earn more interest will generate the best results.

Paper Clips

Although some bonds still come in a certificate form, most issuers now keep track of them electronically, meaning they exist as a computer record. You will receive written confirmation and periodic communications, but the bond itself exists electronically.

Bonds Away

Bonds are savings instruments that many people use to prepare for retirement, but you can also use them to meet other financial goals. Governments from the federal level on down—as well as corporations—issue bonds to finance a variety of needs. Although they come in many flavors and from an assortment of issuers, all bonds share some common elements. Many bonds are issued electronically, but you will still find plenty that are in paper form.

U.S. Treasury Bonds

The U.S. Treasury offers a wide variety of bills, bonds, and notes ranging from $25 to tens of thousands of dollars and with maturities of 4 weeks to 30 years. Some pay interest every six months; other only pay interest at maturity.

Although the terms may differ, your bond has some items in common with all bonds. These key elements define how you want the bond to fit in your financial life, so it is important that you understand how they work. The Treasury issues its bonds either electronically or in paper form, although some bonds are only issued in electronic form. This distinction is important because there are key elements unique to each form. In addition, the size and type of bond dictates certain features.

(A) Date bond was issued

(B) Face value of the bond

(C) The stated interest rate or coupon rate

(D) The amount of interest you earn annually

(E) The date the bond matures

(F) Registration options for bonds bought directly from the U.S. Treasury

(G) For an individual owner

(H) First owner and secondary owner

(I) Owner and beneficiary

(J) For an individual owner

(K) For two equal owners

Primary Elements	
(A) Date of Issue:	02/01/06
(B) Principal:	$5,000.00
(C) Stated Interest:	4.2%
(D) Coupon Payment:	$210.00
(E) Maturity:	02/01/16

(F) **Registration Options for Bonds Bought Directly**

TreasuryDirect Bonds Option 1:

(G) Sole Ownership:	Jane Doe 333-33-3333

TreasuryDirect Bonds Option 2:

(H) Primary Ownership:	Jane Doe 333-33-3333 with John Doe 444-44-4444

TreasuryDirect Bonds Option 3:

(I) Owner:	Jane Doe 333-33-3333
Beneficiary:	John Doe 444-44-4444

Paper Bonds Option 1:

(J) Single Ownership:	Jane Doe 333-33-3333

Paper Bonds Option 2:

(K) Co-Ownership:	Jane Doe 333-33-3333 or John Doe 444-44-4444

Paper Bonds Option 3:

L Beneficiary: Jane Doe 333-33-3333
POD
John Doe 444-44-4444

M **Registration Options for Notes/Bills Bought at Auction**

N Single Ownership: Jane Doe 333-33-3333

O Joint Ownership with
Right of Survivorship: Jane Doe 333-33-3333
and John Doe 444-44-4444
with right of survivorship

P Joint Ownership Without
Right of Survivorship: Jane Doe 333-33-3333
and John Doe 444-44-4444
without right of survivorship

Q Co-Ownership: Jane Doe 333-33-3333
or John Doe 444-44-4444

R Beneficiary: Jane Doe 333-33-3333
POD
John Doe 444-44-4444

S Natural Guardian: Jane Doe 333-33-3333

T Custodian: Jane Doe 333-33-3333

U Estate Representative: Jane Doe 333-33-3333

V Trustees: Jane Doe 333-33-3333

W Individual Retirement Accounts: First National Bank, Custodian

X Private Organizations: Amalgamated Kumquats, Inc.

Y Government Entities and Officers: Anytown, Texas

L Owner and beneficiary

M Registration options for bills and notes bought at auction

N For an individual owner

O Two owners with Right of Survivorship registration

P Two owners without Right of Survivorship registration

Q Two owners, but not equal

R Owner and beneficiary

S For a guardian for a minor

T Custodian of a retirement account

U If the owner is an estate

V For a trust

W Custodian of an IRA

X For a private company

Y For a governmental body

Bonds in Detail

The paperwork associated with U.S. Treasury bonds is as varied as the number of different types of bonds, notes, and bills our government offers. Despite those differences, I have created a selection of key data elements that you need to know.

Primary Elements

A Date of Issue: 02/01/06

B Principal: $5,000.00

C Stated Interest: 4.2%

D Coupon Payment: $210.00

E Maturity: 02/01/16

A Date bond was issued

B Face value of the bond

C The stated interest rate or coupon rate

D The amount of interest you earn annually

E The date the bond matures

Principal

The principal, also known as the face value, is the amount of the note, bond, or bill. In most cases, you will buy a new security from the U.S. Treasury for that amount. Some U.S. Treasury products are sold at a discount off the face value.

For example, short-term Treasury bills are sold at a discount, so you might pay $9,500 for a $10,000 26-week Treasury Bill. The $500 is the interest you earn when the bill matures, and you receive $10,000. In that case, the principal or face value would be $10,000, even though you only paid $9,500 for the security.

Stated Interest Rate

Your bond will earn this interest rate, also known as the coupon or coupon rate, until maturity. The rate will not change for most U.S. Treasury products. If you buy a product that features a variable interest rate, such as a Treasury Inflation-Protected Securities (TIPS), this interest rate changes on a scheduled basis as explained in the security's documentation.

Coupon Payment

The coupon payment is the annual interest you receive from your bond. For this bond, it amounts to $210 per year paid in two payments of $105 each every six months. For most bonds, this payment continues unchanged until the bond matures.

Maturity

The security's maturity date marks the time when most notes and bonds quit paying interest. In most cases, you have the option to receive the principal or face amount at maturity or you may reinvest it in another U.S. Treasury security. However, you cannot reinvest some notes and bonds.

Corporate Bonds

Corporations use bonds to finance large projects because it is usually cheaper than going to the bank for a loan. Corporate bonds come in $1,000 denominations and carry a variety of maturities.

Some corporations still issue paper bonds, although many are moving to electronic bonds. You buy corporate bonds through a broker as new issues or as previously issued.

Ⓐ Date bond was issued

Ⓑ The date the bond will mature

Ⓒ Amount you will receive at maturity

Ⓓ Interest rate the bond pays

Ⓔ Annual interest payment

Key Corporate Bond Elements	
Ⓐ Date of Issue:	02/01/06
Ⓑ Date of Maturity:	02/01/26
Ⓒ Face Value:	$1,000.00
Ⓓ Coupon Rate:	5.2%
Ⓔ Coupon Payment:	$52

Additional Corporate Bond Elements	
Callable:	02/01/08
Convertible:	02/01/10
Coupons:	None
Registered	Your information

F The date the bond is eligible to be called

G The date the bond may be converted

H Indicates there are no coupons attached

I Identifies the bond as registered

Corporate Bond Elements

Whether you receive a paper bond or an electronic version, several key pieces of information will be common to all. This information identifies key elements about the bond.

Key Corporate Bond Elements	
Date of Issue:	02/01/06
Date of Maturity:	02/01/26
Face Value:	$1,000.00
Coupon Rate:	5.2%
Coupon Payment:	$52

A Date bond was issued

B The date the bond will mature

C Amount you will receive at maturity

D Interest rate the bond pays

E Annual interest payment

Dates of Issue and Maturity

These two dates identify when the bond was issued and when it matures. The maturity date is especially important because bonds typically don't pay interest after that date. You will want to cash in the bond at maturity. Owners of registered bonds, which includes most bonds, are notified prior to maturity.

- **Face Value.** The face value on the bond indicates how much you will receive when the bond matures. In most cases, it is also what you paid for the bond. However, corporations sometimes issue what are known as zero-coupon bonds. These bonds pay no interest, but sell at a deep discount, so you pay much less than the face value for them.

- **Coupon Rate.** The coupon rate is the interest rate paid throughout the life of the bond. It is figured annually and paid semi-annually in most cases.

- **Coupon Payment.** The coupon payment is the annual income generated by the bond. The bond usually pays interest semi-annually; so in this example, you would receive two checks for $26 each.

- **Additional Elements.** Beyond the basics, some key items need your attention on corporate bonds. These items contain important information about your bond that affect how you use them in your finances.

F The date the bond is eligible to be called

G The date the bond may be converted

H Indicates there are no coupons attached

I Identifies the bond as registered

Additional Corporate Bond Elements	
F Callable:	02/01/08
G Convertible:	02/01/10
H Coupons:	None
I Registered	Your information

Callable

Some corporate bonds, but not all, are callable by the issuing corporation. This means that past some stated date, the corporation has the right to call or buy back the bonds without your permission. The corporation will do this if it believes it can borrow the money it needs somewhere else at a lower rate than the bond was paying.

This is an important item to check before you buy a bond, because it could be called away from you and you may be forced to reinvest the money at a lower interest rate. Some corporate bonds may also contain a "put" provision that allows you to redeem the bond before maturity on or after a certain date.

Convertible

Corporations also issue convertible bonds. You can convert these bonds to shares of common stock after a certain date and under certain circumstances. The company sets the terms of conversion, so you will know how many shares your bond can buy. The company can also force a conversion and make you redeem your bond if it is in their interests.

Coupons

Years ago, people called bondholders "coupon clippers" because of the coupons attached to bonds that needed to be mailed in to receive interest payments. Some bonds, particularly older bonds, still carry coupons that you must present to receive interest payments.

Registered

Most bond issuers and trustees register the owners of bonds. This registration provides a record of ownership and a means of contacting the owner with notices of information about the bond.

Bearer bonds have no registered owners. They must be presented, with or without coupons, for payment. Bearer bonds are almost as good as cash because the person in physical possession of the bond is considered the owner.

Municipal Bonds

Governmental entities, such as cities, counties, school districts, and so on, issue bonds to fund a wide variety of projects and activities. These bonds offer the advantage of freedom from federal income tax and, in some cases, freedom from state and local taxes.

Governments issue municipal bonds (or munis) in $5,000 denominations. The bonds come in two types. The first type is a revenue bond that finances projects such as a toll road or housing project, and the bond is repaid from fees or rents. The second type is a general obligation bond that the government repays with taxes and so on.

CAUTION

Form Alarm

If you find your grandmother left you some old bearer bonds, it is a good idea to get them to a safe place, such as a bank safe deposit box, until you can establish their worth. Anyone can cash bearer bonds, including a burglar.

Key Municipal Bond Elements	
Ⓐ Date of Issue:	02/01/06
Ⓑ Date of Maturity:	02/01/36
Ⓒ Face Value:	$5,000.00
Ⓓ Coupon Rate:	4.2%
Ⓔ Coupon Payment:	$210
Additional Municipal Bond Elements	
Ⓕ Callable:	02/01/08
Ⓖ Put:	02/01/10
Ⓗ Insured:	Yes
Ⓘ Coupons:	None
Ⓙ Registered:	Your information

Ⓐ The date bond was issued
Ⓑ The date the bond will mature
Ⓒ Amount you will receive at maturity
Ⓓ Interest rate the bond pays
Ⓔ Annual interest payment
Ⓕ The date the bond is eligible to be called
Ⓖ The date you may redeem the bond prematurely
Ⓗ The principal and interest insured by a third party
Ⓘ Indicates no coupons attached
Ⓙ Identifies the bond as registered

Municipal Bond Elements

Municipal bonds come in a wide variety of issues from a wider variety of issuers. You need to know some important facts about all municipal bonds.

Key Municipal Bond Elements	
Ⓐ Date of Issue:	02/01/06
Ⓑ Date of Maturity:	02/01/36
Ⓒ Face Value:	$5,000.00
Ⓓ Coupon Rate:	4.2%
Ⓔ Coupon Payment:	$210

Ⓐ The date bond was issued
Ⓑ The date the bond will mature
Ⓒ Amount you will receive at maturity
Ⓓ Interest rate the bond pays
Ⓔ Annual interest payment

Dates of Issue and Maturity

These two dates identify when the bond was issued and when it matures. The maturity date is especially important because bonds typically don't pay interest after that date. You will want to cash in the bond at maturity. Owners of registered bonds, which includes most bonds, are notified prior to maturity.

Face Value

The face value on the bond indicates how much you will receive when the bond matures. In most cases, it is also what you paid for the bond. However, governmental units sometimes issue what are known as zero-coupon bonds. These bonds pay no interest, but sell at a deep discount, so you would pay much less than the face value for them.

You can also buy municipal bonds on the secondary market. What you pay depends on a variety of factors, including the relationship of the bond's coupon rate and the current market interest rate, along with the time remaining until maturity, among other factors.

Coupon Rate

The coupon rate is the interest rate paid throughout the life of the bond. It is figured annually and paid semi-annually in most cases. One type of municipal bond offers a variable interest rate. Popularly known as floaters, these bonds have a formula for calculating the change in the interest rate.

Coupon Payment

The coupon payment is the annual income generated by the bond. The bond usually pays interest semi-annually; so in this example, you would receive two checks for $26 each. The exception would be the zero-coupon bonds that pay no interest until maturity.

Additional Elements

Beyond the basics, some key items need your attention on municipal bonds. These items contain important information about your bond.

Additional Municipal Bond Elements	
F Callable:	02/01/08
G Put:	02/01/10
H Insured:	Yes
I Coupons:	None
J Registered:	Your information

F The date the bond is eligible to be called

G The date you may redeem the bond prematurely

H The principal and interest insured by a third party

I Indicates no coupons attached

J Identifies the bond as registered

The definitions used earlier in this chapter for callable, put, coupons, and registered apply to municipal bonds as well.

Municipal bonds are generally safe, but some governmental entities go to extra lengths and insure the principal and interest payments. Expect a lower interest rate for this extra safety.

Chapter 4

Credit Where It's Due

In This Chapter

- ◆ Avoiding misleading information
- ◆ Paying attention to the little details
- ◆ Monitoring advances and offers
- ◆ Verifying everything

Credit cards are a convenient way to pay for a variety of goods and services. They are also an easy road to financial trouble. The warning signs, if you know where to look, are on your monthly statement.

Credit Cards

It's hard to imagine living without the convenience of credit cards. Yet that convenience can quickly get out of hand if you're not careful. Consumers in the past found credit card statements confusing and difficult to understand. The credit card companies have made some progress in simplifying statements, but you still need to read yours carefully.

(A) The billing cycle covered by this statement

(B) Balance carried forward from last statement

(C) Total of payments

(D) Total of purchases

(E) Your cash advances

(F) Balances transferred from other credit cards

(G) Finance charges added to your account

(H) New account balance for this billing period

(I) Date payment is due without penalty

(J) Minimum payment due to avoid penalty fees

(K) Your credit limit

(L) Amount of credit available

(M) Your limit on cash advances

(N) How much you have left on cash advance limit

(O) Payments posted to account

(P) Purchases posted

(Q) Cash advance taken on this date

(R) Balance transferred to this account

(S) The average daily balance of the account this cycle

(T) The interest rate on a daily basis

(U) The annual interest rate

(V) Finance charges this cycle

(W) Transaction fees charged

(X) Number of days in current billing cycle

Account Summary

(A)	Billing Cycle	01/01/06 – 02/01/06
(B)	Previous Balance	$9,384.39
(C)	Payments and Credits	- $900.00
(D)	Purchases	+ $345.34
(E)	Cash Advances	+ $500.00
(F)	Balance Transfers	+ $1,000.00
(G)	Finance Charges	+ $136.32
(H)	New Balance	= $10,463.05
(I)	Payment Due Date	03/01/06
(J)	Minimum Payment Due	$210.94
(K)	Credit Limit	$15,000.00
(L)	Credit Available	$4,515.00
(M)	Cash Credit Limit	$7,200.00
(N)	Cash Credit Available	$6,000.00

(O) Payments

Date	Posted	Amount
01/08/06	01/12/06	$900.00

(P) Purchases

Date	Vendor	Amount
01/11/06	ABC Books, Anytown, WI	$45.29
01/16/06	Bills Gas, Anytown, WI	$38.90
01/16/06	Amazon.com	$45.98
01/24/06	Bills Gas, Anytown, WI	$32.83
01/25/06	Elegant Jewelry, Anytown, WI	$156.78
01/27/06	Bills Gas, Anytown, WI	$25.56

Advances and Transfers

Date	Source	Amount
(Q) 01/15/06	Cash Advance	$500.00
(R) 01/20/06	Balance Transfer Visa #1111-111-1111	$1,000.00

Finance Charges

	(S) Ave. Daily Balances	(T) Daily Periodic Rates	(U) Annual Percent. Rates	(V) Periodic Finance Charges	(W) Trans. Fees Charges
Purchases	$9,876.64	0.04175%	15.24% V	$127.83	none
Cash Adv.	$500.00	0.05477%	19.99% F	$8.49	

(X) (Current billing period is 31 days)

Statement Detail

Although they come in different formats, credit card statements all contain the same basic information. It is important that you understand how the credit card companies structure the statements and learn to read the interest disclosures. The generic credit card statement I have created includes most of the major transactions you are likely to use, but maybe not all in one month.

	Account Summary		
A	Billing Cycle	01/01/06 – 02/01/06	
B	Previous Balance	$9,384.39	
C	Payments and Credits	- $900.00	
D	Purchases	+ $345.34	
E	Cash Advances	+ $500.00	
F	Balance Transfers	+ $1,000.00	
G	Finance Charges	+ $136.32	
H	New Balance	= $10,463.05	
I	Payment Due Date	03/01/06	
J	Minimum Payment Due	$210.94	
K	Credit Limit	$15,000.00	
L	Credit Available	$4,515.00	
M	Cash Credit Limit	$7,200.00	
N	Cash Credit Available	$6,000.00	

A The billing cycle covered by this statement

B Balance carried forward from last statement

C Total of payments

D Total of purchases

E Your cash advances

F Balances transferred from other credit cards

G Finance charges added to your account

H New account balance for this billing period

I Date payment is due without penalty

J Minimum payment due to avoid penalty fees

K Your credit limit

L Amount of credit available

M Your limit on cash advances

N How much you have left on cash advance limit

Account Summary

The account summary captures all the important summary information on the statement. Most credit card statements present this information all together, or the bottom portion beginning with Payment Due Date may be off to the side. Although it is important to review this information, don't stop here. The real problems, if there are any, will likely show up in the details below the summary on the statement.

Billing Cycle and Balances

The billing cycle dates and the previous and new balance numbers bracket the account summary. The billing cycle dates show you when the account closed to transactions for this statement. Any charges after the closing date will show up on the next statement, as will any payments.

The previous balance simply picks up the balance from the previous cycle and begins the process again. The new balance is the sum of all the transactions in the account summary applied to the previous balance.

Form Alarm

Review the transactions section carefully. Not all credit card thieves will try to run up a huge bill. Some hope to slip by a few charges each month.

Transactions

The transactions in the middle of the account summary represent totals from the detailed reports that follow. These list payments, purchases, cash advances, balance transfers, and interest charges. It is convenient to have the information presented in this summary form; if you have an active account, however, it's not very helpful. You really need to dig into the details. Remember, credit card companies do make mistakes. People will rip you off if they have access to your credit card number.

Payment Due Date and Minimum Payment Due

You don't want to overlook a couple of important items. The payment due date is the date your payment must be in the credit card company's hands. In most cases, having it postmarked by this date won't cut it. If you miss this date, the credit card company will sock you with a big transaction fee (see below). If you want to know how they calculate this fee, the credit card company should disclose it to you in one of those documents printed in tiny type.

The same thing is true for the minimum payment due. Keep an eye on this figure, because it changes from month to month, depending on your balance. Don't assume it will be the same as last month. If you don't pay the minimum due, you'll pay a fee.

Credit and Limits

The remainder of the account summary is devoted to revealing how much credit you have left in your account and how much cash you can still take out in advances. This not-so-subtle reminder of how much shopping is left on your card also serves a useful purpose as a red flag if your spending is getting out of hand.

Ⓞ Payments posted to account
Ⓟ Purchases posted
Ⓠ Cash advance taken on this date
Ⓡ Balance transferred to this account

Ⓞ **Payments**

Date	Posted	Amount
01/08/06	01/12/06	$900.00

Ⓟ **Purchases**

Date	Vendor	Amount
01/11/06	ABC Books, Anytown, WI	$45.29
01/16/06	Bills Gas, Anytown, WI	$38.90
01/16/06	Amazon.com	$45.98
01/24/06	Bills Gas, Anytown, WI	$32.83
01/25/06	Elegant Jewelry, Anytown, WI	$156.78
01/27/06	Bills Gas, Anytown, WI	$25.56

Advances and Transfers

Date	Source	Amount
Ⓠ 01/15/06	Cash Advance	$500.00
Ⓡ 01/20/06	Balance Transfer Visa #1111-111-1111	$1,000.00

Finance Charges					
	S Ave. Daily Balances	**T Daily Periodic Rates**	**U Annual Percent. Rates**	**V Periodic Finance Charges**	**W Trans. Fees Charges**
Purchases	$9,876.64	0.04175%	15.24% V	$127.83	none
Cash Adv.	$500.00	0.05477%	19.99% F	$8.49	

X (Current billing period is 31 days)

- **S** The average daily balance of the account this cycle
- **T** The interest rate on a daily basis
- **U** The annual interest rate
- **V** Finance charges this cycle
- **W** Transaction fees charged
- **X** Number of days in current billing cycle

More Details

This section of the credit card statement covers transactions and some other details. You should spend some time here making sure everything is in order. Are all the charges correct? Have all the payments been posted? What about cash advances and balance transfers?

Payments

This is simple enough, but watch for late-posting payments—that is, payments that take many days to post after you mail in your check. This could raise a problem if you mail your check later in the monthly cycle and it takes the credit card company a long time to post the payment.

Purchases

In this example, I have listed only a few transactions; however, in real life most of us run up quite a few more in the course of a month. Take a few minutes and review them for accuracy. Just because the process appears to be electronic with card-swipe machines and so on doesn't mean it's foolproof.

You should also be concerned that someone with access to your credit card number might be making purchases without your knowledge. This is the place to catch unauthorized transactions.

Advances and Transfers

Credit card companies are big on cash advances because they are usually charged a higher rate of interest than regular purchases. If you use this service, be aware of the potential charges and how your credit card figures interest. For instance, some card companies apply all payments to the lower-interest purchases first and only when you pay them off do your payments go to the higher-interest cash advances.

Credit card companies also love balance transfers because it gives them a larger account on which to charge interest. Read the disclosure carefully to see whether an offer of low interest on balance transfers is for a short period followed by a regular interest rate.

Paper Clips

One of the ways credit card companies make money is by charging interest on balances. They want you to pay something each month, but not the whole balance—that way they can collect interest on the unpaid portion.

Finance Charges

The credit card company must disclose to you the interest rate it charges on various parts of your account and how it computes those rates. This section details that information in a rather confusing format. The first thing you notice is that there is a different rate of interest for your purchases and for cash advances. Here's what the columns mean:

- **Average Daily Balance.** The credit card company computes this using your payments, purchases, and other transactions. This is the number they use to calculate the finance charge.

- **Daily Periodic Rates.** This is the interest rate computed on a daily basis. This number is a percentage, so you must convert it to a decimal by dividing by 100 (or, the easier way is to just add two zeros to the right of the decimal point). In this example, you would express 0.04175 as 0.0004175 in a calculation. If you multiply this number times the daily balance times the number of days in the cycle (see Current Billing Period in this list), you get the finance charge.

- **Annual Percentage Rate.** This is the annual representation of the interest rate. You will notice that the two interest rates in the example are different. The rate for purchases is 15.24% followed by *V*, and the rate for cash advances is 19.99% followed by *F.* The *V* stands for variable, meaning the interest rate is subject to change; the *F* means fixed, meaning the interest rate will not change for some predetermined period.

- **Periodic Finance Charges.** This is the result of the previously mentioned calculation. This would be the Average Daily Balance × (Daily Periodic Rate × Days in Current Billing Period) = Periodic Finance Charges.

- **Transaction Fees and Charges.** The credit card company assesses these fees and charges if you miss the due date or fail to pay the minimum due. Other assessments might occur if you write a bad check or reversed a charge, for example. Some credit cards still charge an annual fee, and it will likely show up in this column.

- **Current Billing Period.** This figure tells you how many days are in the current billing cycle. The credit card company uses this number in computing your finance charges.

> **Paper Clips**
>
> Always read the disclosures about interest rates before you decide on taking a cash advance from your credit card. You may find that this quickie loan is way too expensive when you consider the interest rate, which is almost always much higher than the regular card rate. Always check special promotions such as "skip a payment" or "same as cash" financing for what happens to interest. In most cases it accrues during the "specials" and you may end up paying more.

Online Versions

Many credit card companies have made great strides in bringing their statements online. Most of the major card issuers offer a number of interactive services, such as bill paying, balance transfers, and cash advances via their websites. You can also view historical files of transactions and check your available credit at any time during the month.

If your credit card comes from your bank, you may have even more possibilities for interaction. That's one of the benefits banks push to draw new customers and retain existing clients.

Differences, Similarities

Online credit card statements can vary a great deal in format and function. Originally, many credit card companies tried to make the statements look as much like the paper statements as possible. However, as customers became more familiar and comfortable with the Internet and web pages, credit card companies have formatted the statements and websites to be more interactive and less static. Either way, the information is still the same. There will be more access to historical accounts, and increased functionality, as time passes.

Security

Security remains a concern for any transaction on the Internet that involves sensitive financial data and information. Identity theft and credit card fraud are real problems. However, given the total number of users in the system, these problems still only affect a small percentage of customers.

Chapter 5

Keeping the Lights On

In This Chapter

- ◆ Understanding gas and electricity
- ◆ Water vs. waste
- ◆ Following the budget plan

One group of bills you don't want to put off are those monthly love notes from your utility providers. With today's high energy costs, it's more important than ever to monitor your statements. Many consumers find that wildly fluctuating utility bills from season to season are too disruptive to their budget and opt for a stable payment plan. I explain those also.

Utility Bills

In some markets, your gas and electric bill may come from the same provider, whereas in others they will come separately. Your city or municipality usually provides water and sewer services, but these bills also may come from the same utility that brings in the electricity. If you use heating oil in your furnace, the bill will come from a vendor not usually considered a utility. In the interest of simplicity, I have kept electricity, gas, and water/waste water separate. The generic bills I have created may or may not look like the ones you receive, but the important information, how much you have to pay and why, will be the same.

Electricity

Electricity and gas are the two biggest utility costs. Depending on which part of the country you live in, heating or cooling will drive the largest part of your bill. Yes, it helps to turn off lights you're not using, but it's the air conditioning (AC) and furnace that really get the meters spinning.

A States the billing period

B Date of bill

C Amount of last month's bill

D Payment amount and date received

E Previous balance carried forward

F Current charges

G Amount and date of budget payment

H Date and amount budget plan will draft your account

I Beginning meter reading

J Ending meter reading

K KWH consumed

L Billing Code

M Power cost adjustment clause (PCAC) or adjustment for fuel cost to utility

N Public benefits fee funds utility environmental improvements

O Previous balance

P Amount due this month

Q Average kilowatt per hour (KWH) per day

R A measure of relative weather trends shows how hot or cold the billing period was

---

Account Summary

A Billing period 12/20/05 to 01/21/06	
B Bill date: 01/25/06	
C Last month's total bill	$45.70
D Payment through 01/25/06	$53.00
E Previous Balance	-$7.30
F This month's charges	$43.26
G Budget due by 02/13/06	$53.00
H Easy Budget Plan – account is being drafted on 02/13/06 for $53.00	

Consumption Information

Service	Meter No.	Previous Read (I)	Current Read (J)	Consumed (K)	Code (L)	Amount
Electricity	84993	19908	20410	502	RG1	$49.10
M PCAC Charge @ .0011					RG1	$.55
N Public Benefits Fee					PBR	$.91
O			Previous Balance			-$7.30
P Amount Due 2/13/06						$43.26

Conservation Information

	Days	KWH/Used	KWH/Day (Q)	Heating Deg. Days (R)	Cooling Deg. Days
This Year	32	502	15.69	1470	0
Last Year	33	694	21.03	1307	0

Statement Detail

Your statement from the utility company will likely follow something like the generic one I have created. The account summary and usage areas capture the key elements.

A States the billing period

B Date of bill

C Amount of last month's bill

D Payment amount and date received

E Previous balance carried forward

F Current charges

G Amount and date of budget payment

H Date and amount budget plan will draft your account

Account Summary

A Billing period 12/20/05 to 01/21/06	
B Bill date: 01/25/06	
C Last month's total bill	$45.70
D Payment through 01/25/06	$53.00
E Previous Balance	-$7.30
F This month's charges	$43.26
G Budget due by 02/13/06	$53.00
H Easy Budget Plan – account is being drafted on 02/13/06 for $53.00	

Account Summary

The account summary area tells you at a glance where your account stands. This example shows a customer on a "budget payment plan," which I explain in detail later in this chapter. The numbers may look somewhat different from those on a regular payment plan; however, all of the elements remain the same.

Billing Period and Payments

You might notice that the billing period on this account is not an even month. Because this utility physically reads meters, it is not always possible to get a reading that covers a 30- or 31-day period. It may be 33 days or 28 days or somewhere in between. Many utilities are converting to new technology that permits remote meter reading, which should allow more timely charges.

Also notice that the total charges for last month were $45.70, but the payment through 01/25/06 was $53.00, or $7.30 more than was due. This is a reflection of the budget payment plan, which pays a fixed amount each month regardless of usage. More about the budget plan at the end of the chapter.

Paper Clips

You can find the billing period in days without doing the math in the conservation portion of the statement on many bills.

Previous Balance and Current Charges

Because the budget plan paid more than was actually due last month, you have a negative balance carried forward. A negative balance on a bill means they owe you money—a credit in other words. The utility applies that credit toward your current bill, but it will still charge you the current budget amount ($53) even though your new balance is once again under the budget amount. This will make more sense when we look at budget plans in detail.

The statement also notifies you when they plan to draft your account for the next budget plan payment. This gives you a heads-up to make sure your bank account has sufficient funds to cover the draft.

Consumption Information		I	J	K	L	
Service	Meter No.	Previous Read	Current Read	Consumed	Code	Amount
Electricity	84993	19908	20410	502	RG1	$49.10
(M) PCAC Charge @ .0011					RG1	$.55
(N) Public Benefits Fee					PBR	$.91
(O) Previous Balance						-$7.30
(P) Amount Due 2/13/06						$43.26

- (I) Beginning meter reading
- (J) Ending meter reading
- (K) KWH consumed
- (L) Billing Code
- (M) Power cost adjustment clause (PCAC) or adjustment for fuel cost to utility
- (N) Public benefits fee funds utility environmental improvements
- (O) Previous balance
- (P) Amount due this month

Consumption Information

Although some utilities use sophisticated reporting technology, many still send employees around every month to read your electric meter. As in any human

Financial Speak

A **kilowatt hour** is equal to the amount of energy used by a 100-watt light bulb burning for 10 hours.

Financial Speak

Heating and Cooling Degree Days are a measurement of relative weather trends. Heating Degree Days are the sum of all average daily temperatures below 65 degrees, and Cooling Degree Days are the sum of all average daily temperatures above 65 degrees. These measurements give you a relative idea of how warm or cold a billing period was.

Ⓠ Average kilowatts per hour (KWH) per day

Ⓡ A measure of relative weather trends shows how hot or cold the billing period was

endeavor, meter readers can make mistakes. This portion of your statement notes how many KWH or *kilowatt hours* you used since the last time the utility read the meter.

Any unusual change that can't be accounted for by weather patterns (severe hot or cold) or other factors should be reported to the utility. It is possible for them to double-check the reading and check to make sure the meter is not defective.

Charges

The electricity charge is by the KWH. If the rates per KWH are not included in your bill, and some aren't, the utility will provide them to you. Often the charges are "coded" with a reference somewhere on the statement.

The PCAC charge refers to the power cost adjustment clause. This nifty little item lets the utility pass along the increase or decrease in the cost of fuel or power it buys from other utilities. In other words, it is a surcharge passed on to you when the utility's costs exceed what they budgeted. It is possible that this could be a negative number (a credit) if fuel costs for the month come in lower than expected.

The public benefits fee or something like it will show up on most utility bills. This is a small fee assessed customers, usually based on usage, which goes to programs that assist low-income customers with their utility bills.

Previous Balance and Amount Due

The previous balance is applied—in this case a credit—to the charges. The new balance and a due date round out this section of the statement. The balance due appears in the account summary.

Conservation Information				Ⓠ	Ⓡ	
	Days	KWH/Used	KWH/Day	Heating Deg. Days	Cooling Deg. Days	
This Year	32	502	15.69	1470	0	
Last Year	33	694	21.03	1307	0	

Conservation Information

The conservation information, which may not appear on all utility bills, gives you a look at your consumption compared to the same period one year ago. The table shows how many days were in the period, total KWHs used, and the average number of KWHs per day. Based on this example, it appears the consumer was able to cut consumption rather dramatically from the previous year.

The *Heating and Cooling Degree Days* are ways of measuring relative weather trends. Heating Degree Days are the sum of the average daily temperatures below 65 degrees Fahrenheit for the period. For example, if the average temperature for Monday is 44, that number would go in the Heating Degree Days.

Cooling Degree Days is the opposite. It is the sum of the average daily temperatures above 65 degrees Fahrenheit. For example, if the average temperature on Tuesday is 72, that number would go in the Cooling Degree Days.

The Heating Degree Days column reveals a significant factor in the reduction. The difference makes it clear that the current month was much warmer than last year. Higher average daily temperatures pushed the total Heating Degree Days over last year.

Gas

Some utilities provide both gas and electricity; others only provide one. In this example, I am assuming a different company provides the gas, so the bill will have a different format. The important information is still the same regardless of formatting: how much did you consume, what did it cost, and what are the extra charges?

Statement		
A Billing Period	01/18/2006 – 02/16/2006	
B Next Read	03/18/2006	
C Reading 02/16/2006	3844	
D Reading 01/18/2006	-3402	
E Gas Used (CCF)	442	
F Each CCF contains 1.014 therms	448.2 therms	
Local Distribution Service		
G Fixed		$9.50
H Volumetric ($0.19520 per therm)		$87.49
Gas Supply Service		
I Gas Supply Acquisition Service ($0.01989 per therm)		$8.87
J Natural Gas Costs ($0.73307 per therm)		$328.56
K Total Gas Charges:		$434.42
Budget Summary		
Amount Used	$434.42	
L Budget Amount Billed	-$259.00	
M Difference	$175.42	
N Previous Budget Amount	-$34.93	
O New Budget Balance	$140.49	
P **Statement Summary**		
Previous Balance 01/19/2006	$259.00	
Payment 01/26/2006	$259.00	
Beginning Amount	$259.00	
Budget Amount Billed	$259.00	

A Defines the billing period as 29 days

B When the next meter reading is scheduled

C Meter reading on billing date

D Meter reading on previous billing date

E How much gas in one hundred cubic foot units you used

F Measurement of how much heat in one hundred cubic feet

G Fixed portion of cost of gas distribution system

H Charges for gas distribution system based on usage

I A surcharge the company charges customers for purchasing and managing gas supplies

J Actual cost of gas itself based on therms

K Total for this bill

L Budget amount applied to current bill

M Difference or amount still owed to company

N Previous balance applied to current bill

O New balance

P Summary of budget billing and payments

Statement

The first part of the statement defines the billing period and details usage and charges for this statement.

(A) Defines the billing period as 29 days

(B) When the next meter reading is scheduled

(C) Meter reading on billing date

(D) Meter reading on previous billing date

(E) How much gas in one hundred cubic foot units you used

(F) Measurement of how much heat in one hundred cubic feet

(G) Fixed portion of cost of gas distribution system

(H) Charges for gas distribution system based on usage

(I) A surcharge the company charges customers for purchasing and managing gas supplies

(J) Actual cost of gas itself based on therms

(K) Total for this bill

Statement		
(A) Billing Period	01/18/2006 – 02/16/2006	
(B) Next Read	03/18/2006	
(C) Reading 02/16/2006	3844	
(D) Reading 01/18/2006	-3402	
(E) Gas Used (CCF)	442	
(F) Each CCF contains 1.014 therms	448.2 therms	
Local Distribution Service		
(G) Fixed		$9.50
(H) Volumetric ($0.19520 per therm)		$87.49
Gas Supply Service		
(I) Gas Supply Acquisition Service ($0.01989 per therm)		$8.87
(J) Natural Gas Costs ($0.73307 per therm)		$328.56
(K) Total Gas Charges:		$434.42

Fill In the Blank

The Department of Energy has a comprehensive website that covers a variety of energy-related issues. You can find answers to numerous questions at www.eia.doe.gov/.

Details

Although this bill doesn't make it clear, the statement only covers 29 days. Like any utility, meter readers get as close to a month as possible, but your next bill could be for 32 days, depending on where you fall in the schedule.

The previous month's reading and this reading give the company the numbers to compute how much gas you have used. The company measures gas in one hundred cubic foot units (CCF). However, the company sells you gas based on the energy it creates, which they measure in therms.

A therm is equal to 100,000 BTUs, or British thermal units. A BTU is the quantity of heat need to raise the temperature of 1 pound of water by 1 degree Fahrenheit. Each CCF of gas contains 1.014 therms.

Charges

Most gas bills contain two basic charges. One set of charges covers distribution costs, and the other set of charges is for the actual gas.

Distribution charges are usually broken down into two components: fixed and volumetric. Both charges relate to the costs of administering (metering and billing) as well as other costs related to providing service to local customers. The fixed charges, as the name implies, do not change. The volumetric charges apply to therms used and vary from month to month.

Gas supply service charges include the gas supply acquisition service, which covers the purchase and management of gas supplies and the storing of gas in off-peak seasons. Natural gas costs make up the biggest chunk of the costs, and the company bills on a per therm basis.

Add all of these costs together and you get your total gas charges for the month.

Budget Summary	
Amount Used	$434.42
Budget Amount Billed	-$259.00
Difference	$175.42
Previous Budget Amount	-$34.93
New Budget Balance	$140.49
Statement Summary	
Previous Balance 01/19/2006	$259.00
Payment 01/26/2006	$259.00
Beginning Amount	$259.00
Budget Amount Billed	$259.00

L Budget amount applied to current bill

M Difference or amount still owed to company

N Previous balance applied to current bill

O New balance

P Summary of budget billing and payments

Budget Summary

This section shows you how the budget plan worked for this month's bill. The total amount or amount used was $434.42, and the budget amount (for this hypothetical customer) is $259.00, leaving a remaining balance of $175.42. A credit of $34.93 carried forward. A credit results when the budget amount exceeds the monthly usage.

The credit amount reduces the remaining balance to $140.49. This amount will show up on next month's bill as a previous budget balance.

Statement Summary

The statement summary shows you paid the previous balance on 01/26/2006. A new beginning amount of the budget payment of $259.00 and the budget amount billed complete the statement.

If this customer were not on the budget payment plan, this section would record the same information but the numbers would reflect the actual bill and payment amounts rather than the fixed budget amount of $259.00.

Water and Sewer

Utilities bill water and sewer service charges together. Your utility may include them with other services such as gas or electric, or the statement may come by itself. However it arrives, it shares common items with the other utilities previously discussed: a meter reading, a charge based on usage, and additional charges for other services.

Ⓐ Period covered by statement
Ⓑ Date of bill
Ⓒ Beginning meter reading
Ⓓ Ending meter reading
Ⓔ Thousand gallons consumed
Ⓕ Billing code
Ⓖ Charges for water and sewer
Ⓗ Fee for local fire protection
Ⓘ Last month's payment
Ⓙ Current charges
Ⓚ Due date for bill

Statement Information

Ⓐ Billing period 12/20/05 to 01/21/06
Ⓑ Bill date: 01/25/06

Consumption Information

Service	Meter No.	Previous Read	Current Read	Consumed	Code	Amount
Ⓖ Water	30016	75	83	8	MG1	$13.10
Sewage Service Charge				8	SWR	$21.74
Ⓗ Public Fire Protection					FD1	$2.80
Amount Due 2/13/06						$37.84

Account Summary

Last month's total bill	$33.66
Ⓘ Payments through 01/25/06	$33.66
Previous Balance	$0.00
Ⓙ This month's charges	$37.84
Ⓚ Amount due by 02/13/06	$37.84

Statement Detail

If your water bill comes from a provider of either your gas or electricity, that company will likely format it in the same manner. This example shows another format option, although it contains all the important information you will need regardless of formatting.

Ⓐ Period covered by statement
Ⓑ Date of bill
Ⓒ Beginning meter reading
Ⓓ Ending meter reading
Ⓔ Thousand gallons consumed
Ⓕ Billing code
Ⓖ Charges for water and sewer
Ⓗ Fee for local fire protection

Statement Information

Ⓐ Billing period 12/20/05 to 01/21/06
Ⓑ Bill date: 01/25/06

Consumption Information

Service	Meter No.	Previous Read	Current Read	Consumed	Code	Amount
Ⓖ Water	30016	75	83	8	MG1	$13.10
Sewage Service Charge				8	SWR	$21.74
Ⓗ Public Fire Protection					FD1	$2.80
Amount Due 2/13/06						$37.84

Statement Information

This section sets the period for the statement—in this case, 32 days and fixes the date of the bill (01/25/06).

Consumption Information

The utility bases water and sewer charges on consumption. This bill reflects that the consumer used 8,000 gallons during the month for a charge of $13.10.

The utility bases the sewer charge of $21.74 on a usage of 8,000 gallons. Is there a meter on your sewer, too? No, what utilities do is assume that water going into your residence ends up in the sewer system one way or the other. No need to detail the ways water might find its way to the sewer, but I think you can see the logic.

In warm climates, where much more water goes on the lawn than goes into the residence, utilities make adjustments. For example, they might take a three-month reading of water usage in winter months when you are not watering the lawn. The utility uses this average usage as a year-round number to figure sewer charges.

It is not unusual to see sewer charges higher than actual water charges. Utilities struggle to keep up with growing populations and sewage systems that need constant upgrades and maintenance to meet state and federal standards.

The public fire protection charge may not appear on every water bill. Here it is a charge to maintain and build new fire hydrants and other firefighting infrastructure in the community. This fee helps ensure water availability in case of fire.

Form Alarm

Be on the lookout for sudden spikes in water usage. An underground pipe could be leaking and you might not even be aware, but you are responsible for the usage and repairs.

Account Summary	
Last month's total bill	$33.66
Payments through 01/25/06	$33.66
Previous Balance	$0.00
This month's charges	$37.84
Amount due by 02/13/06	$37.84

I Last month's payment
J Current charges
K Due date for bill

Account Summary

This portion of the statement summarizes your account with the utility. Unlike the other statements, this one shows a regular "pay as you go" account.

You paid last month's bill in full, resulting in a previous balance for this statement of $0.00. The current charges are $37.84, and that amount is due by 02/13/06.

Online Versions

I have consolidated my discussion of utility and energy company online bills into one section because most communities have only one or two providers for all of their services. The same utility that provides the electricity often provides either the water or natural gas or both. What distinguishes the online offerings seems to fall between whether the service provider is a municipally owned utility or a private company.

The municipally owned utilities often lag behind in providing comprehensive Internet-based services and information. This is especially true of the many smaller community utilities, which probably don't have the budget or staff to support such an enterprise. Larger municipal utilities offer more comparable web-based services, such as online bill paying.

Private companies that provide energy services to communities, such as natural gas, often have significant web-based services, including online bill paying, account balances, bill forecasting, bill history, and detailed consumer information on energy conservation and related topics. This is in addition to the usual customer service offerings.

Heating Oil and Propane

The vast majority of the residences in the United States use either natural gas or electricity for heat and power. However, there are other sources of energy. Utilities usually do *not* supply these other types of energy sources.

Heating Oil

Heating oil supplies energy for furnaces in colder climates, predominantly in the Northeast. Oil companies deliver their product and sell it by the gallon—not unlike filling up your car's gas tank, except it comes to you. Some co-op type of organizations offer oil at reduced prices, but most vendors are private companies that sell and service oil-burning furnaces.

Most of the vendors also offer budget plans similar to utilities and, because of the life-sustaining nature of the service, participate in low-income assistance programs for customers who need help getting through the winter.

Most oil companies leave a delivery slip with you as a statement, which simply states that they delivered *X* number of gallons on a specific date. You can pay by check, budget, or automatic debit.

Propane Gas

Propane gas is a petroleum derivative that works very much like natural gas. It is common in rural areas and is gaining acceptance in outlying suburbs not served by gas utilities or as an alternative to gas utilities. The gas is stored as a liquid in pressurized tanks, usually above ground and away from the residence.

The propane comes to the residence, just as natural gas does, through pipes. When released from pressure, propane becomes a gas.

The vendor refills the tank when needed or on a regular schedule. The statement is usually fairly straightforward with little that would differ from the previous examples.

Budget Plans

Utilities and companies providing energy products recognize that consumers don't like huge heating bills (if you live in the North) or equally huge cooling bills (if you live in the South). Budget plans address this concern.

How They Work

I live in the Upper Midwest, and my gas bill ranges from $40 in July to more than $400 in January. That makes it hard to manage our budget without a lot of cash flow juggling. The answer is the budget plan, which spreads the cost of our energy out over 12 months.

The utility looks at the history of your residence and, based on what it projects energy is going to cost, estimates your bill for the coming 12 months. It takes that number and divides it by 12. This becomes your monthly payment, regardless of your actual consumption. Some months you pay for more energy than you use, and some months you use more energy than you pay for.

Every six months, the utility reviews your account and makes adjustments if necessary. They may raise or lower your budget amount depending on your consumption to date, energy costs, and other factors. If they make an adjustment, it will stay at that level for at least another six months. You know where you are by the "Previous Budget Amount" or similar item on your monthly statement. As long as this number is negative, you have paid in more than you have used. When this number becomes positive, you are using more energy than your budget is covering.

Most budget plans require a direct debit from your bank account, although some accept a charge on a credit card for the amount.

Pitfall

As long as you remain in the residence (and keep current), the budget plan works fine. Every six months, it is examined and adjusted (or not) depending on conditions.

There can be a problem if you decide to leave while on the budget plan. If you are in one of the periods in which you have used more energy than you have paid for, you will find yourself with a bill to make up the difference.

Paper Clips

Budget plans for utility bills are not just for people who can't afford the cost or don't plan well. They make good sense for anyone who wants to do a yearly budget, because you can plan on fixed utility costs.

Chapter 6

Phone Home

In This Chapter

- ◆ Going beyond the basic land line
- ◆ Long-distance billing varieties
- ◆ Adding the Internet
- ◆ Understanding cell phone bill language

Phone bills used to be straightforward, but things are different now. You may find multiple vendors providing a variety of services all showing up on your phone bill. Don't forget your cell phone: roaming charges, over minutes, ring tones, and whatever.

Few of us could imagine living without some kind of telephone service. There is a growing trend for people to drop their traditional "land line" service and make their cell phone the only phone they use. However you choose to connect with people, you still face one or more bills each month. Despite efforts to make them easier to understand, phone bills still contain a dizzying array of options, services, and fees that are difficult to decipher. This chapter will help you make the connection.

Land Line—Statement Basics

Telephone service statements cover local service, optional services, taxes and fees, and nontelephone options. Depending on your choice of long-distance provider, the bill for that service may appear on your regular statement or the provider may bill you separately. In this example, I construct a typical residential telephone bill. It may not include all of the options you have available, but it has the major ones offered. The bill for long-distance service comes later in the chapter.

Ⓐ Defines the statement period

Ⓑ Amount owed

Ⓒ Amount paid of last bill

Ⓓ Any adjustments to previous bill

Ⓔ Any remaining balance

Ⓕ The amount you owe this month

Ⓖ Amount charged to your credit card

Ⓗ Price for bundled services

Ⓘ Price for provided Internet service

Ⓙ Total for all services

Ⓚ Name of particular service bundle

Ⓛ Caller ID service

Ⓜ Displays name on your phone

Ⓝ Alerts you to another call

Ⓞ Local phone service package

Ⓟ Name of toll service rate

Ⓠ Dialing service

Ⓡ Federally mandated charge

Ⓢ Total charges for plan and services

Ⓣ Local calls included in plan

Ⓤ Local toll calls in your area

Ⓥ Code identifies time call placed

Ⓦ How long call lasted

Ⓧ Supports local 911 service

Ⓨ Federally mandated charge

Ⓩ Total fees

ⒶⒶ Taxes on service

ⒷⒷ Price of DSL service

ⒸⒸ Discount for contract

ⒹⒹ Pass through fee from provider

ⒺⒺ Total Internet services

Account Summary

Ⓐ Billing Period	02/11/2006 – 03/10/2006
Ⓑ Previous Bill	$68.60
Ⓒ Payment	$68.60
Ⓓ Adjustments/Credits	$0.00
Ⓔ Balance	$0.00
Ⓕ Current Charges	$68.89
Ⓖ Amount to be debited to credit card on 04/02/06	$68.69

Billing Summary

Ⓗ Plans and Services	$38.75
Ⓘ Internet Services	$30.14
Ⓙ Total of Current Charges	$68.69

Plans and Services

Ⓚ **Local Economy**	$30.00
Ⓛ Caller Identification	
Ⓜ Calling Name Display	
Ⓝ Call Waiting	
Ⓞ Local Service Package	
Ⓟ Fulltime Rate	

Touchtone Service

Ⓠ Federal Access Charge	$5.06
Ⓢ Total Monthly Service	$35.06
Ⓣ Local Calls	$0.00

Ⓤ Local Toll

Date	Time	Place	Number	Ⓥ Code	Ⓦ Min	Amount
01/02/06	1039A	Anywhere NY	555-555-5555	N	1<o	$.07
01/10/06	407P	Anywhere NY	555-555-5555	D	1<p	$.07
Total Local Toll						$.14

Surcharges and Other Fees

Ⓧ 911 Emergency System	$.27
Ⓨ Federal Universal Service Fee	$.54
Ⓩ Total Surcharges and Other Fees	$.81

ⒶⒶ Taxes

Federal at 3%	$.95
State at 5%	$1.79
Total Taxes	$2.74
Total Plans and Services	**$38.75**

Internet Services

ⒷⒷ Standard DSL Package	$49.95
ⒸⒸ Service Discount	-$23.00
Sales Tax	$1.35
ⒹⒹ Pass Through Fee	$1.84
ⒺⒺ Total Internet Services	$30.14

Statement Detail

Telephone companies offer a bewildering variety of products and services these days. You can purchase them individually, but the phone companies really want you to buy packages of products and services. This example captures some of the common options offered, including DSL Internet service. However, I have not included long-distance service on this statement. I cover long-distance service in the next part of this chapter. If your local bill contains long-distance service, refer to the long-distance bill example and you will find all the same important elements.

Account Summary		
(A) Billing Period	02/11/2006 – 03/10/2006	
(B) Previous Bill		$68.60
(C) Payment		$68.60
(D) Adjustments/Credits		$0.00
(E) Balance		$0.00
(F) Current Charges		$68.89
(G) Amount to be debited to credit card on 04/02/06		$68.69
Billing Summary		
(H) Plans and Services		$38.75
(I) Internet Services		$30.14
(J) Total of Current Charges		$68.69

(A) Defines the statement period

(B) Amount owed

(C) Amount paid of last bill

(D) Any adjustments to previous bill

(E) Any remaining balance

(F) The amount you owe this month

(G) Amount charged to your credit card

(H) Price for bundled services

(I) Price for provided Internet service

(J) Total for all services

Account Summary

This portion of your statement quickly tells you the status of your account. Are you current? Were there any credits or adjustments? You can easily see whether the new charges are way out of line with the previous charges. If they are, do you know why?

This section also notes that the phone company will debit the current charges to a credit card. This payment method is very popular, especially with people who receive and pay their phone bill online. Another popular choice is to have the phone company debit your bank account for the amount of your bill, which avoids your having to write a check and you are never late with a payment as long as there is enough money in your account. If you choose to pay by check, the bill would give you a due date.

Billing Summary

The billing summary simply takes the current charges and breaks them down into two components: your current plans and services and Internet charges. If your long-distance provider bills through your local phone provider, those charges would appear as another line in this section.

Paper Clips

Phone companies offer their services in a variety of packages they claim will save you money. A typical package might include caller ID, call forwarding, call waiting, and several other options. If you want all of the services, the package will probably save you money over buying them individually. However, don't buy a package just to get a few of the services—it may be cheaper to buy them separately.

K Name of particular service bundle
L Caller ID service
M Displays name on your phone
N Alerts you to another call
O Local phone service package
P Name of toll service rate
Q Dialing service
R Federally mandated charge
S Total charges for plan and services
T Local calls included in plan
U Local toll calls in your area
V Code identifies time call placed
W How long call lasted
X Supports local 911 service
Y Federally mandated charge
Z Total fees
AA Taxes on service

Plans and Services

K **Local Economy** $30.00

L Caller Identification
M Calling Name Display
N Call Waiting
O Local Service Package
P Fulltime Rate

Q **Touchtone Service**
R Federal Access Charge $5.06
S Total Monthly Service $35.06
T Local Calls $0.00

U **Local Toll** **V** **W**

Date	Time	Place	Number	Code	Min	Amount
01/02/06	1039A	Anywhere NY	555-555-5555	N	1<o	$.07
01/10/06	407P	Anywhere NY	555-555-5555	D	1<p	$.07
Total Local Toll						$.14

Surcharges and Other Fees

X 911 Emergency System $.27
Y Federal Universal Service Fee $.54
Z Total Surcharges and Other Fees $.81

AA **Taxes**

Federal at 3% $.95
State at 5% $1.79
Total Taxes $2.74
Total Plans and Services **$38.75**

Plans and Services

Phone companies will sell you many of their services one at a time, but they prefer to sell you a package of services. They bundle and price the packages in a manner that makes them less expensive than if you buy the options individually.

Each phone company has their own set of packages for sale with different names and components. This particular bundle I call the Local Economy plan for illustration purposes. Here are the services included in this package:

- **Caller Identification.** With a properly equipped phone, you can see the number calling you when the phone rings.
- **Calling Name Display.** Adds the person listed with the phone number to caller ID on the display.
- **Call Waiting.** Alerts you to another call coming in and allows you to put current call on hold and answer incoming call.
- **Local Service Package.** Gives you unlimited local telephone calls.
- **Fulltime Rate.** Provides toll call service to surrounding areas at a reduced rate.

◆ **Touchtone Service.** Used by virtually all phones today as opposed to pulse dialing.

There is a Federal Access Charge, which you'll find on all phone bills (although it may have a different name, such as Interstate Access Charge, Federal Subscriber Line Charge, or Customer Line Charge). The Federal Communications Commission mandates this fee to hold down the cost of long-distance service. Even if you don't make long-distance calls, you still have to pay. The idea is that the fee helps provide for the nationwide long-distance network.

Your phone service may include any number of other options and services, such as voicemail, callback (*69), call blocking, and other features.

You will notice the line after the Total for Monthly Service that states Local Calls: $0.00. The reason is all local calls are included in the Local Economy Plan. This is not always the case. Some people opt to pay on a per-call basis rather than buy unlimited local calls as part of a package.

Paper Clips

If you make limited local phone calls, a pay per call plan may save you money. With these plans, your monthly charge is quite a bit less, but you pay for local calls on a per-minute basis the same as long-distance calls. Your phone company can help you determine if this will work for you.

Local Toll

Local toll calls are those made to areas in your immediate vicinity that do not fall into the long-distance category, but are outside the local calling area. Some providers consider any call made within the state a toll call; others stick with the more traditional definition.

The sample plan has a fixed price for toll calls at $0.07 per minute. The statement details the calls by date, time, number, and length. In addition, the statement codes the calls by day (D) or night/weekend (N).

Surcharges and Other Fees

The statement records several fees and surcharges that apply to all accounts. The 911 Emergency System Fee supports that service in your community. The Federal Universal Service Fee goes to help low-income and rural customers with phone service. The fee, which may also appear as the Universal Connectivity Charge, also provides discounts on telecommunications services to schools and libraries.

Taxes

What can I say? Your bill may have even more government entities with their hand in your pocket.

Total for Plan and Services

When you finally get through all the lines, you notice that the total is $38.75. However, only $30.14 represents actual services you received ($30 for the Local Economy Plan and $0.14 in toll calls). Some $8.61 goes to fees, taxes, and surcharges. In other words, more than 22% of your bill is going for something other than the service you received.

BB Price of DSL service

CC Discount for contract

DD Pass through fee from provider

EE Total Internet services

Internet Services	
BB Standard DSL Package	$49.95
CC Service Discount	-$23.00
Sales Tax	$1.35
DD Pass Through Fee	$1.84
EE Total Internet Services	$30.14

Internet Services

Phone companies are rapidly rolling our DSL (Digital Subscriber Line) service, which is high-speed Internet access. Phone companies usually partner with a technology company to offer DSL service over their telephone lines. The "always-on" connection is very popular, and prices are very competitive.

This statement reveals a common practice of pricing the service at a high monthly rate, but offering a significant discount for an annual contract. In this example, the discount is almost 50% off the list price.

You pay a sales tax and a pass through fee from the company that provides the technology to the phone company, and these round out your cost for the DSL service.

Like other services, some phone companies offer options such as a higher-speed service for more money each month. They may also offer a service contract and equipment (modem, router, and so one) rental or purchase.

Online Versions

The larger phone companies have taken great strides in moving their statements online. Their bills, for the most part, are identical to the paper versions in content, but offer richer options in terms of viewing other products and services.

Most allow and encourage online payment with credit card or automatic debit of your bank account and alert you by e-mail when they post a new statement. Many have done away with the paper statement altogether for customers who prefer to keep everything online.

The systems, for the most part, are set up as default payments. That is, unless you intervene, the company automatically debits your credit card or your bank account. That makes it doubly important that you review your charges to catch any errors before the debit occurs.

Long-Distance Service

You can buy long-distance services from a variety of vendors. You can choose your local service provider, one of the national providers (MCI for example), or you can use a third-party reseller. Just emerging is telephone service over the Internet via a broadband connection.

The plans all offer the same basic service, but differ in how they bill calls. Some plans have no fee, but a per-call charge. Other plans charge a monthly fee, but have a lower per-call charge. Still other plans offer unlimited calls (with some restrictions) for a flat fee each month. Here is a sample long-distance bill that uses a fee and per-call charge, which seems to cover the many plans.

Paper Clips

Many people are using the free long-distance calling at night and on weekends feature of their cell phones. More about that in the next section of this chapter.

Billing Summary

(A) Billing from 01/22/06 to 02/21/06	
(B) Long Distance Total	$20.19
(C) Other Products and Services Total	$0.00
(D) Total Current Charges	$20.19

Account Summary

(E) Charges Last Statement	$12.26
(F) Payment Received 01/24/06	-$12.26
Adjustments/Credits	$0.00
(G) Past Due	$0.00

Amount Due This Statement

Past Due	$0.00
(H) Total Current Charges	$20.19
(I) Total Due by 03/21/06	$20.19

(J) Itemized Calls

No.	Date	Time	Place	Number	Code	Min	Amount
1	1-23	1039A	Anywhere CA	555-555-5555	F	53.0	$3.71
2	1-25	407P	Anywhere TX	555-555-5555	F	11.0	$1.10
3	2-06	1239A	Anywhere WI	555-555-5555	F	55.0	$3.85
4	2-10	407P	Anywhere TX	555-555-5555	F	11.0	$1.26
5	2-12	1119A	Anywhere CA	555-555-5555	F	1.0	$.10
6	2-13	1000P	Anywhere TX	555-555-5555	F	1.0	$.10
7	2-14	1119A	Anywhere MA	555-555-5555	F	1.0	$.07
8	2-15	905P	Anywhere CO	555-555-5555	F	1.0	$.07
9	2-16	1019A	Anywhere CA	555-555-5555	F	1.0	$1.00
Total Itemized Calls							$11.26

Other Charges

(K) Savings Plus Plan	$4.95

Summary of Long Distance

Long Distance – Total Itemized Calls	$11.26
Long Distance – Other Charges	$4.95
(L) Regulatory and Other Charges Recovery Fee	$ .99
(M) FCC Universal Service Fee	$1.49
(N) Federal Tax	$.56
State Tax	$.94
Total	$20.19

(A) Sets the current billing period

(B) Total for long-distance service

(C) Any other products or services

(D) Total currently due

(E) Charges to account last month

(F) Amount received

(G) Any past due amount

(H) Current charges this bill

(I) Amount and date due

(J) List of calls made during statement period

(K) Name and cost of long-distance plan

(L) Fee to offset cost of complying with federal regulations

(M) Fund assists low-income people with phone service

(N) Federal and state taxes on long-distance service

Statement Details

My example shows you a statement for a typical plan with a monthly fee and a per-call fee. Other plans that simply charge a flat fee would contain many of the same elements, but may lack the itemized call list or one in such detail. Other plans that are strictly on a per-minute basis would also contain most of the same elements.

(A) Sets the current billing period

(B) Total for long-distance service

(C) Any other products or services

(D) Total currently due

(E) Charges to account last month

(F) Amount received

(G) Any past due amount

(H) Current charges this bill

(I) Amount and date due

Billing Summary	
(A) Billing from 01/22/06 to 02/21/06	
(B) Long Distance Total	$20.19
(C) Other Products and Services Total	$0.00
(D) Total Current Charges	$20.19
Account Summary	
(E) Charges Last Statement	$12.26
(F) Payment Received 01/24/06	-$12.26
Adjustments/Credits	$0.00
(G) Past Due	$0.00
Amount Due This Statement	
Past Due	$0.00
(H) Total Current Charges	$20.19
(I) Total Due by 03/21/06	$20.19

Billing Summary

The first part of the long-distance statement tells you everything in summary form. The statement defines the billing period and gets directly to the point. The Billing Summary lets you know at a glance what the current charges are and whether any additional charges are pending.

Account Summary

The account summary also quickly gives you a history of your payments. If you have a pending balance or any adjustments or credits, here's where they will show up. Any credits, such as misdials, also appear in this section.

Amount Due This Statement

There's no mistaking what this section is about. It states directly that you owe this amount. Any past due amount is included in the total.

Itemized Calls

No.	Date	Time	Place	Number	Code	Min	Amount
1	1-23	1039A	Anywhere CA	555-555-5555	F	53.0	$3.71
2	1-25	407P	Anywhere TX	555-555-5555	F	11.0	$1.10
3	2-06	1239A	Anywhere WI	555-555-5555	F	55.0	$3.85
4	2-10	407P	Anywhere TX	555-555-5555	F	11.0	$1.26
5	2-12	1119A	Anywhere CA	555-555-5555	F	1.0	$.10
6	2-13	1000P	Anywhere TX	555-555-5555	F	1.0	$.10
7	2-14	1119A	Anywhere MA	555-555-5555	F	1.0	$.07
8	2-15	905P	Anywhere CO	555-555-5555	F	1.0	$.07
9	2-16	1019A	Anywhere CA	555-555-5555	F	1.0	$1.00
Total Itemized Calls							$11.26

Other Charges

Savings Plus Plan	$4.95

Summary of Long Distance

Long Distance – Total Itemized Calls	$11.26
Long Distance – Other Charges	$4.95
Regulatory and Other Charges Recovery Fee	$.99
FCC Universal Service Fee	$1.49
Federal Tax	$.56
State Tax	$.94
Total	$20.19

J List of calls made during statement period

K Name and cost of long-distance plan

L Fee to offset cost of complying with federal regulations

M Fund assists low-income people with phone service

N Federal and state taxes on long-distance service

Itemized Calls

This section of the statement details the calls made during the billing period. Each call is recorded by date, time, place, number, code, minutes, and amount. This plan bills all of the calls at the same flat (F) rate. Other plans might designate different calling codes that might be associated with different rates. For example, some plans charge a lower rate on nights and on weekends.

You'll notice one difference that suggests not all calls are billed at the same flat rate. There are two calls to California phone numbers of one minute each that cost $0.10 and two other calls to states outside of California also for one minute, but billed only $0.07. Even flat-rate billing plans often have different rates for interstate and intrastate calls. This is part of the unwinding regulatory mess that still exists in the telecommunications industry.

Other Charges

This line on the statement is for the plan fee. In my example, I call the long-distance plan the Savings Plus Plan just for illustration. You will find plans listed under a variety of names. The monthly fee is a way the long-distance carrier subsidizes the cost of service. You pay this fee every month whether you make 5 calls or 500.

CAUTION

Form Alarm

Beware of "cheap" long distance calling plans. There is almost always a hook. For example, the "$0.99 for the first 10 minutes" plans sound great, but if you only talk a minute, it's still $0.99.

Summary of Long Distance

The final detail on the statement sums up your usage and adds in the fees and taxes. Your long-distance total and plan fee lead the way. Next is an item called the Regulatory and Other Charges Recovery Fee. This fee is something phone companies came up with to help them recover the cost of complying with federal regulations. No government or regulatory authority mandates this fee—it goes right into the phone company's pocket.

The Federal Universal Service Fee goes to help low-income and rural customers with phone service. The fee, which may also appear as the Universal Connectivity Charge, also provides discounts on telecommunications services to schools and libraries.

State and federal taxes are just what they say—you can't really ever avoid them. The total for all of this gives you what you owe for the period.

Online Version

Like the local service phone companies, long-distance carriers, at least the larger ones, offer comprehensive websites for viewing your bill. You can pay online with a credit card and set up automatic debits from your bank account for most carriers.

Smaller resellers may not offer the same level of sophistication. If online access is important, check it out before signing on with a long-distance carrier.

Cell Phone

Cell phones have gone from an expensive status symbol to a major traffic hazard almost overnight. The market is very competitive, and providers work hard to get your business. That doesn't mean everything is clear as a bell when you sign a two-year contract for service.

Billing Information

(A) Billing Period   02/24/06 – 03/23/06
(B) Invoice Date   03/24/06
(C) Previous Balance $37.50
(D) Payment on 03/22/06   -$37.50
(E) Total Current Charges $45.54
(F) Amount Due Upon Receipt $45.54

(G) **Account Summary**

Name	Monthly Service Charges	Add. Usage Charges	Other Charges	Taxes, Surcharges and Fees	Total
John Doe	$37.50	$3.25		$4.79	$45.54

Monthly Service Charges

(H) Monthly Service Plan $35.00
(I) Equipment Protection Plan $2.50
    Total $37.70

(J) **Additional Usage Charges**

Roaming Minutes
13 minutes (Off Network @ .25/ min) $3.25

Other Charges

None $0.00

Taxes, Surcharges and Fees

(K) Federal Tax $1.34
(L) Federal Universal Service Fund $1.05
(M) State Tax $1.75
(N) Federal Wireless Number Pooling and Portability $0.25
(O) Federal 911 $0.40
    Total $4.79

Usage Summary

(P) Regular Airtime Minutes   249 $0.00
(Q) Roaming Minutes Off Network   13 $3.25
    Total $3.25

(A) Sets the billing period

(B) Fixes the date of the invoice

(C) Any previous balance appears here

(D) Notes date and amount of last payment

(E) Current charges

(F) What's due upon receipt of bill

(G) Summarizes components of total charge

(H) Cost of selected service plan

(I) Insurance against lost, stolen, damaged phone

(J) Roaming minutes charged at different rate

(K) Federal tax due

(L) Fund assists low-income people with phone service

(M) State sales tax

(N) Covers cost of allowing customers to keep phone number

(O) Pays for federally mandated locating capabilities of cell phones

(P) Minutes used under plan

(Q) Roaming minutes

Statement Details

The cell phone industry is consolidating. However, a number of providers, both regional and national, still offer service. Your statement may not look like my example or it may contain some additional options, but the major components to understand what the cell phone company is offering are the same.

Ⓐ Sets the billing period

Ⓑ Fixes the date of the invoice

Ⓒ Any previous balance appears here

Ⓓ Notes date and amount of last payment

Ⓔ Current charges

Ⓕ What's due upon receipt of bill

Billing Information

Ⓐ	Billing Period	02/24/06 – 03/23/06
Ⓑ	Invoice Date	03/24/06
Ⓒ	Previous Balance	$37.50
Ⓓ	Payment on 03/22/06	-$37.50
Ⓔ	Total Current Charges	$45.54
Ⓕ	Amount Due Upon Receipt	$45.54

Paper Clips

Cell phone companies are usually unforgiving about late bills. Read your agreement carefully so you fully understand exactly when they expect your money.

Billing Information

The first part of the statement sets out the term of the bill and notes the invoice date. Last month's history is noted, including when the company received payment. If there had been a remaining balance, the statement would reflect it here. The bill sets out the current charges and notes that it expects them "due upon receipt."

Ⓖ Summarizes components of total charge

Ⓗ Cost of selected service plan

Ⓘ Insurance against lost, stolen, damaged phone

Ⓙ Roaming minutes charged at different rate

Ⓖ **Account Summary**

Name	Monthly Service Charges	Add. Usage Charges	Other Charges	Taxes, Surcharges and Fees	Total
John Doe	$37.50	$3.25		$4.79	$45.54

Monthly Service Charges

Ⓗ Monthly Service Plan	$35.00
Ⓘ Equipment Protection Plan	$2.50
Total	$37.70

Ⓙ **Additional Usage Charges**

Roaming Minutes 13 minutes (Off Network @ .25/ min)	$3.25

Other Charges

None	$0.00

Taxes, Surcharges and Fees		
K Federal Tax		$1.34
L Federal Universal Service Fund		$1.05
M State Tax		$1.75
N Federal Wireless Number Pooling and Portability		$0.25
O Federal 911		$0.40
Total		$4.79
Usage Summary		
P Regular Airtime Minutes	249	$0.00
Q Roaming Minutes Off Network	13	$3.25
Total		$3.25

K Federal tax due

L Fund assists low-income people with phone service

M State sales tax

N Covers cost of allowing customers to keep phone number

O Pays for federally mandated locating capabilities of cell phones

P Minutes used under plan

Q Roaming minutes

Account Summary

The account summary covers four main areas:

◆ Monthly service charge

◆ Additional usage charges

◆ Other charges

◆ Taxes, surcharges, and fees

Each of these four main areas contributes to the total charges for any month.

Monthly Service Charges

This is the fee you pay for your service plan. Most cell phone companies devise plans around the number of minutes you expect to use in a month. For a fee, you get a certain number of minutes to use anytime you want during peak hours, usually during the workweek from 6 a.m. to 9 p.m. Most include free long-distance and free nights and weekend calling in the plan cost.

Some plans require you to stay within a certain geographical area to use your anytime minutes; others let you use them anywhere.

In addition to the calling plan, you can also buy protection for your cell phone. The protection is an insurance policy of sorts that covers repairs and replacement should you lose your phone or have it stolen.

Additional Usage Charges

Your service plan has some defined boundaries. When you move outside those boundaries, you are "roaming," which means you are using another carrier's network and that's going to cost more. Each cell phone provider has its own schedule for how this works, but there may be two different roaming fees depending on where you are. Many cell phones tell you that you are in a roaming environment before placing a call so you won't be surprised with a nasty charge on your bill. Although anytime minutes are free, roaming minutes can run up a big charge in a hurry.

Paper Clips

Competition in the cell phone industry is intense. Free nighttime minutes start at different times for different providers and are starting earlier and earlier. When looking for a provider, check this feature if it is important to you.

Other Charges

I didn't list any on my example, but if you bought additional equipment from your carrier, here's where it would appear. Some providers might also drop penalties in this category for bad checks and such.

If you access the Internet from your cell phone, those charges will appear here as a separate item. Text messaging, which is an extremely popular feature, may carry charges that also appear here. Both of these features can run into some money depending on your plan, so make sure you understand the terms and limits before you sign up if you are a heavy user of either or both of these services.

Taxes, Surcharges, and Fees

Speaking of penalties. Here is where you once again encounter all the taxes and fees you've come to love about the telecommunications industry. The federal and state taxes are obvious, and you've seen the Federal Universal Service Fund on the previous two bills in this chapter.

What is new are the two entries titled "Federal Wireless Pooling and Portability" and the "Federal 911." The first fee supports the effort to make telephone numbers portable—so when you move, you take your phone number with you. The idea is that your number will stay with you when you physically move or change cell phone providers.

The Federal 911 fee supports the federal mandate to upgrade local 911 services to take advantage of the newer cell phones, which allow 911 operators to locate a caller in an emergency.

Usage Summary

This portion of the statement shows how you are doing on minutes. It lets you know how many of your allotted anytime minutes you used. If you go over the maximum, the cell phone company will charge you a hefty fee. This section also details roaming minutes and the charges associated with those minutes. This is the number reported under Additional Usage Charges on the account summary.

Some providers allow you to roll over minutes that you haven't used to the next month up to a certain number. If you are constantly way over or way under, you may want to change your basic plan.

Online Version

Cell phone providers, except for the small regional ones, provide comprehensive statement detail on the Internet. In fact, if your phone is equipped and you have the service, you can view your bill on your cell phone's screen. Because cell phone service providers position themselves as leading-edge companies, it makes sense that their websites are quite robust. Most of the larger companies let you order cell phone service from their website, too.

Part 2

On Borrowed Time

Sometimes the biggest problems come from the finest print. Loan statements, credit cards bills, home mortgages, and other common debt documents have their own unique way of communicating with you. When the interest rate clock is running on the money you owe, mistakes can be costly. If you understand these documents, you can spot mistakes (yes, they happen more often than you think), and you'll know how to take advantage of the best terms available on your loan payments.

Chapter 7

Cars Forever

In This Chapter

◆ Explaining car loan statements

◆ Understanding car loan interest

◆ Leasing statements

◆ Paying taxes on auto leases

For most of us, a car is the second most expensive item we'll purchase after a house. It is not uncommon to find 60-month (or longer) financing for new cars these days, so it is possible you'll be making car payments for most of your life.

If you fancy a new car sooner, lease options might fit the bill. This chapter looks at the information you'll find on automobile loan and lease statements so you can make sure you know where each dollar of your payment goes.

Automobile Loans

Even with automobile manufacturers subsidizing interest rates, cars are still expensive. If you have less-than-perfect credit, you may find your options narrowed considerably. Still, cars are remarkably easy to finance. If you stick with a reputable car dealer or financial institution, you won't get too badly soaked on interest charges and fees. The following example of an automobile loan statement assumes the loan is from a reputable lender, but the manufacturer does not subsidize the interest rate. The only thing about the statement that would change if the lender subsidized the interest rate would be lower or no interest charges in the case of a 0% loan.

A Billing period covered by this statement		
B Date the statement was mailed or posted		
C Number of payments out of the total number		
D Balance of the last statement		
E Date the payment was received		
F The amount due now		
G When the balance is due		
H The balance of the original note		
I The total amount paid to date		
J Amount that is left to pay		
K The date your note matures		

Billing Summary

A Billing period	01/14/06 – 02/14/06	
B Date of statement		01/05/06
C Payment number		10 of 48
D Previous balance		$349.89
E Payment received	12/06/05	$349.89
F Current Due		$349.89
G Due Date		01/14/06

Account Summary

H Total note	$16,794.72
I Paid to date	-$3,149.01
J Remaining balance	$13,645.71
K Maturity Date	04/14/09

Statement Terms

Automobile note statements are deceptively simple-looking; after all, there isn't that much information to report. However, as we walk through the easy stuff, I think you may be surprised at the end (unless you read your loan agreement very carefully).

A Billing period covered by this statement		
B Date the statement was mailed or posted		
C Number of payments out of the total number		
D Balance of the last statement		
E Date the payment was received		
F The amount due now		
G When the balance is due		

Billing Summary

A Billing period	01/14/06 – 02/14/06	
B Date of statement		01/05/06
C Payment number		10 of 48
D Previous balance		$349.89
E Payment received	12/06/05	$349.89
F Current Due		$349.89
G Due Date		01/14/06

Billing Summary

Like many loans, this automobile note bills for the month in advance. The statement date precedes the month covered by a week to 10 days on many notes. Not all loans are set up this way, however. When we look at the payments, the importance of dates will become clearer. The statement tells you which payment this statement represents out of the total number of statements.

The next section covers your most recent payments, including the amount due, the amount paid, and when the loan company received payment. This particular loan takes advantage of an automatic debit feature, which pays the balance out of the customer's checking account the day after the statement date.

The reason the customer is willing to allow such a prompt automatic payment is the lender gives a small discount on the interest rate.

The statement still has a due date in case the customer terminates the automatic debit and begins paying by check.

Account Summary	
(H) Total note	$16,794.72
(I) Paid to date	-$3,149.01
(J) Remaining balance	$13,645.71
(K) Maturity Date	04/14/09

(H) The balance of the original note

(I) The total amount paid to date

(J) Amount that is left to pay

(K) The date your note matures

Account Summary

The account summary appears to be a simple summary of what you owe, what you have paid, and the remaining balance. It's close, but not quite that simple. In fact, some statements don't provide this information because it causes confusion if you compare two statements. Here's the problem.

Most automobile loans calculate interest on a daily basis. This means if you have a $15,000 balance and a note with 7% interest, each day is costing you about $2.87 in interest ($0.0001917 \times 15,000$). The lender counts the days between when it receives payments to determine the interest for a particular statement period. For example, say you pay by check, and in January your check arrives on the third; in February, it arrives on the seventh. For interest purposes, the lender will count the days (34) and apply interest charges. That interest charge comes out of your payment first, and then what's left goes to the principal of the loan. If you get your check in earlier the next month, you may only have 28 days of interest and more of your payment will go toward principal.

For this reason, you don't know exactly what the remaining balance is on your loan. If you want to pay off the loan early, you have to call the lender, and they will calculate it for you.

Paper Clips

Amortization tables don't work very well with this type of loan because the interest charges are determined by when checks arrive at the lender. Your best bet is to keep the time between payments to a minimum and don't miss any payments.

Online Version

Like so many financial documents, your car loan statement is most likely available online if you've chosen a major lender. Many lenders encourage this form of communication and will stop sending you statements if you use an automatic debit to make your payment. You have to sign a statement saying it's okay for the lender to stop sending paper copies. You may get an e-mail reminder that the debit will occur in a few days, and you will have access to a secure site to view your account if you wish.

Automobile Leases

Leasing is another way to finance a new car. There are many options to consider, but for most people it comes down to whether they want a new car every three years or sooner. If that's the case, leasing usually makes more sense. If you normally drive cars longer, buying will work out best in most cases. Lease statements are usually uncomplicated, but you should know what each item covers. Unless odd charges show up, such as a change in the sales tax charged in some states, the payment should remain the same each month.

(A) Amount of current payment

(B) Date the payment is due

(C) Total amount due

(D) Number of months in lease

(E) How many months are left

(F) Date the lease matures

(G) Date and amount of last payment

(H) Monthly payment due

Account Summary		
(A) Scheduled payment	$375.25	
(B) Due Date	01/15/06	
(C) Total Due	$375.25	
(D) Lease Term	36	
(E) Months Remaining	29	
(F) Maturity Date	06/15/08	
Transactions		
Description	Amount	Total
(G) Payment Activity (Received 12/05/05)	$375.25	$375.25
(H) Current Activity Monthly Payment	$375.25	$375.25

Statement Terms

Lease statements tell their story simply and without much detail. Some leases may include a summary of the lease terms, such as maximum miles per year and so on, but many do not.

Account Summary

The account summary gets to the point and tells you what you owe and when it is due. The reason there may be two categories (current payment and total amount due) is that if you incurred any additional penalty fee or had a credit, it would be inserted between these two numbers, and the second number would be adjusted accordingly.

The next section details the term of the lease, the remaining months of the lease, and the maturity date of the lease.

Transactions

This section records the activity in the account since the last statement, including all payments and the date received. The current amount due is listed with a due date.

Paper Clips

Automatic debit of bills where interest is charged as in loans and leases is a smart move because you'll never miss a payment and most lenders will give you a break on interest.

If you set the account to automatic debit a checking or savings account on a certain date, those transactions show up in this area. You may get a small (very small) break on financing charges by letting the leaseholder debit your account.

Miscellaneous

In some states, you will pay taxes on your lease, such as excise or property taxes. Typically, the lease company, as titleholder, will receive the bill and pay it, and then forward it to you for reimbursement. You may also find situations where states charge sales tax on some leases, although this is less typical.

Another figure you might find on some lease statements is a balance for the lease. This is a confusing number that is not the sum of your lease payments, as such. The reason is a big part of your lease payment, especially the early payments, goes toward depreciation. Cars depreciate rapidly when they are new and this is part of the calculation of your lease price. If you make a $375.25 payment in the early part of the lease, your balance won't drop by that much. Many companies don't include this information because it is so confusing to consumers. Like auto loans, if you want to know the actual balance, you'll need to call the lease company for an up-to-the-minute quote.

Online Version

Like auto financing, auto leasing statements from large vendors are readily available online. If you arrange to pay them with an automatic debit program, you may not need to receive another statement unless there are other charges, such as a tax bill to pay.

> **CAUTION** **Form Alarm**
>
> Be careful of lease companies that want to sell you additional services such as life or disability insurance to cover your lease payments. If you have adequate personal insurance, you probably don't need these expensive add-ons.

Chapter 8

Home on the Range

- Principal, interest, and the escrow fund
- The annual summary of activity
- Watching interest and principal paid amounts
- Checking beginning and ending principal balances
- Tallying up the charges

Home may be where the heart is, but it's also where a big chunk of your money goes each month. Whether you live in a single family home or opt for a condominium or cooperative arrangement, there's plenty of paperwork to sort through. Mortgage statements, escrow funds, management fees, and special assessments are some of the documents that need your attention on a regular basis. If you joined the millions of homeowners who tapped the equity in their homes, you'll need to know what those home equity loan statements are all about.

By far, the largest investment most people make is in a home. You sign your name and commit to payments for the next 30 years. Yikes! Every month you send in a check. What does it cover?

Don't think that just because your lender is some giga-billion-dollar giant that it doesn't make mistakes. It happens all the time. If you know what you're looking for, mistakes won't get by you. This chapter looks at your monthly mortgage statement and the annual statement your lender sends.

Monthly Mortgage Statement

A variety of home mortgages are available from thousands of different lenders, so your mortgage statement may not look like the one I have created. For example, some lenders send a monthly statement that provides detailed information, whereas other lenders send you a book with coupons for each month's payment. My example may have more information than your statement, but it will cover all the important elements of most statements—long or short.

Ⓐ Establishes date of statement

Ⓑ Your mortgage identification number

Ⓒ Your mortgage's interest rate

Ⓓ When the note matures

Ⓔ When the payment is due

Ⓕ The amount due now

Ⓖ Transactions since the last statement

Ⓗ Escrow account pays taxes, insurance

Ⓘ Mail this in with payment

Ⓙ Note extra payment here

Ⓚ Amount of late charge and date

Ⓛ You write in amount paid

Account Information

Ⓐ	Statement Date	02/01/06
Ⓑ	Loan Number	3893898
Ⓒ	Interest Rate	5.50%
Ⓓ	Maturity Date	02/01/32
Ⓔ	Payment Due	03/01/06
Ⓕ	Amount Due	$1,654.00

Ⓖ **Transactions**   Ⓗ

Date	Description	Principal	Interest	Escrow	Fees	Total
02/01	Payment	$344	$1,097	$212		$1,654

Ⓘ **Payment Coupon**

Payment Due	03/01/06
Amount Due	$1,657.61
Ⓙ Extra Amount	$0.00
Ⓚ Late Charge	$55.42
	If received after 03/16/06

Ⓛ **Amount Enclosed**

Statement Detail

This sample mortgage statement assumes a fixed-rate, 30-year note. When other types of mortgages may show variations on the statement, I will note them.

Ⓐ Establishes date of statement

Ⓑ Your mortgage identification number

Ⓒ Your mortgage's interest rate

Ⓓ When the note matures

Ⓔ When the payment is due

Ⓕ The amount due now

Ⓖ Transactions since the last statement

Ⓗ Escrow account pays taxes, insurance

Account Information

Ⓐ	Statement Date	02/01/06
Ⓑ	Loan Number	3893898
Ⓒ	Interest Rate	5.50%
Ⓓ	Maturity Date	02/01/32
Ⓔ	Payment Due	03/01/06
Ⓕ	Amount Due	$1,654.00

Ⓖ **Transactions**   Ⓗ

Date	Description	Principal	Interest	Escrow	Fees	Total
02/01	Payment	$344	$1,097	$212		$1,654

Account Information

The top half of the statement lists details of the mortgage and states how much is due and when. In this example, I am using a fixed-rate mortgage, so the interest rate remains constant throughout the life of the note. If this were an *adjustable rate mortgage (ARM)*, there would be an additional line under the interest rate stating the next date the interest could change.

The maturity date of the note is fixed; however, you can pay off the mortgage early by making extra payments. There is a place on the payment coupon for noting extra payments. Your loan document should detail how to make additional payments to principal to pay off the note early.

Transactions

This summary shows you what the lender has recorded into your account since the last statement. In this period, you can see what part of the payment went to principal, interest, and the escrow account. This note is still young and most of the dollars are going toward interest. The escrow account accumulates throughout the year to pay property taxes and insurance premiums. An *escrow account* or fund is a holding account at a local bank where the mortgage company deposits funds to pay property taxes and insurance premiums on the house. These funds come from your monthly payment.

Payment Coupon	
Payment Due	03/01/06
Amount Due	$1,654.00
Extra Amount	$0.00
Late Charge	$55.42
	If received after 03/16/06
Amount Enclosed	

- ❶ Mail this in with payment
- ❿ Note extra payment here
- Ⓚ Amount of late charge and date
- Ⓛ You write in amount paid

Payment Coupon

The payment coupon in this example is the bottom portion of the statement that you tear off and send in with your payment. It gives you the payment due date and the amount due. There is also space, probably left blank on the actual statement, to write in any extra amount you want to include.

The coupon provides a late charge and the date when the charge applies. Late charges on mortgages vary, but they are all steep. Lenders encourage you to arrange for a automatic debit from your checking account to avoid late fees.

Mortgage Annual Statement

Every year your lender will send you an annual summary of your activity for the year. This report details your payments, the amount applied to principal and interest, the escrow account balance, and in some cases an *amortization schedule* of your note. For simplicity, I have, in most cases, rounded the amounts to whole dollars.

Financial Speak

An **amortization schedule** is a computation of the principal and interest payments over the life of a loan. It shows how the interest decreases and the principal portion increases until the payments retire the principal.

A End of year balances

B Principal balance excludes accumulated interest

C Amount paid to principal of note

D Total interest paid

E Balance in Escrow account

F Taxes due if known

G Fees owed if any

H Amortization schedule for year

I Total of all 12 payments, plus any extra payments

A **Balances as of 12/31/05**

B Principal Balance*	**C** Principal	**D** Interest	**E** Escrow Balance	**F** Taxes	**G** Other Fees
$239,799	$3,990	$13,302	$2,544		

Principal balance is not the amount needed to pay off loan in full.

H **Annual Amortization Schedule**

Date	Principal Paid	Interest Paid	Loan Balance
Jan 2005	$324	$1,117	$243,471
Feb 2005	$326	$1,115	$243,145
Mar 2005	$327	$1,114	$242,817
Apr 2005	$329	$1,112	$242,488
May 2005	$330	$1,111	$242,157
Jun 2005	$332	$1,109	$241,825
Jul 2005	$333	$1,108	$241,491
Aug 2005	$335	$1,106	$241,155
Sep 2005	$336	$1,105	$240,819
Oct 2005	$338	$1,103	$240,480
Nov 2005	$339	$1,102	$240,140
Dec 2005	$341	$1,100	$239,799
I Total payments past 12 months		$19,848	

End-of-Year Balances

The numbers in this section tell you how your payments were directed and the ending principal balance. The principal balance is the remaining principal on the note. It is not what it will take to pay off the loan, because that would include accumulated interest.

You will note that most of your loan payment went toward interest ($13,302) compared to principal ($3,990). That's because the illustration I chose was of a loan in the early years. The more years you pay on a note, the more goes toward principal and the less toward interest. On this particular note, it takes more than 17 years of payments before the principal portion exceeds the interest portion.

You must also pay into an escrow fund, which accumulates money during the year to pay property taxes and homeowner's insurance premiums. The lender sets this figure based on current tax rates and insurance coverage and spreads the cost over 12 months. Taxes and insurance premiums come out of this fund. If there is a shortfall, your house payment will go up the next year. Although a 30-year fixed mortgage payment will never increase, your actual payment probably will change as tax rates go up.

If any taxes had been paid to date, they would be noted here along with other fees, such as late charges and so on.

Amortization Schedule

This *amortization schedule* for the previous years shows how each payment breaks down between principal and interest. The remaining loan balance is in the far right column. You'll note that the principal and interest payments don't add up to the monthly payment of $1,654 ($341 + $1,100 = $1,441). The remainder on the payment is the escrow fund contribution. Your lender will provide a complete 30-year amortization schedule if you want one or there are several places on the Internet where you can generate your own, such as this one at Yahoo! (realestate.yahoo.com/re/calculators/amortization.html).

Online Version

There is not much online support for home mortgages unless your lender retains service of the mortgage. One of the main reasons is that the lender that made the loan almost certainly sold your mortgage to a third party. Many banks and financial institutions don't service the loans they generate. They make more money selling the loans to other companies that specialize in servicing mortgages.

Home, Home on the Equity

Home equity loans are very popular, but your house is on the hook, so you had better know what's on that statement. The competition for this business is fierce and, at times, unethical.

There are two basic types of loans: a straight home equity loan and a home equity line-of-credit loan. Terms and conditions are different for each, so you need to understand what you are signing up for. You don't want to mess up on this bill.

Home Equity Loans

Home *equity* loan statements, like the loans, are simple and straightforward. Some lenders use a statement with a tear-off coupon on the bottom, whereas others opt for a coupon book with minimum information, much like a mortgage loan book. Either way, my example has the important information contained on most home equity loan statements.

Financial Speak

Equity is the difference between what your house is worth and what you owe. For example, if your house is worth $150,000 and your mortgage balance is $70,000, your equity is $80,000.

(A) Regular payment

(B) Past due amount

(C) Late charges from previous statement

(D) Any other fees or charges

(E) Extra payments included

(F) Total due this statement

(G) Date payment due

(H) Late fee and past due date

(I) Amount of principal

(J) Portion of payment going to principal

(K) Portion of payment going to interest

(L) Total of payment

(M) New principal balance

Payment Information

(A)	Payment This Period	$449.41
(B)	Past Due	$0.00
(C)	Unpaid Late Charges	$0.00
(D)	Other Fees and Charges	$0.00
(E)	Extra Payment	$0.00
(F)	Total Due	$449.41
(G)	Due Date	02/15/06
(H)	Late Fee	$25.00
	If paid after 03/01/06	

Account Activity

	Date Effective	Description	Transaction Amount	Principal Balance
(I)	01/15/06	Previous balance		$48,711.95
(J)	01/15/06	Principal Payment	($165.26)	
(K)	01/15/06	Interest Payment	($284.15)	
(L)		Total payments	$449.41	
(M)		Ending Principal Balance		$48,546.69

Statement Terms

The top portion of this home equity loan statement summarizes the current charges, any past due charges, and fees owed.

Payment Information	
(A) Payment This Period	$449.41
(B) Past Due	$0.00
(C) Unpaid Late Charges	$0.00
(D) Other Fees and Charges	$0.00
(E) Extra Payment	$0.00
(F) Total Due	$449.41
(G) Due Date	02/15/06
(H) Late Fee	$25.00
	If paid after 03/01/06

(A) Regular payment

(B) Past due amount

(C) Late charges from previous statement

(D) Any other fees or charges

(E) Extra payments included

(F) Total due this statement

(G) Date payment due

(H) Late fee and past due date

Payment Information

The payment information on this home equity loan is simple and to the point. Your monthly payment is fixed, and unless you miss a payment, have a late fee, or have a bad check, there shouldn't be any other charges on the statement. You have the option of including extra money with your payment if you want to retire the loan early.

Like many mortgage loans, there is not a large window to pay the note (15 days). The late fee in this example is a flat $25. Many loans charge a percentage of the payment due as a late fee.

Account Activity			
Date Effective	Description	Transaction Amount	Principal Balance
(I) 01/15/06	Previous balance		$48,711.95
(J) 01/15/06	Principal Payment	($165.26)	
(K) 01/15/06	Interest Payment	($284.15)	
(L)	Total payments	$449.41	
(M)	Ending Principal Balance		$48,546.69

(I) Amount of principal

(J) Portion of payment going to principal

(K) Portion of payment going to interest

(L) Total of payment

(M) New principal balance

Account Activity

The account activity portion of the statement details what has happened since your last statement. Here you see how your payment was applied to principal and interest. This loan is still reasonably young, so more of your payment is going toward interest than toward principal.

The principal balance is the amount of principal remaining on your note. It is not the amount needed to pay off the loan because it does not include accumulated interest. You'll notice that the amount on this statement decreased by only the amount of your payment that went to principal payment ($165.26).

Annual Statement

The annual statement for a home equity loan is similar to a straight home mortgage. It summarizes the principal and interest paid for the year. However, there is usually no escrow account because that is tied to the primary mortgage.

Ⓐ End of year balances

Ⓑ Principal balance excludes accumulated interest

Ⓒ Amount paid to principal of note

Ⓓ Total interest paid

Ⓔ Fees owed if any

Ⓕ Amortization schedule for year

Ⓖ Total of all 9 payments, plus any extra

Ⓐ **Balances as of 12/31/05**

Ⓑ Principal Balance*	Ⓒ Principal	Ⓓ Interest	Ⓔ Fees
$48,546	$1,449	$2,587	

Principal balance is not the amount needed to pay off loan in full.

Ⓕ **Annual Amortization Schedule**

Date	Principal Paid	Interest Paid	Loan Balance
Apr 2005	$157	$291	$49,842
May 2005	$158	$290	$49,683
Jun 2005	$159	$289	$49,523
Jul 2005	$160	$288	$49,363
Aug 2005	$161	$287	$49,202
Sep 2005	$162	$287	$49,039
Oct 2005	$163	$286	$48,876
Nov 2005	$164	$285	$48,711
Dec 2005	$165	$285	$48,546

Ⓖ Total payments past 9 months $4,044

Paper Clips

Most interest on home equity loans is tax deductible, so you'll want to save this statement for your records. Check with your tax advisor to verify that the interest is tax deductible.

Balances

This summary tells you what was paid into principal and what was paid to interest for the past year. It gives you the ending principal balance, which is not the payoff number for the loan. The payoff number for the loan includes accumulated interest.

Amortization Schedule

The amortization schedule shows this loan has only been active for nine months, which accounts for why more of the monthly payment is going for interest than to principal. You can see the reduction in the principal balance by the amount paid in each month to the principal account. At the end of the statement is the total amount paid for the year.

Form Alarm

Beware of home equity loans that are set up as interest-only loans. At the end of the term, you'll owe the whole principal in a balloon payment.

Online Versions

Major lenders in the highly competitive home equity market have extensive and helpful websites where you can access your account. This is helpful if you want to see when the lender posted a payment, for example. Some offer payoff calculations and other more sophisticated services. Websites are helpful with straight home equity loans, but they are much more so with the home equity line-of-credit loans, which is discussed next.

Home Equity Line of Credit

The other type of home equity loan is a home equity line of credit, or HELOC. This is a more complex reporting arrangement because the loan is not a fixed principal, and the interest rates may vary. A HELOC is a line of credit against the equity of your home accessed by a special credit card or checks. Your monthly payment depends on how much of the credit you use.

Account Summary	
(A) Statement Date	01/15/06
(B) Approved Line of Credit	$60,000.00
(C) Credit Accessed	$8,500.00
(D) Available Credit	$51,500.00
(E) Beginning Balance	$8,539.11
(F) Payment Received 12/15/05	$39.11
(G) Current Charges	$40.42
(H) Ending Balance	$8,540.42
(I) Current Charges	$40.42
(J) Due Date	02/01/06

(K) **Transaction Summary**

Date	Number of days	Average daily balance	Finance charge	Daily rate	Annual % rate
12/15/05	30	$8,500	$39.11	.015342%	5.6%

(L) **Interest Rates**

$0.00 - $24,999.99	5.60%
$25,000 - $49,999.99	5.49%
$50,000 - $100,000.00	5.49%

(A) Date of statement
(B) Total amount you can borrow
(C) How much you have borrowed
(D) Amount of money available
(E) Balance from last statement
(F) Payment
(G) What you owe this statement
(H) Ending balance
(I) What the lender is expecting
(J) Due by this date
(K) Transactions since last statement
(L) Chart of interest rates

HELOC Statement

Although this sample statement may not look exactly like yours, it contains the important elements you need to know to understand your monthly statement.

Ⓐ Date of statement

Ⓑ Total amount you can borrow

Ⓒ How much you have borrowed

Ⓓ Amount of money available

Ⓔ Balance from last statement

Ⓕ Payment

Ⓖ What you owe this statement

Ⓗ Ending balance

Ⓘ What the lender is expecting

Ⓙ Due by this date

Account Summary

Ⓐ	Statement Date	01/15/06
Ⓑ	Approved Line of Credit	$60,000.00
Ⓒ	Credit Accessed	$8,500.00
Ⓓ	Available Credit	$51,500.00
Ⓔ	Beginning Balance	$8,539.11
Ⓕ	Payment Received 12/15/05	$39.11
Ⓖ	Current Charges	$40.42
Ⓗ	Ending Balance	$8,540.42
Ⓘ	Current Charges	$40.42
Ⓙ	Due Date	02/01/06

Account Summary

You will note immediately that this is a different type of loan than the straight home equity loan. In this example, the borrower has $60,000 available, but is only using $8,500 of credit. Some home equity lines of credit require you to use a certain minimum to keep the line open.

Another difference is this loan is not fully amortized, meaning only interest payments are currently being made on the note. Nothing is going toward the principal of the loan. Most lenders are fine with this, but at some point they'll want their principal back.

You may also note two different interest charges. Last month, the interest charge was $39.11, and this month's charge is $40.42. The difference is one day in the billing cycle. Like most loans, the lender computes interest on a daily basis, so there will be some fluctuation in interest charges on this basis.

Ⓚ Transactions since last statement

Ⓛ Chart of interest rates

Transaction Summary

Date	Number of days	Average daily balance	Finance charge	Daily rate	Annual % rate
12/15/05	30	$8,500	$39.11	.015342%	5.6%

Interest Rates

$0.00 - $24,999.99	5.60%
$25,000 - $49,999.99	5.49%
$50,000 - $100,000.00	5.49%

Transaction Summary

The transaction summary reflects activity in the account. It shows how the previous interest rate was calculated using a daily interest rate and the number of days in the billing cycle. When the number of days changes or the interest rate changes, this section will detail that information.

Interest Rates

Many lenders offer an interest-rate break depending on how much you borrow. This chart shows that the first $25,000 borrowed is charged 5.60%. Any sum borrowed over that amount is charged at 5.49%. Your statement may also contain promotional messages encouraging you to borrow more by offering special promotional rates.

Annual Statement

The annual statement for a home equity line of credit may be very simple or more complicated depending on whether you are paying off the note or simply paying interest on the loan. It will look very much like the home equity loan annual statement we have already reviewed if you are paying off the note. If you are only paying interest, the annual statement will drop the amortization schedule.

Online Version

Major lenders that offer home equity lines of credit have robust and helpful websites to assist you in managing your account. Because this is a revolving loan, you will want to stay on top of your current balances and payments. Many people find the online version of their account much more helpful than waiting for a statement every month. This is especially true if you are using a "credit card" to access your credit line. You can stay on top of your balances more easily with online access.

Moving On Up

Condominium or co-operative housing arrangements require you to agree to a monthly maintenance or homeowner's fee. Knowing what's on that statement will help you avoid a nasty surprise.

Condos and co-ops also involve working with a group of other owners. You have many of the advantages of homeownership without the responsibility of exterior maintenance in most cases. However, because you jointly own parts of the building with a group of people it is in your interest to stay involved in the unit's homeowners board. It is a good idea to keep an eye on the board or co-op's finances for your own protection.

Condominium Dwelling

Condominiums are individually owned units in a larger complex. Each owner has a nonexclusive interest in certain *common areas*. A board made up of homeowners manages the complex. Your condominium's homeowners board or whatever you call the group of owners is responsible for managing and maintaining the common areas of the building(s). Each unit of the condominium pays a monthly fee that goes to the homeowners board. Normally, the board works with a management company that actually performs the work.

Financial Speak

Common areas of a condominium or co-op include places in the building(s) available to all the residents, such as lobbies, garages, swimming pools, lawns, recreation rooms, and so on.

Ⓐ Date of notice
Ⓑ Dues for current month
Ⓒ Date due
Ⓓ Balance last statement
Ⓔ Any payments received
Ⓕ Other charges (late fees, etc.)
Ⓖ Balance due this statement

Account Summary	
Ⓐ Date	03/01/06
Ⓑ Homeowner's Dues for March	$325.00
Ⓒ Due Date	03/15/06
Ⓓ Previous Balance	$325.00
Ⓔ Payment Received	-$325.00
Ⓕ Other Charges	$0.00
Ⓖ Balance Due	$325.00

Form Alarm

Special assessments happen when something unexpected occurs, such as a water pipe bursts or there is a fire. However, if your condominium is experiencing one special assessment after another it may be a sign of poor management and certainly should be looked into for the cause.

Statement Details

This sample condominium statement probably has more information than many do. In many cases, you may just receive a note in your mailbox that the homeowner's fee or maintenance fee is due.

Account Summary

This is a simple statement that tells you how much you owe and when it is due. The second part of the statement details the previous month's transaction. If there was a late fee or any other out-of-the-ordinary charge, it would appear here.

Unless something unusual happens, your monthly fee shouldn't change more than once or twice a year, depending on how often the condominium board needs to make adjustments. If some type of emergency (a fire, for example) happens that requires extensive repairs, you might see more frequent increases. These special assessments can run into large sums of money if there is a significant problem.

Financial Statements

Your condominium board should provide you with a financial statement at some regular interval. The homeowner's agreement should spell out the details. At the very least, you will get a statement once a year. However often the board meets, make it a point to attend so you know what decisions are being made about your money. It would be difficult to create a sample financial statement that would cover the many different kinds of condominiums, so here is a list of what should you look for in the financial report:

- **Frequent assessments.** If you have to pay frequent assessments to cover maintenance costs, the board is not managing the budget well. Assuming there have been no unusual circumstances such a fire or flood, the regular monthly fee should anticipate maintenance expenses.

- **No or very low reserve fund.** One of the ways to avoid assessments is to have a reserve fund to cover the unexpected. Part of your monthly fee should go into a reserve fund for emergencies.

- **Huge reserve fund.** The opposite of no fund is a reserve fund way out of proportion to the need. In this case, you (the owners) are losing money by paying too much each month.

- **No insurance premiums.** The homeowners group should have adequate liability and hazard insurance for the property. The board needs to review this coverage on a regular basis.

- **Schedule of major repairs.** Although it may not technically be part of the financial report, there should exist a schedule of major repairs (roofs, carpeting, and so on) and a plan for how to pay for each.

- **Unexplained large changes.** Notice any item that has changed dramatically from the last reporting period. (If you are getting financial statements that don't show a previous period for comparison, demand to know why not.) Large changes in charges by the management company should be accompanied by increased services and should be voted on by the board.

Co-Op Living

Co-operative housing or co-op living arrangements span the spectrum from student housing to very exclusive and expensive New York City dwellings. Financially, they can be very inexpensive or very expensive, depending on how they are organized. In many situations, you have to be voted on by the other residents before you are allowed to join the group. Sometimes exclusive co-ops in places like New York City have terrible fights over who gets in and who doesn't.

Statement Details

Co-op residents don't own their apartment like condominium owners do. They own stock in a corporation that owns the building, which grants them lease

Financial Speak

Co-ops are cooperative housing units where the residents own and manage the complex. They range from low-cost student housing to exclusive high-rise residences.

rights to their apartment. They must pay a monthly fee that includes money for maintenance, but also must cover the mortgage on the building, taxes, utilities, and all other costs of owning and maintaining the building.

Monthly Fee

Your monthly fee covers your portion of all the corporation's costs of owning and maintaining the building. In many cases, this can be more than a condominium owner would pay for a similar-size apartment. It does not cover the cost of your apartment, which is a separate fee.

For simplicity's sake, I am assuming the co-op monthly statement would not be any more complicated than the condominium statement earlier in this chapter.

Financial Statement

Because co-op owners are stockholders, they should get a comprehensive financial statement on a regular basis—monthly would be right. This statement should include an income statement and balance sheet.

It is beyond the scope of this book to do a complete analysis of an income statement and balance sheet of a co-op corporation. However, several resources in Appendix B will help you understand these financial documents. Several areas of each warrant your attention even if you're not an expert in financial analysis.

Income Statement

The income statement details the income and expenses of the corporation. In other words, what came in, what went out, and what the board had left over. This document should show current expenses compared to a budget and to a previous period. This way you can spot troubling items easier. Here are some areas to watch:

- ◆ **Over budget.** If you notice an item that is significantly over budget there should be a good explanation. For example, if you budgeted $20,000 for utilities, but spent $30,000, you should find out the reason for the big difference. Was it bad planning or something else?

- ◆ **Taxes paid.** Make sure all taxes are current on the property. That item will show up on the income statement. Failure to pay taxes may result in losing the property.

- ◆ **Shows a loss.** If the co-op is spending more than it takes in, something needs to change in the process. Either the board must cut expenses or raise dues to get the corporation back to a positive.

- ◆ **No insurance premiums.** The co-op should have adequate liability and hazard insurance for the property. A professional assessment of coverage should be done and the board needs to review this coverage on a regular basis.

Form Alarm

Because a co-op is a corporation and you are one of the owners, you may be liable if one or more of the other owners fails to meet their financial obligations to the corporations.

◆ **Making a profit.** Many, if not most, co-ops are set up as nonprofit corporations. This doesn't mean they can't show a profit on their income
statement. It simply means the board can't distribute the money to shareholders. The "profit" goes back into the corporation for a reserve fund or
to pay off debt or some other use.

The Balance Sheet

The balance sheet gives you an idea of the co-op's financial health and its ability
to meet its obligations. Here is where you will find out whether the board has
been faithful in safeguarding the co-op's future. Here are some areas to watch:

◆ **Reserve fund.** The board should provide an adequate reserve fund for
emergency repairs. The only reason for a depleted fund is if it has just
paid out for an emergency.

◆ **Long-term debt.** Is the long-term debt on the property current? What is
the interest rate? Can (should) it be refinanced at a lower rate?

◆ **Short-term debt.** Has the board taken on any short-term debt need-
lessly? What is the status on any outstanding notes?

◆ **Assets.** Aside from the building itself, what other tangible assets does the
corporation own? Stocks? Cash? Bonds? Short of selling the building,
what could it use to pay off obligations if it had to?

◆ **Accounts receivable.** Are there folks behind in their dues/rent? If so,
how many and why? What are the co-op rules regarding delinquency?

Chapter 9

Buying an Education

In This Chapter

◆ Student loan statements as coupon books
◆ Finding the remaining balance
◆ Get an amortization schedule

It is difficult to get yourself or a child through college without a student loan considering the high cost of higher education. Because these bills follow you long after college is over, it's important to know what they are all about. (If any of that loan money went to English classes, you should know not to end a sentence with a preposition … five points off.)

Student Loans

Your student loan or loans can come from any number of sources, including private lenders, the state you live in, and federally guaranteed programs. There's a good chance you may have a mix of sources. After you get out of school, many people find that consolidating multiple loans into one note makes sense, especially if interest rates are low. Regardless of the source, loan statements and the year-end summary tend to carry the same basic information.

If you can't immediately begin repaying your student loan upon graduation, you may be eligible for a deferment. The deferment postpones the time when you must begin repaying the loan—it does not forgive the loan. You can find more information about deferment and the associated risks at the website listed in the Paper Clips about Sallie Mae.

Paper Clips

The leading provider of college loan funding is Sallie Mae (www. salliemae.com/), which started out as a quasi-government corporation but has transitioned to a completely private company. They have a tremendous website for information on college loans.

A Date statement issued

B Amount of payment

C Date payment due

D Late fee

E Amount including late fee if paid after due date

F Loan balance after this payment

G Number of this payment

Account Summary

A	Statement Date	02/01/06
B	Amount Due	$271.00
C	Due Date 02/15/06	
D	Late Fee	$13.55
E	Due if paid after 02/15/06	$284.55
F	Loan Balance	$29,110
G	Payment	71 of 240

Form Alarm

Defaulting on a student loan is a big no-no. Although enforcement has been lax in the past, it will come back to haunt you and could prevent you from getting a job in the government or qualifying for a home mortgage. Pay it off!

Statement Format

This sample college loan statement may contain much more information than the one you have. Many lenders use a booklet with tear-out coupons for each month's payment. However, the important information you need to know is on this sample.

My assumption with this statement is that you are out of college and paying off the note, which is perhaps a consolidation of several notes. The particulars are as follows:

♦ Original balance of $35,000.

♦ Interest rate is 7%.

♦ Term of the loan is 20 years.

Account Summary

The account summary clearly defines the amount due and the due date. A late fee is figured as 5% of the note payment. Lenders figure this fee using different calculations. The statement also notes the loan balance following this payment and tells you that you have made 71 of 240 payments. You can make extra payments to retire the note early without penalty. Check your loan documents for the proper way to handle extra payments.

Annual Statement

Most lenders send an annual statement summarizing activity for the previous year. This information tells you how you are progressing in terms of paying off the note. Interest on student loans is tax deductible in most cases as of this writing, so you want to note this information for your records. (Always check with competent tax advisers before making decisions concerning deductions.)

Ⓐ Balances as of 12/31/05

Ⓑ Principal Balance	Ⓒ Principal	Ⓓ Interest	Ⓔ Other Fees
$29,312	$1,154	$2,090	$0.00

Principal balance is not the amount needed to pay off loan in full.

Ⓕ Annual Amortization Schedule

Date	Principal Paid	Interest Paid	Loan Balance
Jan 2005	$93	$177	$30,378
Feb 2005	$94	$177	$30,284
Mar 2005	$94	$176	$30,189
Apr 2005	$95	$176	$30,094
May 2005	$95	$175	$29,998
Jun 2005	$96	$174	$29,902
Jul 2005	$96	$174	$29,805
Aug 2005	$97	$173	$29,707
Sep 2005	$98	$173	$29,609
Oct 2005	$98	$172	$29,511
Nov 2005	$99	$172	$29,412
Dec 2005	$99	$171	$29,312

Ⓖ *Total payments past 12 months* $3,252

Ⓐ End-of-year balances

Ⓑ Principal balance excludes accumulated interest

Ⓒ Amount paid to principal of note

Ⓓ Total interest paid

Ⓔ Fees owed, if any

Ⓕ Amortization schedule for previous year

Ⓖ Total of all 12 payments, plus any extra

Statement Details

The annual statement gives you the total principal and interest paid toward the note for the previous year. You may need this information for your tax return, so be sure to keep it. The principal balance will be close to the payoff value, but not exact because there will be accumulated interest in the account.

If you owed any late fees or other charges outstanding or during the year, they would show up under the "Other Fees" column.

The amortization schedule for the previous year lets you see how your principal and interest payments applied to the loan. Thanks to rounding of the numbers, they don't seem to change in a consistent pattern. Lenders figure the amount to the exact penny (many to the tenth of a penny), so when the numbers are rounded for reporting purposes, you get the inconsistent changes.

Online Version

Although student loans can come from a variety of vendors, a great many come from major financial institutions that provide some of the best websites for managing your account. You can update account information, track payments, change repayment options, and find many other helpful activities on these secure websites—including applying for a new loan if you are still in the education market.

Chapter 10

Personally on the Hook

In This Chapter

- Statements list the interest rate and number of payments
- Installment loans have fixed interest rates
- Revolving loans have variable interest rates
- The annual statement summarizes your account activity

You can use a personal loan for that special vacation, to furnish a new apartment, or for an emergency car repair. They aren't as common as in the past, thanks to credit cards, but are still available. However, you definitely want to know exactly what's on that statement and how it affects your repayment.

Personal Loan Statement

There are two types of personal loans: the straight installment loan and a *revolving* or *line-of-credit* loan. The installment loan is the most common and gives you a fixed interest rate and a definite payoff schedule.

Installment Loans

The statement I have created may have more information than lenders provide on statements for personal installment loans (lenders may also call them closed-end loans). There are two common types of statements: the monthly statement with a tear-off coupon on the bottom, and a booklet that has a coupon for each payment. My sample statement should cover all the important information, regardless of the format of your statement.

Financial Speak

Revolving credit is an arrangement that lets you replenish your credit line by paying off outstanding balances. A credit card is an example of revolving credit. You have a limit, and your available credit is determined by how much you borrow and pay back.

Ⓐ Date statement issued
Ⓑ Note payment
Ⓒ Date due
Ⓓ Amount of late fee
Ⓔ Balance with late fee
Ⓕ Loan balance after this payment
Ⓖ Original loan amount
Ⓗ Fixed interest rate

Ⓐ	Statement Date	02/15/06
Ⓑ	Balance Due	$81.00
Ⓒ	Payment Due	03/01/06
Ⓓ	Late Fee	$5.00
Ⓔ	Balance Due if paid after 03/01/06	$86.00
Ⓕ	Loan Balance 03/01/06	$1,756.00
Ⓖ	Original Balance	$2,500.00
Ⓗ	Interest Rate	11%

Fill In the Blank

Back in the mid-1980s, the IRS revised the tax code and eliminated tax deductions for most consumer credit costs, so interest on credit cards and personal loans is not deductible. This is why home equity (Chapter 10) loans are so popular. In most cases, interest from these loans is tax deductible.

Statement Terms

The installment loan sample I created is for a $2,500 loan for 3 years at 11% interest.

Statement Details

You will pay the same $81 for the life of the loan. Most loans have no prepayment penalty, but check the document or ask the lender for clarification.

In this example, I have the lender imposing a $5 late fee. Some lenders may set a higher flat fee or go with a percentage of the payment.

Additional information on this statement includes the loan balance after you make this payment, the original note, and the interest rate.

Annual Report

In many cases, your lender will provide you with an annual summary of activity in the account. Although the interest you pay is not tax deductible (as of this writing), you still need to know where your money is going. Unlike an annual statement on a large loan such as your mortgage, the report is simple.

Balances as of 12/31/05				A
B Principal Balance*	C Principal	D Interest	E Fees	
$1,949	$543	$186	$35	
*Principal balance is not the amount needed to pay off loan in full.				
Total of Payments for 2005		$729		

A End of year balances

B Principal balance excludes accumulated interest

C Amount paid to principal of note

D Total interest paid

E Fees owed if any

Statement Detail

The annual report gives you the remaining principal balance as of the end of the year along with the amounts paid into principal and interest on the note. Because the note is only for three years, you begin significant principal payments immediately.

The fee of $35 is an annual account maintenance fee. (Some lenders may have another name for it.) The fee may be a flat sum as in my example or a percentage. Personal loans are not very profitable for many lenders, and fees help make them more profitable.

Line of Credit

A line-of-credit personal loan lets you draw on an approved amount as you need the money using special checks. You pay a variable interest rate, but at some point you must pay off the principal and interest.

CAUTION

Form Alarm

Be careful of hidden fees and charges, such as an application fee or an early payoff fee that can run the cost of personal loans way up. Also be wary of loan officers who try to get you to borrow more money than you need. (They are probably on commission.)

Account Summary	
A Statement Date	01/15/06
B Approved Line of Credit	$10,000.00
C Credit Accessed	$2,500.00
D Available Credit	$7,500.00
E Note Term	04/01/05 - 04/01/08
F Interest Rate (v)	15%
G Beginning Balance	$2,500.00
H Current Charges	$30.82
I Ending Balance	$2,530.82
J Current Charges	$30.82
K Due Date	02/01/06

A Date of statement

B Total amount you can borrow

C How much you have borrowed

D What's left of the credit line

E Length of note

F Variable interest rate

G Balance from last statement

H What you owe this statement

I Ending balance

J What lender is expecting

K Due by this date

Statement Terms

The sample statement I created summarizes the personal line-of-credit loan. The note is for 3 years with a variable interest rate (currently at 15%) for a total

CAUTION

Form Alarm

Line-of-credit personal loans may ultimately cost as much as a credit card, and you face a fixed payoff date. Be sure to comparison shop before you decide on a credit line.

Ⓐ End of year balances

Ⓑ Principal balance excludes accumulated interest

Ⓒ Amount paid to principal of note

Ⓓ Total interest paid

Ⓔ Fees owed, if any

of $10,000. You can borrow up to that amount during the term of the note, but you must repay all interest and principal at the end of three years.

The loan statement asks for interest-only payments, which are figured on the outstanding amount ($2,500) at the current rate over three years. If the interest rate changes or the amount borrowed changes, your monthly payment will change.

Annual Report

The annual report for a line-of-credit personal loan has much the same format as an installment loan. It lists the principal balance and any payments to principal, interest payments, and fees. Interest is not tax deductible as of this writing.

Ⓐ **Balances as of 12/31/05**

Ⓑ Principal

Balance*	Ⓒ Principal	Ⓓ Interest	Ⓔ Fees
$2,500	$0	$277.35	$35

Principal balance is not the amount needed to pay off loan in full.

Total of Payments for 2005 $277.35

Statement Terms

In this statement, the principal has not been paid down because the borrower is paying interest only. By the end of the three-year term of the loan, the principal and accumulated interest will be due.

This loan also requires an annual maintenance fee for handling. It is the same as an installment loan. However, line-of-credit loans tend to carry larger balances, despite my example. Lenders make more money on larger balances and may reduce the fee or waive it under certain circumstances.

Online Version

Personal loans are low-profit businesses for most lenders. As such, you may not find much in the way of online support for the product. Major lenders that are still in this business will likely be the exception with account maintenance functions and online application and approval services.

Part 3

Got You Covered

You can pay insurance bills for years and never file a claim. However, when you need insurance, you're very glad it's there. From your car to your home to your life to your health and more, insurance is the safety net we all hope we don't need. Health insurance in particular is complicated, and the communications from insurance companies often contain errors. No one wants to spend hours each week deciphering payment forms, but if you have to argue with the insurance company, you should at least have some information to help you.

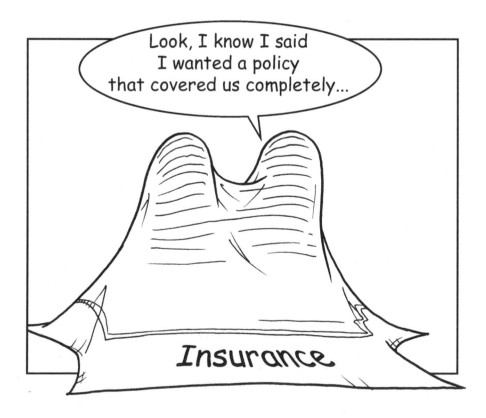

Chapter 11

Fender Benders

In This Chapter

- The automobile insurance declarations page
- Auto insurance coverage details
- Using a preferred method of payment
- Having no bills

Automobile insurance is not only smart, it's required in most states. What type of coverage you get beyond the basics is up to you. The declarations page details your coverage and what it costs. The premium statement is the actual bill. This chapter shows you examples of both.

The Declarations Page

The declarations page is the insurance company's statement of your coverage. It details coverage on your car(s) and itemizes the coverage by premium.

Ⓐ Policy period of 6 months

Ⓑ Identifies insured car

Ⓒ Sets limits on payments per person

Ⓓ Sets limits on payments per accident

Ⓔ Sets limits on payments for property damage

Ⓕ Sets medical payments limit

Ⓖ The deductible is $250 for comprehensive

Ⓗ The deductible is $1,000 for collision

Ⓘ Cost of towing, storage, etc., coverage

Ⓙ Cost of car rental insurance

Ⓚ Coverage if hit by uninsured motorist

Ⓛ Total for 6 months' premium

Ⓜ Identifies lien holder

Ⓐ **Policy Period**			**03/22/06 – 09/22/06**		
Ⓑ **Year**	**Make**	**Model**	**Body Style**	**Vehicle ID Number Class**	
2002	Saturn		4Dr	1DK884Q84093W8983	

Coverage	Premiums
Bodily Injury Liability Ⓒ Each Person Ⓓ Each Accident $250,000 $500,000	$138.03
Ⓔ Property Damage $200,000 Each Accident	
Ⓕ Medical Payments Limit Each Person $25,000	$15.91
Ⓖ $250 Deductible Comprehensive	$30.70
Ⓗ $1,000 Deductible Collision	$48.33
Ⓘ Emergency Road Service	$3.40

Ⓙ Car Rental/Travel Expenses
  Each Day   Each Occurrence
  80% $500
	$7.20

Ⓚ Uninsured Motor Vehicle
  Each Person   Each Accident
  $100,000 $300,000
	$6.33

Ⓛ Total premium for 03/22/06 – 09/22/06 This is not a bill	$255.89
Ⓜ Exceptions: Financed by First State Bank, Anywhere, USA	

Declaration Details

Note that the declarations page and the renewal notice, which comes twice a year on most policies, contain virtually the same information. In the interest of space, I present only a sample of a declarations page, but the same explanations hold true for your renewal notice. The main difference between the two documents is the declarations page is technically part of your policy, whereas the renewal notice is not.

You should also know that each state regulates personal insurance, which includes automobile insurance. This means that all 50 states have different sets of rules and guidelines for the insurance companies to follow. If my sample doesn't quite look like your declarations page or renewal notice, you can thank your state regulators.

Policy Period				03/22/06 – 09/22/06	
Year	Make	Model	Body Style	Vehicle ID Number	Class
2002	Saturn		4Dr	1DK884Q84093W8983	

Coverage	Premiums
Bodily Injury Liability	$138.03
Each Person Each Accident	
$250,000 $500,000	
Property Damage	
$200,000 Each Accident	
Medical Payments Limit	$15.91
Each Person $25,000	

Ⓐ Policy period of 6 months
Ⓑ Identifies insured car
Ⓒ Sets limits on payments per person
Ⓓ Sets limits on payments per accident
Ⓔ Sets limits on payments for property damage
Ⓕ Sets medical payments limit

To make it somewhat easier to discuss, I've arbitrarily sliced the declarations page in half. Many auto policies cover six months at a time, as this one does. The top half identifies the car covered by year, make, model (if applicable), body style, and vehicle ID number. Insurance companies also report the class code assigned to the car for rating purposes.

The coverage section lays out what the policy covers, the limits of the company's liability, and the premiums. In each case, down the declarations page, you can see what the coverage costs, which is helpful.

Injury and Property Damage

This section sets out the limits the insurance company will pay on claims against you from persons injured in a wreck. For bodily injury, they will pay up to $250,000 per person or no more than $500,000 total per accident.

Property Damage

This portion of the coverage pays for any damage you or any covered driver does to another person's property up to the limit set in the coverage ($200,000 in this case).

Medical Payments Limit

Medical payments limit coverage generally refers to money for immediate payments to persons injured in your vehicle. There is no deductible on this payment because the insurance company wants small injuries attended to quickly. These payments may also cover you if you are a passenger in another car or if a car strikes you while walking or on a bike.

Form Alarm

Some insurance experts say you do not need the medical payments coverage if you have health insurance because it duplicates coverage provided under that policy. Check with an advisor before making that decision.

G	The deductible is $250 for comprehensive	
H	The deductible is $1,000 for collision	
I	Cost of towing, storage, etc., coverage	
J	Cost of car rental insurance	
K	Coverage if hit by uninsured motorist	
L	Total for 6 months' premium	
M	Identifies lien holder	

G $250 Deductible Comprehensive $30.70

H $1,000 Deductible Collision $48.33

I Emergency Road Service $3.40

J Car Rental/Travel Expenses $7.20

    Each Day   Each Occurrence

    80% $500

K Uninsured Motor Vehicle $6.33

    Each Person   Each Accident

    $100,000 $300,000

L   Total premium for 03/22/06 – 09/22/06 $255.89

    This is not a bill.

M Exceptions: Financed by First State Bank, Anywhere, USA

Comprehensive and Collision Coverage

Comprehensive and *collision* coverage are often confused. Comprehensive is not coverage for accidents in the regular sense. It covers everything else, such as theft, flood, fire, vandalism, and so on.

Financial Speak

Comprehensive coverage is insurance that covers your vehicle for incidents other than accidents, such as theft, fire, vandalism, weather-related damage, and so on.

Collision coverage covers your vehicle in accidents involving other vehicles or stationary objects, such as trees, poles, houses, and such.

Collision is just what it says: coverage for repairing your car regardless of who was at fault. This sample policy carries a high deductible ($1,000) as a way to hold down the cost of insurance. You might want to set a high deductible and fix small "dings" without filing a claim. You'll be out of pocket in the short term, but over time you won't pay more in higher premiums.

Emergency Road Service

Policies differ on all the features covered under emergency road services, but it is essentially towing. If your car is in a wreck 50 miles from where you want it fixed, the towing charge to move it can be substantial. Some policies may cover towing over a certain distance if your car has a mechanical failure. Your policy may also pay to have your wrecked car stored for a short period while insurance claims are being processed.

Car Rental/Travel Expense

This coverage provides for a rental car and other expenses if your car is in the shop for repairs. This coverage proves especially handy if you need your car for work or if you travel frequently. Some policies pay up to policy limits for a hotel room while stranded on a trip.

Uninsured Motor Vehicle

This is insurance for the person who hits you but has no insurance to pay his share of the costs of damages to your car or injuries you suffer. Insurance is mandatory in most states, but that doesn't stop people from driving without it. If a person without insurance hits you, there's a good chance that person does not have any resources to pay for the damage caused.

Premium Summary

This summary totals the premiums for all the coverages you have for this particular car and gives you a premium total for six months of coverage. As noted earlier, policy renewals contain the same information, including this premium summary.

The difference in most states between the declarations page and the renewal notice is this sheet becomes an official part of your policy.

Exceptions

This space notes special conditions of ownership. For example, in this sample, the lien holder is listed. If you lease the car, the titleholder will be here. Most lenders and leasing companies require adequate insurance to cover their investment. Your lease or lien should contain a clause stating the amount of insurance the leaseholder or lender requires. It will also state that they are the payee for the insurance.

CAUTION **Form Alarm**

Don't assume the policy covers you for some condition or circumstance just because it seems obvious. Always check your policy or call the company or your agent to verify this. For example, if you plan to take the car out of the country (such as Mexico or Canada), find out what your policy covers before you leave. You may not be covered for international travel, so check first before you plan that road trip.

Amendments

Although there are none listed, the declarations page may come with amendments to your policy. Usually these define or redefine terms or conditions. For example, I recently received an amendment that said my insurance company was not going to pay for any damage to me or my car caused by fungi or nuclear reaction. So, I suppose if mushrooms armed with weapons of mass destruction attack, I'm out of luck.

Fill In the Blank

If you have a travel club membership, some or all of the benefits covered under Emergency Road Service and Car Rental/ Travel Expense may already be covered. Check with your insurance carrier to find out whether this is the case.

Automobile Insurance Bill

Your auto insurance bill may come every month or once every six months or something else. With so many different insurance companies and 50 different state's regulations to factor in, it's difficult to come up with the "typical" bill. However, it is likely that many of you will find the information on this sample the same, whether it comes every month or once every six months.

A Date payment due

B Balance at last statement

C Payment received

D Any remaining balance

E Amount and date due this statement

F Car covered on this policy

A	Due Date	04/22/06
B	Previous Balance	$42.65
C	Payment 03/22/06	-$42.65
D	Balance Forward	$0.00
E	Balance Due By 04/22/06	$42.65
F	Policy on Account 2002 Saturn	$42.65

Statement Detail

I've kept my sample simple for the sake of clarity. However, if you have multiple cars and other policies with the same company (even including home or rental insurance), it is likely you will receive a consolidated bill rather than a bill for each policy.

Activity Summary

The top part of the statement lets you know when the bill is due and recaps last month's activity. Usually your payment on one car will not change during the six-month cycle. However, if you have multiple policies included on the statement, it is possible that one of them may have a change so that your payment might differ from the previous month.

Current Charges

The current charges and due date complete the statement. The car covered is listed at the bottom. If you have more than one vehicle insured, this summary is a handy reminder of what each costs for insurance.

Payment Options

When it comes to paying, insurance companies usually offer several alternatives. Most companies bill you monthly, if you choose, with a tear-off section to return with your payment. However, many companies charge a monthly fee for this type of payment.

The preferred payment option is the automatic debit from your bank account for the premium amount. With this option, you get a notice at renewal (usually every six months) of any premium changes. You arrange in advance with the company for them to draft on a certain date. If you use this option, the company may not send you any monthly statements unless there is a change in the premium amount.

Actually, the third option is the one the insurance companies like the best, and that's if you pay the full six-month premium at once.

Online Version

Major insurance companies offer complete online support for their products, including automobile insurance. In addition to doing account updating (change of address and so on), many offer calculators to show you what optional coverages will cost. Many let you apply online for new coverage, although most want an agent to contact you. Many insurance companies offer more than just automobile insurance and want to sell you multiple lines of coverage. You may even get a discount for the extra business.

Chapter 12

Homeland Security

In This Chapter

- ◆ Homeowner's insurance
- ◆ Major points on the declaration page
- ◆ Paying for your homeowner's insurance
- ◆ Special coverage floaters and what they mean

Protecting your most significant investment—your home—is money well spent. Besides, you won't get a mortgage without it. However, not all coverage is equal. Here's what to look for in a policy declarations page and what special coverage floaters mean.

Types of Coverage

Homeowner's insurance covers everything from typical residences to condominiums to farms and other dwellings in between. Like automobile insurance, each of the 50 states regulates homeowner's insurance separately. Although there are basic policy types, each state and company may change details. Fortunately, the policy declarations page (also known as the policy sheet) summarizes your coverage in one convenient place.

The Policy Sheet

The policy sheet or declarations page captures your coverage in a summary form that makes it easy to see what is covered. For specific questions, you may want to refer to the policy itself or talk to the company or your agent. There are many different formats for these pages, but my example captures the important sections you'll find on most forms.

Ⓐ Insurance on the house

Ⓑ Covers outbuildings

Ⓒ Personal property replacement coverage

Ⓓ If someone is hurt on your property

Ⓔ Covers hotel and meals while out of your house for repairs

Ⓕ An additional coverage

Ⓖ Coverage over standard policy

Ⓗ Deductible is 1.5% of structure

Ⓘ Cost of policy

Section I		
Coverage of the Structure		
Ⓐ Main residence		$250,000
Ⓑ Outbuildings (garage, sheds, etc.) @ 10%		$25,000
Section II		
Ⓒ Coverage of Personal Property		
Personal property covered at 60% of structure		$150,000
Section III		
Liability Protection		
Ⓓ Protection against lawsuits (each occurrence)		$300,000
Section IV		
Additional Living Expenses		
Ⓔ Out-of-house living costs at 20% of structure		$20,000
Section V		
Ⓕ Floaters		
Home office/computers		$10,000
Section VI		
Ⓖ Level of Coverage		
Guaranteed replacement cost		
Section VII		
Ⓗ Deductible		1.5%
Ⓘ Policy Premium		$2,234.23

Financial Speak

Market value is the price at which buyers and sellers agree and a sale occurs.

Policy Sheet Overview

This undoubtedly doesn't look like your policy sheet, but it does contain the most important elements about your homeowner's insurance policy. Each company reports these in a different manner, but they still mean the same thing.

Section I—Coverage of Structure

This section details the repairing and rebuilding of your house in the event of a fire or other covered disaster. The value set on the dwelling ($250,000 in this case) does not include the property the house sits on, which is normally not insured. When you buy a house, you pay for the dwelling and the property, so the price you pay is more than the *market value* of the dwelling alone.

Your homeowner's insurance also covers any detached structures such as a garage or work shed. Most policies assign a percentage of the main structure (20% in this case) to those dwellings. If you have an outbuilding that is worth more—a pool house or guest cottage, for example—you may want to buy additional coverage.

Section II—Coverage of Personal Property

Most homeowner's policies assign a percentage of the structure value to the contents. In this example, it is 60%, or $150,000. That may seem like an adequate amount. However, you need to know about certain limits. For example, some policies cover only a fixed amount for home office equipment. If you have several computers, you may want to purchase extra coverage called a floater (see Section VII).

The other key issue is how replacement is determined. If you lose a three-year-old television in a fire, do you want a brand new TV or the cash value of a three-year-old set? The answers to these types of questions determine the level of coverage (see Section VI) and how much premium you'll pay.

Your homeowner's insurance also may cover your property off-premises. The company may insure your property up to 10% of the structure.

Section III—Liability Protection

We live in a world where no incident is too trivial to warrant a lawsuit. Someone slips and falls on your sidewalk, and you end up with a personal injury lawsuit. Homeowner's insurance policies provide some protection for you, although many people believe the standard $100,000 is way too low. You can buy extra coverage as my example shows ($300,000). Many insurance experts urge their clients to buy even more through a personal umbrella policy.

Your policy may also provide "no-fault" medical payments of up to $5,000 for minor injuries on your property. If a neighborhood child falls on your property and needs stitches in the emergency room, the parents can submit the bill to your insurance company without filing suit against you.

Section IV—Additional Living Expenses

If fire or some other disaster damages your house and you can't live in it while repairs are underway, your policy provides funds to cover hotel and living expenses while you wait. Many companies tie this benefit to about 20% of the insurance on your house. You may be able to buy more coverage from your company.

Section V—Floaters

A floater is special coverage that you purchase with your policy. They may increase existing coverage or add coverage not normally present in the policy. Typical floaters include the following:

- Home office/computers
- Jewelry, furs, and so on
- Works of art, collectibles
- Special outbuildings

Section VI—Level of Coverage

Insurance companies offer three levels of coverage for homeowners. These levels of coverage define how and at what cost the insurance company replaces or rebuilds your possessions and/or your house. As you might guess, the more coverage you buy, the higher the premium.

The first level of coverage is the actual cash value of your house or possessions minus a deduction for depreciation. For example, if you lose your three-year-old television in a fire, this level of policy pays you the value of a three-year-old television. What is the depreciated value of your house and possessions? The answer is nowhere near the replacement cost.

The second level of coverage is replacement value. This coverage pays to replace your possessions or rebuild your home without a deduction for depreciation up to the limits of your policy. This is why you need to make sure the values on your policy are correct and current.

The third level of coverage is guaranteed or extended replacement cost. Guaranteed coverage pays to replace your possessions or rebuild your house even if the costs exceed your policy limits. This could happen in times of extraordinary high construction costs due to a widespread disaster or other circumstances. This is the most expensive option, but it protects you against events you can't anticipate.

Some companies offer extended coverage instead of guaranteed coverage. Extended coverage adds an extra 20% to 25% to your coverage for extraordinary circumstances, but caps the coverage there.

Section VII—Premium and Deductible

The final section lists the deductible (1.5%) and the premium ($2,234.23) for the policy. You can choose the deductible, which comes out of your pocket before the company begins paying. A higher deductible lowers your premium.

Special Coverage

Insurance companies offer a wide variety of options to cover all types of situations and circumstances. Rather than list them all on my sample policy sheet, I highlight the more common ones you may want or find on your policy.

Inflation Guard

This feature automatically adjusts the coverage on your house to reflect the rising costs of construction in your area.

Older Dwellings

Some insurance companies will not insure older homes for replacement cost because the expense of duplicating the features of older homes is too high. In addition, if the home is in poor repair, the company doesn't want to pay to upgrade it. You can buy a modified policy that substitutes modern building materials to make sure the house meets modern codes. Insuring older homes takes some thought concerning the cost of replacement.

Building Codes

Most homeowner's policies won't pay for bringing your house up to new codes that exceeds the cost of simply replacing your home. If you live in an area where strict building code changes may affect how your house might be rebuilt or repaired, consider a special endorsement that pays extra to cover these costs. Endorsements are additions to your basic policy that cover specific needs and are usually effective upon payment of the additional premium.

Special Policies

Homeowner's insurance isn't limited to traditional single-family dwellings. Condominium, co-op, mobile home, and farm owners also need and use homeowner's insurance. Each of these situations has some unique features, but most of the policy remains the same as a standard homeowner's policy.

Condominium and Co-Op

Condominium and co-op owners usually need two separate policies. The first covers their personal possessions and liability, much like those items on a standard homeowner's policy. The second policy covers the common areas of the building, such as the roof, mechanical components, and so on. The condo/co-op board usually provides this policy. You need to know specifically what the policy covers within your unit in terms of remodeling and so on. Here are some other considerations:

- **Assessment coverage.** Reimburses you for your share of the cost to all owners if there is a covered loss, such as a fire in a common area. Owners must pay for the cost of the repair.
- **Water backup.** Covers your property if water or sewage backs up into your unit.
- **Earthquake or flood.** Homeowner's policies don't cover either of these disasters, but you can buy the coverage if you live in an area where one or both of these are probable.
- **Floaters/endorsements.** Add typical floaters and endorsements (see above) to cover special circumstances.

> **CAUTION**
>
> **Form Alarm**
>
> Be sure the agent you're dealing with understands the special needs such as assessment coverage, water back-up and such of condominium/co-op owners so that you get the insurance coverage you need.

Mobile Homes

Most mobile homes without wheels and on a permanent location qualify for homeowner's insurance in many states, with all the same features of regular dwellings. In some states, mobile homes may fall under automobile insurance policies. Check with your local agent to determine the status of mobile homes in your state.

Farms and Ranches

Farms and ranches qualify for homeowner's insurance in many states, although in some cases they fall under special policies. Some policies allow the insuring of farm equipment along with your dwelling. Insurance may be higher because fire protection might be some distance from the farm.

Homeowner's Statement

You have two different ways to pay for your homeowner's insurance. Depending on your lender, you may not have a choice but to pick the first option, which is to have them pay the premiums directly. Part of your monthly house payment goes toward the insurance premium. The second way is to pay the premium yourself. Either way, if a lender is involved, they will want proof you have purchased adequate insurance.

(A) Homeowner's policies are one-year terms

(B) Insurance on house and out-buildings

(C) Personal property coverage

(D) Liability protection

(E) Covers additional living expenses while out of your house for repairs

(F) Any extras

(G) The level of replacement costs

(H) Your deductible and premium

(I) Single payment, no charges

(J) Quarterly payment carries finance charge

(K) Monthly payment carries finance charge

Policy Statement	
(A) Policy period	12 months
Effective date	01/15/06
Expiration date	01/15/07
(B) Section I—Structure	
Main residence	$250,000
Outbuildings @10% of residence	$25,000
(C) Section II—Personal Property	
Personal property at 60% of structure	$150,000
(D) Section III—Liability Protection	
Protection against lawsuit (each occurrence)	$300,000
(E) Section IV—Additional Living Expenses	
Out-of-house living expenses @ 20% of structure	$50,000
(F) Section V—Floater/Endorsements	
Home office/computers	$10,000
(G) Section VI—Level of Coverage	
Guaranteed replacement cost	
(H) Section VII—Deductible and Premium	
Deductible as percentage of structure	1.5%
Policy premium	$2,234.23
Payment Options	
(I) Single premium due 01/10/06	$2,234.23
(J) Quarterly payments beginning 01/10/06 of	$563.56
(K) Monthly payments beginning 01/10/06 of	$192.86

Statement Details

You'll notice immediately that the statement and policy sheet contain most of the same information. This is obviously not an accident, because the policy sheet defines the coverage and the statement bills you for that same coverage. Your actual statement may come in a different format, perhaps without this much detail.

I won't go over all the areas that are identical in the policy sheet and policy statement. However, you need to understand some major additions on the policy statement.

Differences

The policy statement notes that this is an annual policy, which is typical of homeowner's policies. The dates mark the beginning and expiration of coverage. The other major difference is in the payment options.

Payment Options	
Single premium due 01/10/06	$2,234.23
Quarterly payments beginning 01/10/06 of	$563.56
Monthly payments beginning 01/10/06 of	$192.86

I Single payment, no charges

J Quarterly payment carries finance charge

K Monthly payment carries finance charge

Payment Options

Most insurance companies give you several options for when you can pay your premium, but some charges may apply. If you choose to pay a single premium at the beginning of the term, you can usually do so without any extra charges.

In my example, the insured has two other options, quarterly and monthly to pay the premium. If you are handy with math, you will quickly see that each of those options includes an extra charge for the privilege of spreading your payments out. The quarterly payment includes a $5 charge, and the monthly payment includes a $4 charge.

Where Your Money Goes

Your homeowner's premium may go one of two places. You may send it directly to the insurance company under one of the options described above. However, for many homeowners the premium is part of their monthly house payment to the mortgage company. The lender holds the money in an *escrow* account and pays the insurance company directly. The lender does this to make sure their investment is adequately insured. If insurance premiums rise, expect to see your house payment go up.

> **Financial Speak**
>
> **Escrow** is a special account where the lender deposits a portion of your monthly house payment. From this account, the lender pays property taxes and homeowner's insurance premiums.

Renter's Insurance

Renters have the same insurance needs as homeowners, but without the need to insure the physical dwelling. You still need coverage for your possession and liability protection. The statement terms are very much like those for homeowners.

A	Renter's policies are one-year terms	
B	Insurance on possessions	
C	Liability protection	
D	Covers additional living expenses while out of your apartment for repairs	
E	Any extras	
F	The level of replacement costs	
G	Your deductible and premium	
H	Single payment, no charges	

A **Policy Statement**
Policy period — 12 months
Effective date — 01/15/06
Expiration date — 01/15/07

B **Section I—Personal Property**
Personal property — $30,000

C **Section II—Liability Protection**
Protection against lawsuit (each occurrence) — $300,000

D **Section III—Additional Living Expenses**
Out-of-apartment living expenses up to — $5,000

E **Section IV—Floater/Endorsements**
Home office/computers — $10,000

F **Section V—Level of Coverage**
Replacement cost

G **Section VI—Deductible and Premium**
Deductible as percentage of structure — $500
Policy premium — $162.00

H **Payment**
Single premium due 01/10/06 — $162.00

Statement Terms

Renter's insurance is an affordable way to protect your possessions while in rental housing. The property owner's insurance will not cover any of your stuff if the apartment suffers a fire, for example.

Personal Property

One of the main differences between renter's insurance and homeowner's insurance is that the personal property is a fixed figure rather than a percentage of the dwelling value. This means you need to be thoughtful about setting the value to accurately reflect the value of your contents.

Additional Living Expenses

Renter's insurance may offer assistance if you must move out of your apartment or house for repairs after an accident. The usual coverage is the difference between what you have to pay in additional costs and your normal rent.

Level of Coverage

Most companies offer either actual cost or replacement cost with no deductible. As with homeowner's insurance, replacement is more expensive, but worth it if you have to replace a significant portion of your worldly possessions. As with homeowner's insurance, companies may cap reimbursement for individual items. If you have expensive items (jewelry, furniture, collections, etc.), be sure to check with your agent about special floaters to extend coverage for these items.

Payment Options

Renter's insurance is an annual premium. Most companies let you pay with the same options as homeowners. Of course, there is no mortgage company involved in this transaction, so the renter makes all payments directly to the insurance company.

If you have more than one policy (auto, for example) with the same company, they will probably consolidate all of your premiums on one bill and encourage you to set up an automatic bank draft program.

Special Insurance

The standard homeowner's policy does not cover earthquakes and floods. These potential disasters obviously don't imperil everyone. If you live on a mountain-top, the threat of flood is slight, so why pay for insurance? On the other hand, in many places, floods and/or earthquakes are real threats. Check your community for any requirements concerning these coverages.

Flood Insurance

The Federal Flood Insurance Program (1-800-427-4661, www.fema.gov/nfip) provides flood insurance. You can buy it from your agent. The policy provides replacement cost for your house, but not your possessions, for which you can get actual cash value. Renters can get flood insurance, too. There is a 30-day waiting period before coverage takes effect, so don't wait until the creek starts rising to call for coverage. This is coverage for a natural flood, not your pipes breaking, which would be covered under a regular homeowner's or renter's policy.

Earthquake Insurance

Some insurance companies offer earthquake insurance as an endorsement, whereas others make you buy a separate policy. In shaky California, you can get it from the California Earthquake Authority (www.cea.gov). In earthquake-prone states, expect to pay a high deductible.

Fill In the Blank
Before you buy or rent a place to live, determine whether it is in a flood plain (an area prone to flooding) or whether the area is geologically active (do they have earthquakes). This information will help you determine the quality of dwelling you need and any special insurance concerns.

Chapter 13

Life or Death

In This Chapter

♦ Your life insurance policy coverage and limits

♦ Naming a beneficiary

♦ What type of life insurance you own

♦ The limitations, if any, on your life insurance policy

You can use life insurance to accomplish a number of financial goals, but its main function is to ease or prevent a financial burden on survivors upon your death. Do you understand the coverage sheet? If not, how do you know what you are paying for on the statement? This chapter explains how to read your coverage and its various options along with the different types of insurance available.

Life Insurance

Life insurance policies come in many different varieties with a wide assortment of options and bells and whistles. It is not surprising that the selling and servicing of life insurance is a huge industry. Broadly speaking, there are two types of life insurance:

♦ Term life

♦ Whole life or permanent life

Term life insurance is a policy for which you pay fixed premiums for a certain number of years, usually 10 to 30, and then the policy ends. If you die during the term (hence the name) of the policy, your *beneficiary* (the person you name in the policy) receives the face amount of the policy. However, if you live through the term, the policy ends.

Financial Speak

The **beneficiary** is the person (or organization) you named to receive the proceeds of your life insurance policy.

Whole life insurance products typically don't have a practical "end" date like term insurance. They keep you covered as long as you pay your premiums. At some point, they become "paid up," which means you no longer need to pay into the policy to retain coverage. The other big difference between whole life and term is that whole products build cash value, which you can borrow against.

Common Features

Although it would be impossible to detail each different life insurance product in this book, they all share some common features, including the following:

- Named insured
- Named beneficiary
- Amount of coverage
- Premium
- Limitations

Term Life Insurance

Term life is the simplest and usually the cheapest insurance you can buy. The product has evolved over the years, but the basics are still the same. Here are the main points you need to understand about your term policy. You will find these on the policy sheet and possibly on the annual report.

A Date policy in force	**A** Policy Effective Date	01/15/06
B Length of policy term	**B** Term	15 years
C End date of policy	**C** Policy End Date	01/15/21
D Product type	**D** Product	Term Level
E Death benefit	**E** Benefit	$250,000
F Identifies insured	**F** Insured	John Smith, Male, 45, Nonsmoker
G Names beneficiary	**G** Beneficiary	Mary Smith, wife
H Annual premium	**H** Premium	$642
I Is policy convertible to whole life	**I** Convertible	Yes
J Exclusions or limitations to policy	**J** Exclusions	Suicide in first two years

Coverage Sheet

Term life insurance coverage sheets list the basics of your policy. For the fine details, refer to the policy itself or talk to your agent, because there are many different types of term policies.

Ⓐ	Policy Effective Date	01/15/06
Ⓑ	Product	Whole Life 65
Ⓒ	Benefit	$100,000
Ⓓ	Insured	John Smith, Male, 45, Nonsmoker
Ⓔ	Beneficiary	Mary Smith, wife
Ⓕ	Premium	$985
Ⓖ	Exclusions	Suicide in first two years

Ⓐ Date policy in force

Ⓑ Product type

Ⓒ Death benefit

Ⓓ Identifies insured

Ⓔ Names beneficiary

Ⓕ Annual premium

Ⓖ Exclusions or limitations to policy

Policy Sheet or Summary

This sample sheet or summary covers the items that will be in common with almost every type of term life insurance policy. Although the different varieties have their own particular options, you will find these basic terms describing the policy on all policy sheets.

Important Dates

The effective and end dates of the policy appear near the top on most term documents along with the term in years. Most term policies come in 1-, 5-, 15-, 20-, or 30-year terms, although you will find other terms.

Product Name and Benefit

Each company has names for their products. Some of the names are descriptive of the product (as in my example, Term Level, which indicates this is a level product, which means the benefit and premium do not change for the life of the policy). Some companies come up with snappy marketing names that tell you nothing about the product, so you may have to do some research to find out what a Modified Classic 500 policy really is.

Insured and Beneficiary

The insured (this is usually, but not always, the owner of the policy) is identified, often by their smoking or nonsmoking status. The beneficiary is also identified along with his or her relationship to the insured. For example, a man might take out a life insurance policy on himself and name his wife as beneficiary.

Premium and Convertibility

The policy sheet states the premium for the product on an annual basis. Like most insurance products, life insurance quotes are for a 12-month period. Convertible refers to whether the insurance company will let you convert the policy to a whole life product before the expiration date (of the policy, not you).

> **Fill In the Blank**
>
> One-year policies are often called annual renewal term policies because they automatically renew at the end of each year; however, the premium changes on renewal. Each year you grow older the premium increases.

Exclusions

Some policies may have exclusions to how or when they will pay a benefit. Suicide in the early part of the policy is the most common exclusion. A one- or two-year wait is the most common suicide exclusion. If you participate in a high-risk sport such as sky diving or you have a high-risk job such as test pilot, you may find that companies impose exclusions on your coverage. During this waiting period, the company will not pay a benefit if you die under certain circumstances.

Whole Life or Permanent Insurance

Whole life, also called straight, permanent, or cash value, insurance does not end as long as you keep it in force. Unlike term life, whole life builds cash value, which you can access through a loan to yourself. If you die, your beneficiary receives the face value of the policy. There are some very complicated whole life policies tied to investment products, but the death benefit portion remains much the same from the simple to the complex product.

The Product

The world of whole life insurance is very crowded and competitive. A popular product is a life policy that is "paid up" when the insured reaches his or her sixty-fifth birthday. This means that at age 65, you no longer need to make premium payments to keep the insurance in force—a good financial-planning device for people about to retire.

Fill In the Blank

Other exclusions that may or may not be included are a war exclusion and an aviation exclusion for private pilots. Soldiers who die in combat situations may be eligible for benefits from the government. Not all private insurance companies have war exclusions.

- **A** Date policy in force
- **B** Product type
- **C** Death benefit
- **D** Identifies insured
- **E** Names beneficiary
- **F** Annual premium
- **G** Exclusions or limitations to policy

A	Policy Effective Date	01/15/06
B	Product	Whole Life 65
C	Benefit	$100,000
D	Insured	John Smith, Male, 45, Nonsmoker
E	Beneficiary	Mary Smith, wife
F	Premium	$985
G	Exclusions	Suicide in first two years

Product Features

The other product features are identical in definition to the term policy. The insured and beneficiary, the premium, and the exclusions are all spelled out on the policy sheet.

Policy Statements

Life insurance companies bill policies annually unless you request a different option, which most are glad to accommodate. The statement, for the most part, contains little information beyond the policy number and the amount due. If you want to pay monthly, most companies will strongly urge you to set up an automatic withdrawal from your checking account so they can debit it each month; they may charge you a fee for this.

Online Version

Life insurance companies offer much information online, including marketing and educational resources. However, for term and simple whole life products, there is not much you can accomplish online with your account beyond change of address and so on. Some of the more complicated investment life products offer robust online access to your financial accounts for updates.

Chapter 14

To Your Health

In This Chapter

◆ Mapping out your coverage

◆ What's covered and what's not

◆ Deducing the deductible

◆ Auditing your bills

If you think health insurance is way overpriced, try paying a hospital bill without it. An overnight stay and a few tests at a hospital for our college freshman was $6,000. Of course, even if you have health insurance, you may not be able to figure out what's covered and what's not.

In this chapter, we look at the key points on your summary of benefits, which tells you what the insurance company covers and what they expect you to handle. Also we show you how to decipher those statements that show what the insurance company has paid and what you owe.

Health Insurance

Health insurance can be incredibly complicated, and dealing with the health-care system may be as stressful as many illnesses. However, given how expensive health care is, insurance is a welcome lifeboat when you need it. The sad fact is that up to 50% of the personal bankruptcies filed are due to medical bills. No matter how frustrating or expensive it is, health insurance is a basic protection millions of Americans don't have.

Types of Health Insurance

Most of us probably get health insurance through our employer in a group policy. Individual policies are essentially the same, although the coverage may be more restrictive and the cost is much higher. The health insurance market is very competitive, and numerous products vie for market share. You can begin making a distinction at a high level by separating the policies into two types: individual providers and *health maintenance organizations* (*HMOs*).

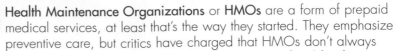

Financial Speak

Health Maintenance Organizations or **HMOs** are a form of prepaid medical services, at least that's the way they started. They emphasize preventive care, but critics have charged that HMOs don't always approve necessary but expensive treatments. Patients pay a fixed fee for most services, but must use doctors and facilities that belong to the HMO.

Individual Providers

Individual provider insurance plans allow you to see a particular doctor. The doctor may be one you pick, or you may have to choose a doctor from a list of "preferred providers." Generally, the more flexibility you have in selecting a doctor, the more expensive the insurance.

HMOs

The HMO health-care option is usually the least expensive. However, you are limited to doctors who are members of the HMO. Your choice of where you go for treatment is limited to the HMO's facilities. When you enroll, you select a primary care physician (PCP). This doctor coordinates all of your health care. If you need to see a specialist, your PCP refers you to a doctor in the HMO. See a summary of HMOs later in this chapter.

The Summary of Benefits

The summary of benefits states what the insurance covers, what it pays, and what you must pay. It describes the deductible under different circumstances and defines terms where appropriate. The following example is for a group preferred provider policy (PPO).

Ⓐ Annual deductible before most benefits are paid

Ⓑ What you pay per visit

Ⓒ Maximum you or the family pays per year out of pocket

Ⓓ Lifetime limit of coverage dollars

Ⓔ Penalty for not calling

BENEFIT	IN-NETWORK	OUT-OF-NETWORK
Who Pays What		
Ⓐ Annual Deductible	$250 Individual $500 Family	$750 Individual $1,500 Family
Ⓑ Co-Pay	$20 Routine Visit $40 Specialist Visit	$20 Routine Visit $40 Specialist Visit
Ⓒ Annual Out-of-Pocket Maximum	$1,500 Individual $3,000 Family	$4,500 Individual $9,000 Family
Ⓓ Lifetime Maximum	$2,000,000	$2,000,000
Ⓔ Pre-Certification Penalty	50% up to $1,000	50% up to $1,000

WHAT'S COVERED AT THE HOSPITAL

(F) Inpatient
Semi-private room — Covered 80% after $250 inpatient co-pay* — Covered 70% after $500 inpatient co-pay*

(G) Inpatient Mental Health — Covered 80%; 45 days per calendar year* — Covered 50%; 45 days per calendar year*

(H) Inpatient Substance Abuse and Detox 30 calendar days — Covered 80%; Detox 7 days; Rehab 30 days per calendar year — Covered 50%; Detox 7 days; Rehab 30 days per calendar year

(I) Outpatient Ambulatory surgery Pre-surgical testing — Facility: 80% covered Physician: 100% after $20/$40 co-pay — Facility: 70% covered Physician: 70% covered

(J) Emergency Room/ Facility (waived if admitted within 48 hours) — $100 co-pay

COVERAGE AT OTHER HEALTH-CARE FACILITIES

(K) Home Health Care 200 visit max. — 80% covered — 70% covered

(L) Hospice 210-day lifetime — 80% covered — 70% covered

(M) Skilled Nursing Facility 60 days per year — 80% covered — 70% covered

NORMAL MEDICAL COVERAGE

(N) Home/Office Visits — $20 co-pay: Routine $40 co-pay: Specialist — Routine not covered Nonroutine: 70%

(O) Annual Physical One per year — $20 co-pay: Routine $40 co-pay: Specialist — Not covered

(P) Well Child Care — $20 co-pay: Routine — Not covered

(Q) Well Woman Care — $20 co-pay: Routine $40 co-pay: Specialist — Not covered

(R) Immunizations — $20 co-pay: Routine $40 co-pay: Specialist — Not covered

(S) Diagnostic Screenings & Mammography — 100% Routine — Not covered

(T) Maternity — $20 co-pay first visit only, then 100% outpatient only — 70% covered

(U) Anesthesiology — 80% covered — 80% covered

(V) Lab & X-Ray — 100% Routine 80% nonroutine — 70% covered

(W) Outpatient Mental 40 visits per year — $40 co-pay — 50% covered

(X) Allergy Testing & Treatment — Testing: $20 co-pay: Routine; $40 co-pay Specialist Treatment: 100% — 70% covered

---

(F) Terms for hospital room
(G) Confined mental health treatment
(H) Confined substance abuse treatment
(I) Surgery done outpatient
(J) Emergency room coverage
(K) Health care at home
(L) Hospice coverage
(M) Skilled (with nurses) nursing home stay
(N) Visit to or from doctor
(O) Physical
(P) Preventive care for children
(Q) Preventive care for women
(R) Vaccinations
(S) Certain tests and mammograms
(T) Pregnancies
(U) Anesthesiology for surgery, etc.
(V) Lab work and x-rays
(W) Outpatient counseling
(X) Allergies

Y	Second Surgical Opinion	$20 co-pay: routine $40 co-pay: specialist	70% covered
Z	Physical Therapy 30 visits	$20 co-pay: routine $40 co-pay: specialist	70% covered
AA	Other Therapies (Occupational, Speech, vision) 60 visits	$20 co-pay: routine $40 co-pay: specialist	70% covered
BB	Infertility Testing & Treatment	Testing: 80% covered; Treatment not covered	Testing: 70% covered; Treatment not covered
CC	Durable Medical Equipment	80% covered	80% covered
DD	Ambulance	80% covered	80% covered
EE	Chiropractic Care 25 visits	$40 co-pay	70% covered

Notes: Unless stated otherwise, percent coverage is after you have met the deductible. Number of visits for a service refers to a calendar year.

Sidebar items:
- **Y** Getting a second opinion
- **Z** Physical therapy
- **AA** Speech, occupational, other therapies
- **BB** Infertility testing, but not treatment
- **CC** Durable equipment (wheelchair, for example)
- **DD** Ambulance service
- **EE** Visits to chiropractor

Your insurance policy's statement of benefits (assuming it's not an HMO) probably looks something like this. The top-of-the-line policies that don't restrict you to any particular doctor don't have the In-Network and Out-of-Network columns. Other policies may have more or fewer details, but my sample covers most of the major areas. I chose this format not because this form of health insurance is necessarily the best, but because it reveals the most categories and calls for a fuller explanation of the document.

Summary Details

Most companies divide their summary of benefits into sections. I divided this example into four sections so that we can look at like items. Those sections are as follows:

- What you pay
- What's covered at the hospital
- What's covered at other health-care facilities
- Normal medical coverage

We look at each section separately so it will be easier to digest the insurance talk. I refer to numbers only in the In-Network column to keep things simple.

BENEFIT	IN-NETWORK	OUT-OF-NETWORK
Who Pays What		
(A) Annual Deductible	$250 Individual $500 Family	$750 Individual $1,500 Family
(B) Co-Pay	$20 Routine Visit $40 Specialist Visit	$20 Routine Visit $40 Specialist Visit
(C) Annual Out-of-Pocket Maximum	$1,500 Individual $3,000 Family	$4,500 Individual $9,000 Family
(D) Lifetime Maximum	$2,000,000	$2,000,000
(E) Pre-Certification Penalty	50% up to $1,000	50% up to $1,000

(A) Annual deductible before most benefits are paid

(B) What you pay per visit

(C) Maximum you or the family pays per year out of pocket

(D) Lifetime limit of coverage dollars

(E) Penalty for not calling

The Network Concept

The first thing you notice about this plan is two schedules of benefits: one called In-Network and the other, creatively named, Out-of-Network. This particular insurance plan relies on you using physicians and facilities that are part of their network, which means they have a financial arrangement.

Some doctors, hospitals, clinics, and so on in a community are part of the network, and others aren't. You get to choose any one you want, as long as they are members of the network. If you choose to use a health-care service that is not a member of the network, you will pay a higher price and, in some cases, the insurance won't pay anything.

Who Pays What?

On the surface, it seems a simple concept: You pay the deductible first, then the insurance kicks in to pick up a percentage of the costs, and so on. However, with insurance, nothing is that simple. My example calls for a $250 individual *deductible* and a $500 family deductible. So, which is it, $250 or $500? If you're single, the answer is easy.

Financial Speak

The **deductible** is the dollar amount you pay each year up to the plan limit per individual or family. Some expenses don't apply toward the deductible, so check your policy for details. When at least two members of the family have met the family deductible, no other members need meet the individual deductible.

Many insurance companies say you have met the family deductible when at least two family members have deductible expenses that equal the family deductible. For example, if Papa Bear has deductible expenses of $200 and Mamma Bear has deductible expenses of $300, the family has met its deductible and Baby Bear doesn't have to worry about any deductible for the rest of the calendar year.

Of course, you may find your insurance company doesn't count some expenses toward your deductible, in which case you will spend more than the stated dollar amount. This is why you need to look at every piece of paper you get from the insurance company and question each item that you believe is wrong.

Out of Pocket

Even after the deductible, you are still paying some percentage of most medical costs and co-pays for office visits. Most health-care insurance caps your annual out-of-pocket expenses, so you have a limit in sight. In my example, the out-of-pocket cap per individual is $1,500 and $3,000 for the family. This deal works the same way as the deductible. When at least two family members have out-of-pocket expenses that add up to the family out-of-pocket cap, the rest of the family is at the limit.

Although this summary of benefits doesn't state it specifically, the effect of this benefit is that the insurance company pays 100% of all expenses for the rest of the calendar year, although some caveats such as limits on days of certain services still exist. You still are responsible for services with a fixed cost, however, such as office visits, emergency room services, and so on.

Lifetime Maximum

The insurance companies put in lifetime maximum benefits to protect themselves from being responsible for horrendous illnesses or injuries that require lengthy hospitalization and treatment. The lifetime limit puts an end to their obligation.

Pre-Certification Penalty

Many of the services involving hospital stays, surgery, inpatient mental-health services, substance abuse, and other longer-term care services require pre-certification from the insurance company or its representative. The phone number for pre-certification is usually on the back of your insurance card.

If you fail to get a service or hospital stay pre-certified, the insurance company may cut your benefits by 50% up to a maximum of $1,000 under this example. This is an excellent reason for you to spend some time with the summary of benefits so you completely understand your responsibilities. The insurance company won't take, "I didn't know I needed to do that," for an answer.

CAUTION

Form Alarm

Many insurance plans require you to notify them within a certain period (24–48 hours) if a doctor admits you or a covered family member to a hospital or you receive some form of emergency care. If you fail to notify the company, you could pay a stiff price.

WHAT'S COVERED AT THE HOSPITAL		
Inpatient Semi-private room	Covered 80% after $250 inpatient co-pay*	Covered 70% after $500 inpatient co-pay*
Inpatient Mental Health	Covered 80%; 45 days per calendar year*	Covered 50%; 45 days per calendar year*
Inpatient Substance Abuse and Detox 30 calendar days	Covered 80%; Detox 7 days; Rehab 30 days per calendar year	Covered 50%; Detox 7 days; Rehab 30 days per calendar year
Outpatient Ambulatory surgery Pre-surgical testing	Facility: 80% covered Physician: 100% after $20/$40 co-pay	Facility: 70% covered Physician: 70% covered
Emergency Room/ Facility (waived if admitted within 48 hours)	$100 co-pay	

F Terms for hospital room

G Confined mental-health treatment

H Confined substance-abuse treatment

I Surgery done outpatient

J Emergency room coverage

Hospital Expenses

A hospital room is the most expensive place most of us will spend the night. Whether it is for medical, mental health, or substance-abuse problems, you must pre-certify all stays under most health insurance plans. Unless it is an emergency admission, you should contact your insurance company as soon as possible.

Semi-Private Room

Most plans cover a semi-private room. If you want a private room, you have to pay the difference, which may be substantial. Notice in my example that there is a $250 co-pay. This is due even if you have met your deductible.

Inpatient Mental Health

Hospital stays for mental-health treatment have a 45-day limit for the calendar year. Note that this is coverage for the facility only and not any therapy or doctor charges. Inpatient mental-health treatment can be very expensive. Check with your insurance company before admission, if possible, to discuss all the details of what your policy covers.

Inpatient Substance Abuse

Coverage for these treatments is limited by days per calendar year. Like the mental-health coverage, this coverage doesn't include doctors or medication or therapy charges. The same caution about contacting your insurance company for details on inpatient mental-health coverage applies to inpatient substance-abuse coverage.

Outpatient Ambulatory Surgery

Thanks to advances in surgical techniques, many procedures that once required several days in the hospital can now be done in the morning and have you out that same afternoon. Obviously, insurance companies like this because it keeps costs down, which is one reason you don't see a co-pay on the facility. If something goes wrong in outpatient surgery and you have to stay, then your insurance company will need to be informed of the change in events.

K Health care at home

L Hospice coverage

M Skilled (with nurses) nursing home stay

COVERAGE AT OTHER HEALTH-CARE FACILITIES		
K Home Health Care 200 visit max.	80% covered	70% covered
L Hospice 210-day lifetime	80% covered	70% covered
M Skilled Nursing Facility 60 days per year	80% covered	70% covered

Other Health-Care Facilities

You can receive health-care services at facilities other than hospitals. In some cases, it is preferable both financially and medically to deliver these services in an alternative environment.

Home Health Care

Home health-care services are an alternative to hospital care for many people who have chronic or long-term illnesses. Health-care professionals deliver services to the patient on a regular or as-needed basis. Most plans set an annual limit for such services and pay a percentage of the costs.

Hospice

Hospice care focuses on palliative rather than curative care for patients with six months or less to live. A variety of providers, including licensed hospice organizations, can deliver the services.

Skilled Nursing Facility

Most plans cover a short amount of time at a skilled nursing facility. Skilled nursing facilities are not the same as nursing homes. They fall under particular guidelines in terms of the level of care they deliver, the qualifications of the staff, and the medical supervision.

A person might need to be in a skilled nursing facility if he or she requires 24-hour monitoring by licensed nurses who administer medications under a doctor's supervision.

CAUTION Form Alarm

Check with your insurance company before counting on them to pick up some of the expense at a skilled nursing facility. The facility must have certification from a variety of agencies.

NORMAL MEDICAL COVERAGE

N	Home/Office Visits	$20 co-pay: Routine $40 co-pay: Specialist	Routine not covered Nonroutine: 70%
O	Annual Physical One per year	$20 co-pay: Routine $40 co-pay: Specialist	Not covered
P	Well Child Care	$20 co-pay: Routine	Not covered
Q	Well Woman Care	$20 co-pay: Routine $40 co-pay: Specialist	Not covered
R	Immunizations	$20 co-pay: Routine $40 co-pay: Specialist	Not covered
S	Diagnostic Screenings & Mammography	100% Routine	Not covered
T	Maternity	$20 co-pay first visit only, then 100% outpatient only	70% covered
U	Anesthesiology	80% covered	80% covered
V	Lab & X-Ray	100% Routine 80% nonroutine	70% covered
W	Outpatient Mental 40 visits per year	$40 co-pay	50% covered
X	Allergy Testing & Treatment	Testing: $20 co-pay: Routine; $40 co-pay Specialist Treatment: 100%	70% covered
Y	Second Surgical Opinion	$20 co-pay: routine $40 co-pay: specialist	70% covered
Z	Physical Therapy 30 visits	$20 co-pay: routine $40 co-pay: specialist	70% covered
AA	Other Therapies (Occupational, Speech, vision) 60 visits	$20 co-pay: routine $40 co-pay: specialist	70% covered
BB	Infertility Testing & Treatment	Testing: 80% covered; Treatment not covered	Testing: 70% covered; Treatment not covered
CC	Durable Medical Equipment	80% covered	80% covered
DD	Ambulance	80% covered	80% covered
EE	Chiropractic Care 25 visits	$40 co-pay	70% covered

Notes: Unless stated otherwise, percent coverage is after you have met the deductible. Number of visits for a service refers to a calendar year.

N Visit to or from doctor
O Physical
P Preventive care for children
Q Preventive care for women
R Vaccinations
S Certain tests and mammograms
T Pregnancies
U Anesthesiology for surgery, etc.
V Lab work and x-rays
W Outpatient counseling
X Allergies
Y Getting a second opinion
Z Physical therapy
AA Speech, occupational, other therapies
BB Infertility testing, but not treatment
CC Durable equipment (wheelchair, for example)
DD Ambulance service
EE Visits to chiropractor

Normal Medical Coverage

This lengthy section details coverage for most of the routine medical benefits such as office visits, lab work, and so on. You will note in the Out-of-Network column that the plan doesn't cover some of the preventive care items.

Routine vs. Specialists

You will see two co-pays under many items, one for Routine and the other called Specialist. Most plans define routine providers as follows:

- General medicine
- Internal medicine
- Family practice
- Pediatrics
- OB-GYN

Other providers (a neurologist, for example) would fall in the Specialist category.

Home/Office Visits

This benefit holds on to the quaint notion that a doctor would actually come to your home for a checkup. For the rest of us, office visits fall into this category.

One item you need to check on your policy is how it treats walk-in health-care centers. These clinics see patients without appointments, and many people use them in place of a family physician. However, some policies may not treat them the same way as a trip to the family doctor. You may be stuck paying a bigger portion of the bill, which can be higher than a normal physician visit.

Fill In the Blank

How your doctor's office codes your visit may determine whether it is an annual exam or something else. Be sure to discuss your insurance coverage when making the appointment. If you're not sure, the doctor's office may be able to find out from the insurance company directly what they cover.

Annual Exam

My example allows one per year and comes with a co-pay. Other plans may pick up 100% of an exam up to a fixed amount. This item usually does not cover infants and children. The Well Child Care section makes provision for their care.

Well Child Care

Well child care begins at birth and follows the child through their teen years. Many plans set a coverage schedule of visits that provides fewer visits as the child gets older. Infants from birth to age 1 are eligible for the most visits, and then the number begins to drop.

Services typically include routine medical exams, some lab work, certain immunizations, and developmental assessment. The focus is preventive care given in a routine environment.

Well Woman Care

Most plans cover one routine annual gynecological examination.

Immunizations

Immunizations fall under the co-pay rules in most cases. However, many doctors will tell you that for older children and adults it is cheaper to go to your county health department for immunizations.

Diagnostic Screening and Mammography

Many plans define diagnostic screening tests for conditions or diseases that don't present any apparent symptoms. High cholesterol is an example of a condition or disease that doesn't present any apparent symptoms.

Your plan will specify which screenings it will pay for at what point and under what circumstances. For example, mammograms follow the recommended procedures for establishing a baseline at a certain age, then following up on a regularly scheduled basis.

Maternity

Maternity benefits vary from plan to plan, but most cover the doctor visits fairly completely. Check your policy for provisions. This is a good example of the difference between staying with a doctor in the network and choosing a doctor outside the network.

> **Fill In the Blank**
>
> Your insurance company may offer special programs for maternity care. Check your policy or the company's website.

Anesthesiology

This is one of those bills you'll get after surgery that will shock you. You probably met the anesthesiologist just before your surgery, but you may not remember his or her name. Depending on the complexity and length of your surgery, this fee may be a big one. Many plans pay only 80%, but will also negotiate a lower fee.

Lab and X-Ray

For normal lab work and x-rays, most plans pay all or most of the cost after the deductible if you have the work done within a certain period after an examination (usually 30 days). If the doctor sends you to an off-site lab for the tests, make sure it is part of the "network" or you may pay more.

Outpatient Mental Health

Insurance companies define outpatient mental-health services as counseling performed by trained therapists and counselors at their offices or other facilities. The plan caps the number of visits per year, and the plan considers the provider a specialist for co-pay purposes.

Allergy Testing and Treatment

Most insurance plans cover allergy testing and treatment in a similar manner, although not all plans cover 100% of treatment. Being allergic to your boss doesn't count under most plans.

Second Surgical Opinion

If you want a second opinion on whether a surgical procedure is necessary, you can get a second opinion from another doctor. Most insurance plans cover this like a regular office visit, although there may be some limits in your policy related to what a "normal charge" would be for this service.

Physical and Other Therapies

Physical, occupational, speech, and vision therapy all have number-of-visit limits per calendar year. The total visits include the combined numbers from in-network and out-of-network providers. Check your policy for the limits on visits per calendar year for each type of therapy. Some plans do not cover occupational therapy; you need to read your policy carefully before going.

If your doctor or mental-health professional recommends music therapy or play therapy or some other type of therapy other than those listed in your policy, check with the insurance company first. Don't assume the policy will cover a treatment just because a health-care professional recommended it.

Infertility Testing and Treatment

It is unlikely that your policy covers infertility treatment, which can run into tens of thousands of dollars very quickly. However, most plans cover infertility testing at a percentage after you meet your deductible.

Durable Medical Equipment

Durable medical equipment includes items such as wheelchairs, hospital beds you may need at home, and other equipment. Most plans cover the rental of such equipment unless it would be cheaper to buy the item.

Ambulance

Ambulance services for insurance purposes means either air or ground transportation. However, you must meet a medical-needs test, which means it truly must be an emergency or a medical necessity.

Chiropractic Care

Many insurance policies cover chiropractic care up to a limited number of visits per calendar year. In my example, chiropractors fall into the specialist's category and command a $40 co-pay. That may or may not be true for your policy.

Form Alarm

Infertility testing and treatment can be emotionally challenging as well as financially difficult. Your policy may have different conditions than the ones listed in my example. Be sure you know what to expect before you begin.

Prescription Drugs

Many health-care policies do not cover prescription drugs but handle them under a separate program. You typically do not receive a monthly bill from the program, but a card to present to the participating pharmacy. The card allows you to buy prescription drugs at a discount: one price for name-brand drugs and another lower price for generic drugs. If you are on "maintenance" medication (drugs you take every day), the plan may have you ordering those through a mail-order system. Some plans, based on the category of the drug coverage, have four different price lists. Many also offer the ability to order a three-month supply online at a further discounted rate.

Vision Plan

Likewise, many health plans do not cover normal eye exams and glasses, but have a separate vision plan. The plan allows for an eye exam at participating facilities for a fixed price and discounts on frames, lenses, and contacts. Neither the health-care plan nor the vision plan covers "laser" surgery for your eyes in most cases. Anything other than routine glasses and contacts may not be covered, so check with the policy first.

Fill In the Blank
Vision plans may or may not actually save you money. There have been times when vision centers offered sales that were better deals than the insurance I carried.

Explanation of Benefits (EOB)

If you visit a health-care professional and flash your insurance ID card, you trigger a claim process that will ultimately result in a form showing up in your mailbox. The insurance industry calls it an explanation of benefits, but that's a stretch. Figuring out what the policy is paying for and why can be an exercise in frustration. At times, logic seems to be a handicap in your efforts. However, most of the issues are clear if you know what your plan pays and how the plan discounts charges. Where trouble begins is when the insurance company denies coverage without an explanation. Then it's time to get on the phone and talk to someone at the company for some answers. Many companies have an HR person who can help or get the insurance broker involved.

Ⓐ Patient name, not name of primary insured

Ⓑ You need this number if you have a question

Ⓒ Provider information

Ⓓ Date you got treatment, etc.

Ⓔ Abbreviation of service (in this case, lab work)

Ⓕ What provider billed insurance company

Ⓖ Discount off amount billed

Ⓗ Plan doesn't cover this; you must pay

Ⓘ Deductible you must pay

Ⓙ Co-insurance you must pay

Ⓚ Co-payment you must pay

Ⓛ Amount insurance will pay

Ⓜ Charges for lab work

Ⓝ Charge for exam

Ⓞ Charge for Test

Ⓟ Totals

Ⓠ What you are responsible for

Ⓐ Patient Name: Joe Smith
Ⓑ Claim Number: 480840804
Date Claim Received: 04/15/06
Ⓒ Provider Name: Physicians Center
Provider Address: 123 Left St.
Ⓗ Anywhere, USA

Ⓓ Dates of Service	Ⓔ Service	Ⓕ Amount Charged	Ⓖ Discount Amount	Charges Not Covered	Ⓘ Deductible	Ⓙ Co-Insurance	Ⓚ Co-Payment	Ⓛ Payable by Company
Ⓜ 04/02/06	Path.	11.75	1.17	0.00	0.00	2.11	0.00	8.47
04/02/06	Path.	129.25	12.92	0.00	0.00	23.26	0.00	93.07
04/02/06	Path.	35.75	3.57	0.00	0.00	6.43	0.00	25.75
04/02/06	Path.	78.75	7.87	0.00	0.00	14.17	0.00	56.71
04/02/06	Path.	20.00	2.00	0.00	0.00	3.60	0.00	14.40
Ⓝ 04/20/06	Exam	81.90	28.85	0.00	0.00	0.00	20.00	33.05
Ⓞ 04/20/06	Med. Test	72.50	7.25	0.00	0.00	13.05	0.00	52.20
Ⓟ	Total:	$429.90	$63.63	$0.00	$0.00	$62.62	$20.00	$283.65
Ⓠ	Your total responsibility:		$82.62					

Not a Bill

It is important to understand that the explanation of benefits is not a bill. It is a form showing you what the policy has (or has not) paid the provider and what is left for you to cover. When you receive the final paperwork, you should have a bill from the provider that matches the explanation of benefits. In this case, it would show you owe the provider $82.62. It is possible that you will get a bill from the provider for the entire amount indicating they have filed a claim with your insurance company. In most cases, they will wait until the insurance company settles before expecting any money from you. However, if the company is slow in paying or there is a problem, the provider will hold you responsible for the bill.

CAUTION **Form Alarm**

If there is a problem with your claim—the health-care provider wants its money, but the insurance company doesn't want to pay for some reason—avoid damaging your credit rating. If you can, go ahead and pay the bill. If the issue is resolved in your favor, the doctor will send you a refund. Be careful doing this; sometimes it takes years to get paid on these. Many doctor offices will work with you to get paid, but if you pay them there is no incentive for them to work with you.

Statement Details

The top portion of the statement identifies the patient, assigns a claim number, and verifies the provider. Don't skip over this portion, especially if two family members have similar names (a Jr., for example). When the provider submits a claim to your insurance company, there is the possibility of an error. This can screw up your deductible and many other benefits.

	Dates of Service (D)	Service (E)	Amount Charged (F)	Discount Amount (G)	Charges Not Covered (H)	Deductible (I)	Co-Insurance (J)	Co-Payment (K)	Payable by Company (L)
(M)	04/02/06	Path.	11.75	1.17	0.00	0.00	2.11	0.00	8.47
	04/02/06	Path.	129.25	12.92	0.00	0.00	23.26	0.00	93.07
	04/02/06	Path.	35.75	3.57	0.00	0.00	6.43	0.00	25.75
	04/02/06	Path.	78.75	7.87	0.00	0.00	14.17	0.00	56.71
	04/02/06	Path.	20.00	2.00	0.00	0.00	3.60	0.00	14.40
(N)	04/20/06	Exam	81.90	28.85	0.00	0.00	0.00	20.00	33.05
(O)	04/20/06	Med. Test	72.50	7.25	0.00	0.00	13.05	0.00	52.20
(P)		Total:	$429.90	$63.63	$0.00	$0.00	$62.62	$20.00	$283.65
(Q)		Your total responsibility:		$82.62					

- **D** Date you got treatment, etc.
- **E** Abbreviation of service (in this case, lab work)
- **F** What provider billed insurance company
- **G** Discount off amount billed
- **H** Plan doesn't cover this; you must pay
- **I** Deductible you must pay
- **J** Co-insurance you must pay
- **K** Co-payment you must pay
- **L** Amount insurance will pay
- **M** Charges for lab work
- **N** Charge for exam
- **O** Charge for Test
- **P** Totals
- **Q** What you are responsible for

Charges Detail

The detail of charges is where things can get confusing. The first two columns are easy enough—they list the date of the service and an abbreviation of the service. When the provider filed the claim, it included a detailed description of the service in the form of a medical code.

The next column lists the charges for this particular service and a column listing a discount off that service follows it. For most of the items on this bill, that discount is 10%. Does that surprise you? This is part of the price of being an in-network provider.

What You Must Pay

The four columns with an asterisk (*) above them are charges you are responsible for paying. If the provider gave you services that your plan does not cover, the full cost would appear in the column titled Charges Not Covered, and you must pay those charges.

The next column is the deductible. If you have not met your deductible and any of the charges apply toward the deductible, they would appear in this column. The next column is co-insurance, which is the portion you pay after the insurance company pays their share. For example, in this explanation of benefits, the insurance company takes a 10% discount off the initial charge, and then pays 80% of the remainder. What's left is the co-insurance you must pay.

Fill In the Blank

People without insurance lose more than one way. Not only do they have to pay the whole amount, they also have no one negotiating a discount for them.

The co-payment is a straight $20 per office visit per your policy. In this case, the original charge was $81.90, and the company discounted it by $28.85. Regardless of how that math works, you still only pay your $20 co-pay, and the insurance company owes the balance. At the bottom of the columns is a balance that is your total responsibility. Many have signed contracts with doctors that state they will pay $XX.XX for X procedure.

What the Insurance Company Must Pay (Kind Of)

The last column seems to indicate the balances the insurance company will pay. At the bottom of the column is a total of $283.65 of all the charges. Most statements carry a footnote indicating that the actual amount may be a negotiated amount. You can translate that to mean that the provider is probably going to get less than the amount that shows up on the explanation of benefits.

Health Maintenance Organizations (HMOs)

HMOs have come a long way since their beginnings many years ago. Today, most HMOs work on the primary care physician (PCP) concept. You pick a doctor off their list for your PCP, and that doctor coordinates all of your health-care needs. Each member of your family can have a different PCP to meet his or her individual needs. If you need a specialist, your PCP will refer you to one in the HMO. If you need to go to the hospital, your PCP will send you to one in the HMO.

The Benefits

There are definite benefits to the HMO system for many people. For one thing, you don't have to find several different specialists if you need those services—the PCP will provide them for you. You can also change your PCP if it's not working out or you move.

The Drawbacks

When you join an HMO, you join a network of specialists, hospitals, and other facilities, whether you like them all or not. The HMOs are rigid on this point. If you decide to use a doctor or hospital that is not part of the HMO, they may not pay anything.

The Financial Benefits

The costs of being in an HMO may not be a whole lot cheaper than regular insurance programs, but many people find the hassle factor far lower. A typical plan's summary of benefits will list many of the same items as my example above, but instead of percentages covered by the insurance company, an HMO has flat co-pays for everything. For example:

- **Office visit.** $25 co-pay
- **Inpatient hospital services.** $100 co-pay per day (up to $500 maximum)

- ◆ **Lab & x-ray.** Covered 100%, no co-pay
- ◆ **Same-day surgery.** $200 co-pay

The other big benefit is there are no forms, no claims to file, and, other than your co-pay, no bills.

Dental Plans

Dental insurance is notoriously expensive relative to what it covers—at least that's my opinion. It works the same basic way as health insurance with some plans. There is a co-pay, deductible, and co-insurance. However, one of the big differences is many dental plans have an annual benefit cap ($1,200, for example). This means that's all they are going to pay in a calendar-year period.

How It Works

A dental plan's summary of benefits looks very much like a health insurance plan's summary. Depending on the plan, there may be in-network and out-of-network providers. Other plans are less restrictive about the dentist you use, but always check your policy to see whether you must choose from an approved list.

Because dental plans cover only a narrow area of health care, their summary of benefits tends to be very specific and full of dental language (Gingival Curettage, for example). The plan may cover certain services and procedures by 50%, whereas others by 80%.

What to Do

The best course of action if you need significant (or even a little) dental work is to visit a dentist approved by your insurance. Based on their exam, most dentists can work up an estimate for what you need done. They can submit this to the insurance company and get back a report that details what the company will pay and what you will have to cover.

The Big Qualifier

The insurance plans and coverage discussed in this chapter may or may not look like your plan. What I have presented is for illustration only, and you should not construe it as definitive insurance counseling. The health insurance market is dynamic and highly competitive. Many plans offer features I have not touched on. The purpose of this chapter is to give you some basic understanding of how to read a summary of benefits and understand an explanation of benefits. When you get a grip on these two examples, the documents that come with your insurance will be easier to understand even if they don't look like my examples.

> **Fill In the Blank**
>
> Dental care is among the most successful health-care treatments in terms of reducing dental problems in the overall population. Good dental health is a factor in your overall health. However, it is still possible to run up a big bill in a hurry if you need special care.

Making the Best

In This Chapter

- ◆ Long-term care insurance policy sheet
- ◆ Reading your statement
- ◆ Disability insurance policy sheet
- ◆ Explanation of benefits

For many people, the thought of going into a nursing home or being permanently disabled is more frightening than just about any other crisis they might face. Insurance that provides some relief when you or a loved one needs long-term care or faces a disability can be expensive and difficult to understand. Here are some tips on identifying the key areas of each policy and statement.

Long-Term Care Insurance

Long-term care insurance helps you cover the cost of providing care for yourself or a loved one if you are unable to perform some of the normal activities of daily living. This insurance provides a cash benefit to pay for nursing home expenses or help in your own home.

Types of Policies

The long-term care insurance industry is highly competitive and not without its critics. Consumer groups complain about the high cost and difficulty of securing the benefits of some policies. However, there are many well-known and reputable companies in the business with excellent financial stability.

You can buy this insurance as part of a group policy through some employers or as an individual. As with most insurance, the group policy will be cheaper, but may end when you leave the company or retire, which may be just the time you need the coverage.

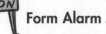

Financial Speak

Long-term care is day-to-day care that you receive in a nursing home, adult daycare facility, or your home following an illness or injury, or in old age.

Benefits

Most policies pay a cash benefit after you have met certain conditions. The benefit may continue for life or be fixed for a certain number of years. The amount of the benefit, which the insurance company pays monthly, may rise by a predetermined amount or by a factor such as the inflation rate.

Summary of Benefits

Because there are so many different plans, the example I have constructed touches on the major benefits found on most policies. You should refer to your policy for specific instructions on when you are eligible to begin receiving the benefit.

Ⓐ Date of policy issue

Ⓑ How long the policy pays benefits

Ⓒ How many days you must pay for

Ⓓ Amount per month

Ⓔ Total policy will pay plus inflation

Ⓕ Home-care benefit

Ⓖ Annual inflation increase

Summary of Benefits

Ⓐ	Date of Policy:	02/15/02
Ⓑ	Duration of Benefit:	4 years
Ⓒ	Elimination Period:	60 days
Ⓓ	Benefit Amount per Month:	$4,000
Ⓔ	Lifetime Maximum Benefit:	$192,000*
Ⓕ	Professional Home Care:	50%
Ⓖ	Inflation Protection:	5% annually

Summary Details

My example of a summary of benefits may not have all the options your policy offers, but it touches on the main points of most long-term care policies. These policies are expensive to own and expensive for the insurance companies to pay out. Your policy book is packed with concerns about how and when the company will pay benefits.

The top part of the summary of benefits lists two important periods:

◆ The duration of the benefit
◆ The elimination period

Duration of the Benefit

Long-term care policies have no set length. You can generally buy them in any yearly increment you wish or you can buy policies that will last your lifetime. Statistics indicate that if you enter a nursing home at age 65 or older, the average stay is two and a half years.

The longer duration you buy, the more expensive the policy. On the other hand, you don't want to outlive the benefit either. Long-term insurance is the biggest guessing game in the profession. You buy protection for something you don't know if you'll need, and if you do need it, you don't know what it will cost or how long you will stay.

Form Alarm

Recent studies indicate nursing home costs may run from $45,000 and up per year. You can bet the costs will go nowhere but up in the future.

The Elimination Period

The elimination period is your deductible. You spend this time in the nursing home or under home health care if your policy covers that, before the policy pays anything. All of this expense comes out of your pocket, and the insurance company does not reimburse you for it.

The elimination period is another item that is subject to some negotiation with some policies. You may be able to get a shorter elimination period, but it will cost you in higher premiums. Most health insurance will not cover nursing home expenses unless you are in a skilled nursing home.

Benefit per Month

The benefit per month is usually an amount you pick. It represents what the insurance company will pay after you have met all the conditions of the policy. Obviously, the higher the amount, the more expensive the premium. The insurance company pays the benefit directly to the nursing home or designated facility.

Lifetime Benefit

This amount caps the benefit the policy pays. The exception is if you purchase an inflation option, which automatically increases your benefit each year.

Professional Home Care

This is an example of an optional care package you can purchase with some policies. In this example, the policy pays a benefit if you choose to receive care in some place other than a nursing home, such as an adult daycare center and/or your home with a licensed home health-care provider.

Your policy spells out the qualifications an adult daycare center must meet (such as a licensed registered nurse on premises) and what licenses in your state a home health-care provider needs.

The policy pays 50% of the nursing home benefit on a daily basis for this type of care. For example, my sample policy would pay $66.66 per day for these services ($4,000 × 50% = $2,000 / 30 = $66.66).

CAUTION | **Form Alarm**

When dealing with agencies and companies that provide home health-care services, don't let their name or a list of organizations they belong to fool you. Your policy should spell out the exact qualifications providers must meet to qualify for the benefit.

Inflation Protection

The inflation protection benefit adds a factor to your coverage for the increases in all health-care costs. Some policies add a flat 5% compounded annually, whereas others look to actual inflation numbers for a factor. Either way, your monthly benefit increases.

Premiums

Long-term insurance is expensive. The older you are, the more expensive it is. The more coverage you want, the more expensive it is. Your premium is a factor of your age, health, how large of benefit you want, the duration of the benefit, how short the elimination period is, and what options you choose.

Disability Insurance

Disability insurance replaces lost income when you are unable to perform your job due to sickness or injury. Many companies offer this coverage as part of their benefit package, and it is also available for individual purchase. Many self-employed professionals use disability insurance to protect their main asset, which is their ability to perform their service.

Policy Options

Paper Clips

Some insurance companies specialize in insuring certain professionals. Check with your agent for companies that can tailor a product that fits your particular needs.

You have a wide range of policies and options to consider. However, the basics of disability insurance are the same for all plans. Factors include the following:

- ◆ Income to be replaced
- ◆ Elimination period
- ◆ Duration of benefits
- ◆ Optional riders

The following summary of benefits highlights the main provisions in disability insurance plans, and the discussion that follows touches on some of the options.

A Date policy is in force
B Specific definition for insurance purposes
C Can't lose protection
D Deductible
E When benefits end
F Optional riders
G Pays if only partially disabled
H Allows for benefit increases

Summary of Benefits	
A Policy Date:	02/15/98
B Definition of Disability:	Own Occupation
C Guaranteed Protection:	Noncancelable, Guaranteed Renewable
D Elimination Period:	90 Days
E Benefit Period:	Until Age 65
F Optional Riders:	**G** Residual Disability Insurance
	H Future Increase Option

Form Alarm

It is so important to read the policy and marketing material before deciding on a particular policy. Just a few words can mean the difference between a good policy and a so-so policy.

Definition of Disability

You may find several definitions of disability if you look at different policies. Own Occupation is the most liberal definition. Here's what the policy will say (or something like this):

> The inability to perform the material and substantial duties of your regular occupation, the insurance company will consider your occupation to be the occupation you are engaged in at the time you become disabled, they will pay the claim even if you are working in some other capacity.

This means you get the benefit even if you decide you don't want to sit around the house and go find a different job. As long as your disability prevents you from performing your occupation, the policy will continue to pay.

A more common definition is one called "Income Replacement." This definition is similar to Own Occupation with one major difference. It adds a clause that says it will pay as long as you are not working or earning income from any source. If you take another job, you may lose some or all of your benefits under this definition.

The worst definition from your perspective is one that uses the phrase *gainful occupation* or something similar. This definition says the policy won't pay if you are able to perform any job you are reasonably qualified and able to do, regardless of whether you want to or not. A surgeon might not find flipping burgers an acceptable substitute for his or her profession, but theoretically could be denied benefits under this definition if he or she was able to cook hamburgers.

Guaranteed Protection

Noncancelable, guaranteed-renewable policies offer the best protection that the coverage will be there when you need it the most. Most policies put an age limit on this benefit of 65, but that is a reasonable limit for insurance that won't go away and premiums that won't go up.

Other forms of renewals fall short of this ironclad protection. However, it doesn't make much sense to risk losing your disability insurance just when you may need it.

Elimination Period

Like long-term care insurance, the elimination period for disability insurance is your deductible. The standard is 90 days, although you can buy a shorter or longer period.

A shorter period will drive your premiums up, and a longer period may put a financial strain on your family. Most policies work best with the 90-day elimination period.

Fill In the Blank

Although 90 days is the standard elimination period, this may be tough on you financially. If that is the case, begin now to sock away emergency cash to get you through such a period if needed. Most financial professionals believe you should have six months' worth of readily available cash on-hand to cover your living expenses during emergencies such as this. The cash should be in accounts you can get to without paying a penalty, such as money market mutual funds or U.S. Treasury Bills. Even though you might only need cash for three months of living expenses, an extra three months' worth would provide a margin of safety for those situations other than disability, such as unemployment when you might need more time to find another job.

Benefit Period

You can buy different benefit periods, but because this is catastrophic insurance for a worst-case scenario, most people pick the retirement age of 65 for benefits to end. Unless you have other financial resources, this is probably the best option.

Optional Rider—Residual Disability Insurance

Residual disability insurance addresses the issue of a partial disability that doesn't prevent you from working but impairs your ability to earn the income you previously enjoyed. Some total disabilities end as residual disabilities when the person returns to work, but at a reduced pace.

For example, a salesperson on commission may not be able to make as many calls or see as many clients. A professional may not be able to bill as many hours as before. When these people suffer a 20% or more loss of income, they are eligible for this rider.

Optional Rider—Future Increase Option

This rider protects future income by guaranteeing insurability up to a certain age—normally 55. You can buy additional disability insurance by just verifying the income you want to insure. This means if you took a small policy when you were in your 30s, but wanted to increase it because you had substantially grown your income by age 45, you could do so without proof of insurability. Without this rider, a health condition might prevent you from buying additional disability insurance.

Premiums

Insurance companies price disability insurance based on the amount of income you wish to insure, your occupation, your age, and your health. If you engage in any risky behavior, such as skydiving, that might affect your premium also. If you buy a policy like my example (I'm not suggesting you do), the premiums will not go up unless you exercise the future increase option and buy more coverage in the future. Make sure you can afford the premium.

Form Alarm

Carefully budget your premium for disability insurance. If you are self-employed or a small business owner or someone whose livelihood depends on you showing up every day, disability insurance is a necessity.

Part 4

Taking It Easy

Several retirement plans will help you save for those years of well-earned fun, but they can't help you if you don't participate. One of the most cited reasons for not participating is a lack of understanding of the plans and the mounds of paperwork they generate. These plans can really make a difference; don't let their confusing documents stand between you and the retirement you deserve.

Chapter 16

Golden Years—You Pay

In This Chapter

- ◆ 401(k), 403(k) plan provisions
- ◆ Quarterly statements
- ◆ Funds list
- ◆ Asset allocation

Employer-sponsored 401(k) or 403(b) retirement plans are an excellent way to save for those golden years. This chapter details the key provisions of the plans you need to focus on and how to read plan statements.

The Plans

401(k) and 403(b) are defined contribution plans. This means you have some degree of control over how much money goes into the accounts. (Incidentally, the only significant difference between these two retirement programs named for their respective chapters in the tax code is that 403(b) plans are for employees of nonprofit organizations.) The programs offer employers some flexibility in what benefits they offer, so some plans are more generous than others. What follows is an example of a summary sheet that describes a typical 401(k) program. It works for a 403(b), too. Although it might not look like what you receive from your employer, the key topics will be the same.

A Date you can enroll

B Max you can contribute

C Employer matches part of your investment

D Matches first dollar

E Vesting schedule for keeping company match

F You bring money from another plan

G Terms for loans

H Where you can invest your money

I Online access available

J Investment help available

PLAN SUMMARY

A Eligible for Enrollment: 90 days after hire

B Maximum Contribution: 12% of salary

C Employer Match: 50% of first 5% of gross pay

D Match Begins: Immediately

E Vesting Schedule: End of year 1—33%

End of year 2—66%

End of year 3—100%

F Rollovers Accepted: Yes, under certain conditions

G Loans: Loans discouraged, but available in cases of hardship or to buy a home. Loans must be repaid through payroll deduction at market rates. See full plan for complete details.

H What are the investment choices: 8 mutual funds:

Large-Cap Growth Fund

Income Fund

Value Fund

Small-Cap Fund

Technology Fund

Foreign Markets Fund

High-Yield Bond Fund

Money Market Fund

I Online Access to Check Funds: Yes

J Help with Asset Allocation: Yes

The Plan Summary

Many employers provide participants a summary of their 401(k) or 403(b) plans. They will also provide you with a booklet that explains the plan in more detail. Usually, a third party administers the plan and acts as a resource for questions about the plan and investments.

A Date you can enroll

B Max you can contribute

C Employer matches part of your investment

D Matches first dollar

E Vesting schedule for keeping company match

A Eligible for Enrollment: 90 days after hire

B Maximum Contribution: 12% of salary

C Employer Match: 50% of first 5% of gross pay

D Match Begins: Immediately

E Vesting Schedule: End of year 1—33%

End of year 2—66%

End of year 3—100%

Plan Details

The plan summary covers the important points of your 401(k) or 403(b) plan. The first part of the example I created lists some of the requirements and limits of the plan. For easier discussion, I cut the plan summary in half.

Enrollment

Employers can set the enrollment eligibility at any date they choose. Most employers, especially those with high turnover, pick some days after employment to avoid the expense of setting up an account for a worker only to have that worker leave. However, employers don't want it too far out; otherwise the plan loses value as an incentive.

Maximum Contribution

The IRS sets maximum amounts that you can put into your retirement plan, although it adjusts the limits for inflation. Given the concern over Social Security, it is possible that Congress will push further increases in contribution limits.

Most employers cap the percentage of your salary you can contribute, regardless of the IRS limits. Your contribution may fall short of the maximum allowed by law because of this employer-imposed limit.

Employer Match

The employer match is the best part of a 401(k) or 403(b) plan. The employer establishes a percentage of your salary it will match as a contribution to your plan. A typical match might be the employer matches 50% of up to the first 5% of your salary you contribute. Here's how the math works:

If you make $48,000 per year, your 5% contribution is $2,400. Your employer matches 50% of that amount or $1,200. This makes the total contribution $3,600 for the year to your plan. You've made an automatic 50% return! That's free money!

Some companies make the match in the form of company stock, which may not be a very good deal at all, because you have no investment options with the contribution.

Not all plans offer a match. It is not required, and some employers can't afford it. My example has the employer match beginning immediately. This is probably more generous than some plans, so your plan may have a waiting period before the employer match kicks in.

Vesting Schedule

From the employer's perspective, the 401(k) or 403(b) plan is an incentive to help attract and retain good employees. To that end, employers often build in incentives to make it worth your while to stick with the company. One of the ways they do this is through a vesting schedule.

A vesting schedule is a timetable for "earning" the benefits of your retirement plan. The major benefit, as we just learned in the previous section, is the employer

---

Fill In the Blank

If you are a senior executive at a company, special rules may govern how much you can contribute to the retirement plan. Check with your human resources or a qualified tax adviser for details.

Paper Clips

Regardless of the vesting method your plan uses, your contributions are always yours to keep and can never be taken from you.

match. A vesting schedule is a way for employees to earn that matching contribution over a period of employment.

A three- or four-year schedule is common. It usually works that you earn a percentage of that matching contribution each year of employment. The match is in your account earning interest for you; if you leave before fully vested, however, you won't get the full match. Using my example, this plan would fully vest you at the end of three years. All of the employer's contributions for the past three years and any future contributions are yours to keep even if you leave the company.

F You bring money from another plan

G Terms for loans

H Where you can invest your money

I Online access available

J Investment help available

F	Rollovers Accepted:	Yes, under certain conditions
G	Loans:	Loans discouraged, but available in cases of hardship or to buy a home. Loans must be repaid through payroll deduction at market rates. See full plan for complete details.
H	What are the investment choices:	8 mutual funds: Large-Cap Growth Fund Income Fund Value Fund Small-Cap Fund Technology Fund Foreign Markets Fund High-Yield Bond Fund Money Market Fund
I	Online Access to Check Funds:	Yes
J	Help with Asset Allocation:	Yes

Some employers may cap contributions. IRS rules as of writing, but maximums rise each year. Check with your provider for current limits.

Rollovers Accepted

Changing jobs means you may have a retirement plan that has a balance. You can usually roll the balance into an IRA. However, some employers let you roll your balance into their 401(k) or 403(b) plan. The advantage is having your retirement assets in one account. Employers are not obligated to do this, and you can't expect a match on your rollover.

Loans

Most 401(k) and 403(b) plans allow loans for hardship cases or to help with the purchase of a home or to finance a college education. However, unless it is an emergency and you have no alternative, borrowing from your retirement plan defeats the purpose of the plan.

Most plans require a payback in 3 to 5 years for personal loans and within 10 years for loans to buy a home. The plan will charge market rates in most cases for the loans, and payments will come out of your paycheck.

Investment Choices

Your investment choices depend on the firm your employer hires to administer the plan. Typically, 8 to 10 mutual funds make up your investment choices. However, some plans may have only a few, whereas others have dozens of choices.

One option that is common for publicly traded companies is stock in the company. Companies offer their own stock, often at a discount, to employees through their retirement plan. Although this sounds like a good deal on the surface, you should be very careful about loading your retirement account with company stock (or any single investment). No single stock should account for more than 10% to 15% of your retirement portfolio.

Help

Large financial services companies that administer most 401(k) and 403(b) programs offer significant online support in the form of customer service, account balances, and educational material.

If you work for a large company, there may be someone within the organization who can answer your questions about the plan. If not, most plan administrators offer toll-free customer service in addition to online access.

Your company will probably not provide investment help with your plan. For that, you need to talk to representatives of the plan administrator. They will probably not give you specific financial advice, but provide some general investment guidance and educational material.

The Quarterly Statement

Each quarter and at the end of the year, you will get a summary report of how your 401(k) or 403(b) did for the period. The report will show contributions, withdrawals, and earnings (or losses) in your investment choices. Included with the earnings will be an asset allocation report that shows the split of your money between the different funds.

CAUTION

Form Alarm

Financial advisers generally frown on loans from your retirement plan. Even though you are "paying yourself," it's not a good idea to borrow from your future to finance your present unless there is no other way. Your retirement account works because it earns interest over a long period. If you pull money out, it's not working for your retirement.

Fill In the Blank

You may find investment advice, beyond general financial education, hard to come by. Many employers worry that if you get financial advice from the investment manager and things don't go well, you'll blame them.

Ⓐ Period covered by the statement

Ⓑ Total paid in

Ⓒ 50% match

Ⓓ Total invested

Ⓔ Fund and percent allocation of contribution

Ⓕ Balance at beginning of quarter

Ⓖ Total of contributions

Ⓗ Growth or loss in fund

Ⓘ Balance at end of quarter

Ⓙ Percent change for quarter

Ⓚ Fund percentage change for quarter

Ⓛ Percent change year to date

Ⓜ Totals for quarter

Ⓝ Allocation of assets among funds

Ⓞ Allocation of assets by stock size

Account Summary

Ⓐ	Statement Period	07/01/06 - 09/30/06
Ⓑ	Employee Contributions:	$1,440
Ⓒ	Employer Match:	$720
Ⓓ	Total Contribution:	$2,160

Ⓔ **Funds and Contributions**

Fund (%)	**Ⓕ** Beginning Balance	Contri-bution	**Ⓗ** Growth	**Ⓘ** Ending Balance	**Ⓙ** % Chge	**Ⓚ** Fund % Chge	**Ⓛ** YTD% Chge
Growth (40%)	$13,384.34	$864	$334.60	$14,582.94	8.9%	2.5%	8.2%
Income (40%)	$11,390.08	$864	$85.43	$12,339.50	8.3%	0.5%	5.3%
Technology (20%)	$5,804.32	$432	-$596.83	$5,639.49	(2.8%)	(10.3%)	9.8%
Ⓜ TOTALS:	$30,578.74	$2,160	-$176.80	$32,561.94	6.4%	(0.05%)	7.4%

Asset Allocation

Ⓝ Growth Fund	44%
Income Fund	37%
Technology Fund	19%
Ⓞ Large-Cap Stocks	78%
Small-Cap Stocks	22%

Statement Detail

Depending on the investment company that manages your 401(k) or 403(b) plan, the quarterly or annual statement may contain more or less information than this example. However, this example captures the important information that you need to note about your plan. Some providers may include educational material about how to structure your plan for your particular life situation. This information may be helpful, but you need to understand where you are before knowing where you need to go.

Account Summary

The top portion of the statement should identify you and your employer (even though I didn't list that information on my example). It is important that you check this information because most large investment companies manage a number of retirement plans. It doesn't happen often, but there is a chance your records could get confused with another client's.

The other important information is the total of your contributions and your employer's contribution (if they provide a match). The total of these two numbers is the sum of the contributions for the quarter. These contributions will be made to your accounts as you are paid.

Ⓔ Funds and Contributions

Fund (%)	Ⓕ Beginning Balance	Contri-bution	Ⓗ Growth	Ⓘ Ending Balance	% Chge	Fund % Chge	YTD % Chge
Growth (40%)	$13,384.34	$864	$334.60	$14,582.94	8.9%	2.5%	8.2%
Income (40%)	$11,390.08	$864	$85.43	$12,339.50	8.3%	0.5%	5.3%
Technology (20%)	$5,804.32	$432	-$596.83	$5,639.49	(2.8%)	(10.3%)	9.8%
Ⓜ TOTALS:	$30,578.74	$2,160	-$176.80	$32,561.94	6.4%	(0.05%)	7.4%

Asset Allocation

Ⓝ Growth Fund	44%
Income Fund	37%
Technology Fund	19%
Ⓞ Large-Cap Stocks	78%
Small-Cap Stocks	22%

Ⓔ Fund and percent allocation of contribution

Ⓕ Balance at beginning of quarter

Ⓖ Total of contributions

Ⓗ Growth or loss in fund

Ⓘ Balance at end of quarter

Ⓙ Percent change for quarter

Ⓚ Fund percentage change for quarter

Ⓛ Percent change year to date

Ⓜ Totals for quarter

Ⓝ Allocation of assets among funds

Ⓞ Allocation of assets by stock size

Funds and Contributions

The real meat of the statements is in the portion that lists the funds and how they performed for the last quarter. To keep the example simple, I have used only three funds in the plan. You may have more, but the important points remain the same.

When you first set up your account, and at any time after, you can allocate a percentage of your contribution and employer match to a grouping of funds. However, some plans limit the number of times per year you can change your allocations. In this example, the first column indicates the plan contains three funds. You allocate a percentage of your contribution to each fund, which is the number following the fund name on the report. Each paycheck the investment company takes money from your account and your employer's match and invests it according to the percentages you establish.

Contributions and Growth

The report lists a beginning balance for each fund, the contribution allocated to that fund, and any growth or loss the fund experienced during the quarter. Some reports may break the growth number down into capital appreciation (share prices), dividend reinvestment, and other income.

Percentage Changes

The first percentage change computes the increase or decrease of the fund's total from the beginning of the quarter (beginning balance) to the end of the quarter (ending balance). This number is valid, but misleading, because you may believe you have "earned" this amount. This percentage change includes the contribution allocated to this fund, which may be much larger than any growth generated by the fund itself.

CAUTION   Form Alarm

Exercise caution when changing funds in your retirement account. Even though you don't suffer any tax consequences by switching, there is seldom any gain in frequently jumping back and forth between funds. Evaluate your account twice a year and make changes then if needed.

Fill In the Blank

To annualize a return, multiply the given return by whatever number needed to reach 12 months. For example, multiply a quarterly report by 4 to annualize it. Multiply a monthly report by 12 to annualize it. Annualizing is a way to estimate returns over longer periods.

The second percentage change—the Fund Percentage Change—shows you the growth (or loss) the fund generated for your investment. You'll notice, for example, that the Growth Fund experienced a 2.5% increase of actual growth during this quarter. On an annual basis, this works out to a 10% return, which is not bad.

The year-to-date percentage change brings your account up to date through the current year. Some reports may also list a trailing 12 months' percent change, which is a way of looking at the fund's performance over a longer period.

Totals and Performance

The final line of the chart totals the columns to give you a bottom line. In my example, you'll notice a good showing by the Growth Fund, a flat performance by the Income Fund, and a terrible quarter for the Technology Fund resulted in virtually no growth.

The account growth came almost exclusively from contributions. Does this mean it's time to bail out of the Technology Fund? Not necessarily, but you'll want to ask yourself whether this fund mix is accomplishing your goals.

Asset Allocation

Asset allocation is the distribution of your investments across different asset classes to achieve your financial goals within acceptable risk limits. Most investment companies provide an asset allocation report with their quarterly and/or annual reports.

The summary may be as simple as the listing I've used in my example or an elaborate chart with color graphics depicting the different asset classes. If you invest in five or six funds in your 401(k) or 403(b) program, the asset allocation portion will be more meaningful.

My example shows that the three funds are not far off the allocation of funds. If you want to keep your funds balanced at these levels, it may become necessary to reallocate percentages. For example, if the Technology Fund keeps dropping and the Growth Fund continues to grow, they both will soon be way off their respective 40% and 20% allocations.

The statement also shows that your account is dominated by large-cap stocks (78%). This is neither good nor bad, but the allocation should fit your investment goals.

Online Version

Most major investment companies offer some level of online access to your retirement account. This may include monitoring performance, account maintenance (address changes and so on), or educational material to help you make more-informed investment choices.

Chapter 17

Golden Years—Company Pays

In This Chapter

- What your pension looks like
- Defining the benefit
- Vesting and cashing out
- Cash balance plans

For many years, the only type of retirement plan was the company pension. These are disappearing rapidly, but quite a few are still around. If you have one, what you need to know is what to expect when you retire. This chapter looks at the pension benefit statement and a new form of the traditional pension called "cash balance plans."

The Company Pension Plan—Defined Benefit

The traditional pension plan defines the benefit you will receive when you retire. In its purest form, employees do not contribute to the plan—it is the employer who funds the entire program. Many of the remaining pension plans exist between companies and unions.

Settlement

When you retire under a traditional pension plan, you normally receive an offer of a lump sum of cash or a paid-up annuity that will provide you an income stream for however long you want. If you are offered a choice, consult with a qualified financial planner to decide which is best for you.

Summary Plan Description

Each pension plan is required to provide participants an easy-to-understand summary of their pension called a summary plan description. This document describes the benefits and structure of the plan, usually in a narrative format. In the interest of space, I have picked out the important points from a typical summary plan description and listed them in a table format. This will allow you to quickly see where you need to focus your attention. The following narrative adds detail you will find in your plan summary.

Paper Clips

Your employer is required to publish a plan summary in plain, easy-to-understand language that describes the important features of the pension plan. If you still have trouble understanding parts of your benefit, check with the benefits or human resources department for help.

(A) Type of pension plan
(B) Who pays
(C) When employee begins
(D) How benefits increase
(E) How credit calculated
(F) Defines retirement age
(G) Payout options
(H) Vesting requirements
(I) Death benefits

Summary Plan Description

(A)	Plan Definition:	Defined Benefit Plan
(B)	Cost to Participant:	None
(C)	Participation Begins:	After 1 year of service with at least 1,000 hours Automatically enrolled
(D)	Benefits Increase:	More years you work, the higher your total pension
(E)	Pensions Credits:	Pension credits based on salary of last 5 years of work
(F)	Retirement Age:	Age 60 with 5 years of service or reach 25 years of service
(G)	Retirement Pay:	Lump sum or different monthly annuity options
(H)	Vesting:	5 years of 1,000 hours worked
(I)	Death Benefits:	Your spouse may be entitled to benefits under this plan even if you die

Summary Details

This pension plan is a "defined benefit" plan, which means the end benefit rather than the contribution is set out in the plan. Part of the plan's legal structure is the formula for defining how it calculates your retirement benefit. Unless the company formally alters the plan, it can't change that formula.

The other part of most traditional defined benefit plans is that the employees do not contribute to the fund. The employer is responsible for funding the entire program.

Participation

Most companies have a window of at least one year before employees join the pension plan. This acknowledges the fact that in some jobs there is a high turnover in the first year and companies don't want the expense of setting up pension accounts for people who work only a few months.

There is usually an hour minimum, too. In my example, which is probably not unusual, the minimum is 1,000 hours. This describes a half-time employee (20 hours per week).

The actual plan will have a number of qualifications to describe all sorts of circumstances, such as employees who have "breaks" in service, employees called to active military duty, and so on. The plan booklet covers all of these circumstances and others. If you fall in some category other than a full-time employee or have unusual breaks in service, check the full plan booklet or talk to a human resources person to clarify how your circumstances may affect your pension.

Benefits and Pension Credits

This pension plan rewards employees for longevity by increasing their retirement pay by a benefits multiplier. The plan summary notes that the increase becomes significant when you have accumulated a number of years of service with the company.

Your retirement pay is based on the following:

- Final average compensation, which is the highest 60 consecutive months of compensation of the last 120 months before you retire (base salary only)
- Years of credited service
- A multiplier that increases with years (1.3% for years 1–4; 1.4% for years 5–9; and 1.6% for years 10–35)

For example, if your final average compensation was $50,000, and you retired at age 65 with 30 years of service, the plan calculates your retirement pay this way:

First 4 years:	.013 × $50,000 = $650 × 4 = $2,600
Years 5–9:	.014 × $50,000 = $700 × 5 = $3,500
Next 21 years:	.016 × $50,000 = $800 × 21 = $16,800
Add these together:	$2,600 + $3,500 + $16,800 = $22,900

This is your annual pension benefit.

Retirement Age

Most pension plans define retirement age differently than Social Security, which fixes an age for benefits. Many pension plans let you retire whenever you want after you meet a couple of conditions. My example may be more liberal than some, but would not be out of the norm, especially for a public, nonprofit, or governmental organization.

Under my example plan, you could retire after 5 years of continuous, 1,000-hour-plus service years and your sixtieth birthday. Of course, you aren't going to receive the longevity bonuses that we saw previously.

Paper Clips

Be sure and see how maternity leave affects your pension, especially if you are medically required to be off work longer than normal.

Form Alarm

Taking early retirement may sound like a great deal, but do the math first. Your benefit is reduced if you retire before 60 in most cases. However, you can retire early and delay your benefit until you reach the age needed to get the full benefit.

The other way to retire is to reach 25 years of service years (1,000 plus hours). In theory, you could retire in your 40s if you started with this organization in your 20s and didn't have any gaps in your employment. If you take early retirement (before 65), you can choose to delay retirement pay or begin receiving your retirement pay now. If you want to receive retirement pay early, it will be lower than if you wait until age 65 because the plan assumes a normal retirement age.

Retirement Pay

The plan will pay you your retirement benefit either in a lump sum or as a paid-up annuity. The lump sum automatically rolls over into an Individual Retirement Account (IRA). This preserves the tax-deferred status until you begin withdrawing money.

The normal payout is a paid-up annuity that guarantees you a monthly income for life. There are some options for this payout. If you stick with a single-pay annuity, you receive the largest check, but the payments stop when you die. The other alternative is an annuity with your wife or husband as a joint survivor. This way, if you die, he or she will continue to receive the payment. Your monthly check will be lower, but the benefit continues after your death. Check the plan booklet for complete payout options and discuss them with your tax adviser.

Vesting

Most plans require you to work for so many years to "earn" your way into the pension plan. This is another way to encourage employees to stay with the organization.

Times vary among plans, but many companies use five years of continuous service as a schedule for vesting. If you have breaks of service before vesting is complete, you may lose some of the time and need to start over on earning vesting credits. See the full plan booklet for complete details.

If you leave the company before you are vested, you lose all of your benefits in the pension plan.

Form Alarm

Even if you are vested, if you leave the company your retirement benefit stays with the company. You do not lose the benefit and can usually access it when you are ready to retire. Some companies may offer to "buy" you out of your plan with a settlement that you can convert to an Individual Retirement Account (IRA) or an annuity. Either way, the money remains tax-deferred as long as you meet the requirements.

Death Benefits

Your spouse is entitled to certain death benefits depending on when you die and whether you had begun receiving benefits or not. The amount of benefits a surviving spouse receives depends on the payout option if the employee has already retired and is receiving benefits.

If you die before you retire, the pension will pay your spouse the beneficiary's part of a 50% joint and survivor annuity. This means your spouse will receive 50% of the benefit that the plan would normally have paid to you.

If you die after you retire, what your spouse receives depends on the payout you selected. If you chose the single life annuity, all payments stop with your death. You could also choose one of the other annuity options that would continue payments at some level to your spouse as long as he or she lived.

It is possible to name someone other than your spouse as a beneficiary. Check with the benefits office for details.

Summary of Annual Report

The other piece of information you will receive is a summary of the plan's annual report. This is usually a one- or two-page narrative that gives you the starting balance, the expense, the income, and the ending fund balance. You cannot tell much from this unless some of the numbers seem way out of line.

Annual Report Summary	
(A) Report period:	04/01/05 - 03/31/06
(B) Beginning Balance:	$523,262,000
(C) Total Expenses:	$18,590,000
(D) Administrative Expenses:	$412,000
(E) Investment Management Fees:	$1,457,000
(F) Benefits Paid:	$16,721,000
(G) Investment Income:	$10,641,000
(H) Ending Balance:	$515,313,000

An actuary's statement shows that enough money was contributed to the plan to keep it funded in accordance with the minimum funding standards of ERISA.

(A) Fiscal year of plan
(B) Balance at start
(C) Total expenses
(D) Administration costs
(E) Fees related to buying and selling securities
(F) Retirement pay
(G) Growth of investments and contributions
(H) Ending balance after income and expenses

Summary Detail

In most cases, the company does not distribute the annual report to all employees. The company must make a copy available to you for your review, although they may charge a copying fee. If you are not familiar with reading detailed financial statements, I wouldn't waste my money, unless you suspect something amiss with the pension fund. In that case, take the report to a friend (a CPA, for instance) who is familiar with financial statements. They should be able to tell you if there's something to worry about.

Fill In the Blank

If you are concerned about your company's pension plan, you can request a full copy of the annual report. The company must provide one to you. You can also get a copy from the U.S. Department of Labor (www.dol. gov/ebsa/publications/ wyskapr.html).

Expenses

Without some frame of reference, it will be hard for you to know whether the expenses are too high. However, if administrative expenses are running 5% of the total expenses, you might be correct in wondering why they are so high.

Likewise, if the investment management fees are topping the 10% to 12% mark, you might wonder what is costing so much and whether the fund is getting its money's worth.

If you suspect that something funny is going on and can't get a straight answer, report it to the Department of Labor. The federal government takes a dim view of companies that play games with pension funds.

Rest of the Report

The rest of the numbers report out the benefits paid to retirees and the ending balance. There is usually no way for you to know whether these numbers are right or not. If you keep these statements from year to year, you can track changes and notice anything that changes in a dramatic fashion from year to year.

Cash Balance Plans

A relatively new variation on the pension plan theme is the cash balance plan. Many companies are converting their old pension plans to the newer cash balance programs. Although they are both "defined benefit" plans, each approaches retirement in an entirely different way. Depending on how old you are, one plan may be better than the other.

> **Fill In the Blank**
>
> Companies converting to cash balance plans may face pressure from employees. Some employees at companies have sued and won age discrimination suits against employers trying to convert to cash balance plans.

How It Works

The cash balance plan is a defined benefit plan, just like a regular pension. In fact, many of the same conditions, such as vesting, may apply to a cash balance plan. The plan works strictly on your salary by investing a credit in your account. You begin accumulating benefits immediately (after the normal one-year waiting period).

After you are vested (usually five years), the money is yours to keep. If you change jobs, the account balance goes with you, unlike a traditional pension, where the benefit remains with the company. This attribute appeals to younger workers who may switch jobs more frequently in their early years.

Older Workers

Older workers, especially those whose company is switching from a traditional pension to a cash balance plan, will not do as well under these plans. Traditional pension plans reward longevity, because you earn large retirement payoffs after years of service when the benefit multipliers factor in. With cash balance plans, the contribution is a percentage of their salary just like everyone else.

Plan Description

Cash balance plans look very much like traditional pension plan until you come to calculating the benefit. With a cash balance plan, the company contributes a percentage of your salary—say 8%—into an account that it guarantees will earn the same rate as long-term treasury bonds (about 4% at this writing).

After you have satisfied the vesting requirements, which may be shorter than typical pensions, the account belongs to you. If you leave the company, the account balance rolls into an IRA to maintain its tax-deferred status. With traditional pensions, when you leave the company, the money stays there.

Your benefit when you retire is the account balance. Unlike the traditional pension, there is no multiplier for length of service or averaging of salaries. The payouts can be just like a regular pension: a lump sum or various annuities.

Chapter 18

Golden Years–Private Pay

In This Chapter

- Various IRA types
- IRA statements
- Details of different funding vehicles

IRAs (Individual Retirement Accounts), in various forms, are an additional way you can save for retirement. You can invest the money in a number of different financial instruments ranging from bank CDs to mutual funds. The precise format of the statement you receive will depend on that choice; however, some items are common among statements. This chapter walks you through IRA statements.

IRAs

An IRA is technically not a product. It is a part of the tax code that lets you defer (in some cases) income tax on the earnings to a later date. When you invest in an IRA, what you are doing is taking a regular investment product such as a bank CD or mutual fund and putting it inside a special "tax envelope," where it is treated differently for tax purposes.

Types of IRAs

There are several different types of IRAs. The tax code splits them into two major categories:

- Traditional IRAs
- Roth IRAs

The tax code treats these two IRAs quite differently.

Traditional IRAs

Traditional IRAs allow you to deduct the qualified investment from your *gross income* before taxes, thus lowering your current income taxes. The investment grows tax deferred as long as it remains within the IRA. You will pay current income tax on withdrawal during your retirement. Certain distribution rules apply, and penalties apply to early withdrawal.

Financial Speak

Gross income is your salary or wages before any deductions for taxes, insurance, or anything else.

Net income is what you can put in the bank. It is what's left after all of the deductions for taxes, insurance premiums, and so on.

Paper Clips

The Roth IRA came from the Taxpayer Relief Act of 1997 and is named for Sen. William V. Roth, Jr. of Delaware.

Roth IRA

The Roth IRA works differently than its traditional cousin. You get no deduction from your current income, but when you withdraw money from the Roth IRA, it is tax free. It also has certain distribution rules and penalties. For more information on both Roth and traditional IRAs, go to the Retirement Planning site on About.com at this web address: http://retireplan.about.com/od/rothandtraditionaliras/.

IRA Statements

The format of your IRA statement depends on which investment product you choose. If you pick a mutual fund, your IRA statement will come from the mutual fund and will look virtually identical, in most cases, to a regular mutual fund statement. If you pick a bank CD, your IRA statement will look like a bank CD statement. You can have more than one IRA so long as you do not exceed the annual contribution limits. If you have multiple IRAs through one company (a bank, for instance), it may provide a consolidated annual statement with all of your accounts on one report. Whatever format your IRA statement takes, the following tables list some common terms that may appear on your statement.

IRA Common Statement Terms

Terms	Definition
(A) Beginning Balance	Amount in account at end of last statement
(B) Ending Balance	Amount in account at end of this statement
(C) Contributions	What you put in during statement period
(D) Earnings	Interest or price appreciation during statement period
(E) Distributions	Any withdrawals during statement period
(F) Transfers	Any money transferred from another IRA to this IRA
(G) Rollover	Money from a qualified retirement plan distributed to this IRA
(H) Withholding	IRS may require a withholding of IRA distribution
(I) Penalty	You may pay a penalty for an early withdrawal

(A) Balance at end of previous statement

(B) Balance at the end of current statement

(C) Your investment

(D) What the investment earned

(E) Withdrawals

(F) Moving money around

(G) Direct transfer

(H) Taxes

(I) Required by law

Statements

You will receive an annual statement for your IRA from the company that manages the investment you chose. Depending on that investment instrument, you may receive statements more frequently. For specific information on statements from different funding investments, refer to those chapters in this book.

Although your IRA statements will look just like regular statements, they may contain some unusual terms that do not show up on regular statements.

Balances

Your annual (or more frequent) IRA statement should list an opening and closing balance for the period covered by the statement. The closing balance includes all of your contributions and any earnings, less any distributions and penalties.

So long as your investment stays within the IRA, you do not pay any taxes on gains or profits. This includes capital gains that mutual funds might generate in the course of trading stock within the funds. You can sell one investment, buy another all within your IRA, and avoid a tax on the profit.

Your Contributions

The statement should list the contributions to your IRA, if any. You are not required to put money into your IRA every year, although it's a good idea. As of this writing, you have until the deadline for filing your personal income tax to fund an IRA for that tax year.

For example, if you plan to file your income tax return for the 2005 tax year on April 16, 2006 (April 15 is on a Sunday), you can still fund a traditional IRA up to that date. Although you legally have this extra time, it is not a good financial play: you lose 16 months of interest, because you could have opened an IRA in January 2005.

Paper Clips

Keep your IRA statements in a convenient place and organized so that if something happens to you, your beneficiaries will have an idea of where to look for your assets.

Earnings

The earnings portion of your IRA reports how well (or poorly) your investment did over the past year. Unfortunately, many people open IRAs, but then forget about them. These investments need to be monitored for performance goals. If the investment vehicle you initially chose is not performing well, make a change.

You are not helping yourself if you let an IRA flounder with a crummy return. You'll need this money in your retirement, so if you're unfamiliar with the stock market, contact a financial professional to help you decide how to best invest your IRA funds.

Distributions

If you are at retirement age and taking money out of your IRA, the statement notes those distributions here. Before you reach age 59½, there are a few circumstances in which you can withdraw money without penalty. In most cases, however, a withdrawal or distribution results in a penalty, which could be as much as 10%, plus a 20% federal tax withholding.

There is a sneaky way you can take money out of an IRA for a quick, short-term loan. The rules, as of this writing, allow you to withdraw money tax-free and penalty-free if you pay it back in full within 60 days. Check with a competent financial adviser for the latest rules on this maneuver. Once again, it's not really a good idea because the money you take out is not earning interest for you.

Transfers

Limits apply as to how much you can contribute to an IRA in any one year. However, you can combine IRAs if you want to avoid several different accounts. For example, if you have several different IRAs in bank CDs, you can combine them into one IRA.

Transfers can cut down on paperwork and confusion, but you need to handle them correctly. This is not a "do-it-yourself" project. Notify the affected companies and tell them what you want to do; they will provide the proper forms to make the transfer happen. The funds will be transferred from the old account to the new one. It is important that the money never come to you because it could trigger federal income tax withholding rules and a 10 percent penalty.

Rollover

You use a rollover to move or transfer money or assets from a qualified tax-deferred retirement plan to your IRA. A qualified tax-deferred retirement plan allows your investments to grow without taxation until you withdraw them when you retire. A 401(k) and a pension plan are both examples of these types of qualified retirement plans.

Here's how a rollover works. If you work for a company that offers a 401(k) plan and leave before retirement, that account comes with you. Sometimes a new employer will let you place those assets in their 401(k) plan. However, many times you will simply roll over your old 401(k) assets into an IRA. This preserves the tax-deferred status of the assets.

This rollover needs to happen soon after you leave. Like the transfer discussed previously, you don't want to take physical possession of the money in your 401(k). You can roll the money into an existing IRA or open a new IRA. In either case, contact the company that manages the IRA, and they will handle the rollover details.

Form Alarm

The IRS is real picky about you taking possession of assets from a qualified retirement plan. If you asked to have the cash instead of rolling the assets over to an IRA, the company may withhold 20% whether you want them to or not. You're safer having the company transfer the assets directly to an IRA. Rollovers and transfers (mentioned above) can be the source of a quick, short-term loan, because you can take the cash without penalty IF you reinvest it in another qualified account within 60 days. However, this is playing with fire, and if something happens that prevents you from reinvesting the money before the 60-day limit, the IRS will hit you with penalties, late fees, and interest. Not a pretty picture.

Withholding and Penalty

As noted, you may face a federal income tax withholding of 20% if you withdraw money from your IRA under circumstances that do not fit a regular distribution (under age 59½, for example). If you are unsure whether an anticipated withdrawal will trigger a withholding, contact the IRA management company for a ruling.

Financial Speak

Extreme hardship means your disability or the imminent loss of your home due to foreclosure, for example.

The IRS generally frowns on taking money out of your IRA account before age 59½ in what they call a "premature distribution." They sock you with a 10% penalty, plus the income tax on the amount. There are a couple of exceptions:

- You can use the money for college education expenses.
- You can use up to $10,000 toward the purchase of your first home.
- *Extreme hardship cases.*

Consult a competent tax adviser for the full scoop on these qualifications and how they may differ if you own a Roth IRA as opposed to a traditional IRA.

Chapter 19

Golden Years—Annuitize This!

In This Chapter

◆ The annuity benefit statement
◆ Statement for different annuity types
◆ Payout options statement

Annuities can be great investments for retirement. This chapter offers a look at the benefit statement along with the payout statement and what these two documents tell you about your annuity.

Annuities

An annuity is a contract between you and a life insurance company. In the broadest terms, the contract says if you give the life insurance company a certain sum of money, it will pay you back a certain sum based on a payout option you choose. Annuities are popular retirement savings tools for several reasons, one of which is that you can pick a payout option that will provide a monthly check as long as you live. In other words, you can't outlive your money, which is a real concern these days.

Benefit Statement—Fixed Annuities

Your annuity will have a benefit statement, although the issuing company might call it a policy sheet or some other term. This document states what type of annuity you own, the terms of the annuity, and the payout options. It will also list your beneficiary. The following statements are for fixed immediate annuities and fixed deferred annuities. A later section covers variable annuities.

Ⓐ Annuity type

Ⓑ Single deposit

Ⓒ Payout option

Ⓓ Who receives benefit if owner and spouse die

Ⓔ Amount of benefit based on payout option

Ⓕ Annuity owner and spouse

Benefit Statement for Fixed Immediate Annuity

Ⓐ	Type of Annuity:	**Single Premium Immediate**
Ⓑ	Premium:	$100,000
Ⓒ	Payout:	Joint Life Income (100%) with 20-year guarantee payout to beneficiary
Ⓓ	Beneficiary:	Mary Smith, Daughter
Ⓔ	Monthly Benefit:	$503.00
Ⓕ	Owner:	Paul Jones, age 60
	Spouse:	Mary Jones, age 60

Fill In the Blank

Many people use annuities when they get a lump sum from their pension or other retirement plan. Money grows inside the annuity on a tax-deferred basis until you begin withdrawals.

Statement Details—Immediate Annuity

There are two types of fixed annuities: immediate and deferred. This statement covers an immediate annuity. The term "immediate" comes from the timing of the payout, which, as you might guess, is immediate.

The other characteristic of an immediate annuity is the single premium or deposit. People usually buy the single premium immediate annuity with funds from a maturing bank certificate of deposit or a payout from a retirement program or some other source of lump-sum payout. You pay the premium and begin receiving benefits immediately.

Payout

One of the attractive benefits of annuities is the many ways you can structure the payout. At the end of this chapter is a whole section devoted to the various payout options that you can select for any annuity.

For this example, I chose a Joint Life Income with a 20-year guaranteed payout to the beneficiary. This means the annuity will pay the owner, Paul Jones, $503 per month for the rest of his life. When he dies, if his wife, Mary, is still alive, she will continue to receive $503 per month until she dies. However, if both Paul and Mary die before the end of 20 years, the annuity will pay their daughter (the beneficiary) $503 per month until the end of 20 years. If Paul and Mary die after the benefits have been paying for 20 years or more, the payments end and nothing passes to the beneficiary or the estate.

Benefit Statement for Fixed Deferred Annuity

(A)	Type of Annuity:	Deferred Annuity
(B)	Premium:	$10,000 initial, $150/month
(C)	Interest Rate:	4.5%
(D)	Payout:	20-Year Certain
(E)	Beneficiary:	Mary Jones, Wife
(F)	Monthly Benefit:	$350
(G)	Owner:	Paul Jones, age 60
	Spouse:	Mary Jones, age 60

(A) Annuity type

(B) Initial deposit, monthly investment

(C) Interest rate

(D) Payout option

(E) Spouse who receives benefit if one of the owners dies

(F) Amount of benefit based on payout option

(G) Annuity owner and spouse

Statement Details—Deferred Annuity

Deferred annuities put off paying benefits to a later date. Many people use them like savings accounts and set up a regular deposit system. You can also fund them with a single deposit if you wish. The key is that benefits come at a later date. In the meantime, your money is earning interest at some guaranteed rate. There is no specific time limit on deferred annuities, although most require you to begin taking money out by age 85. When you are ready to receive benefits, your deferred annuity changes into an immediate annuity, and your payout option begins.

With a deferred annuity, your monthly benefit is a target rather than known as it is with an immediate annuity. Whether you hit that target depends on your continued funding and a stable interest rate. When you buy the annuity, the life insurance company can tell you what it will take to hit the target in terms of your investment, interest rates, and time.

Payout

All of the payout options discussed later in this chapter work for this annuity. For this example, I chose 20-Year Certain. This payout guarantees the owner, Paul Jones, will receive the monthly benefit for 20 years. If he dies before the 20 years is up, the beneficiary, Mary Jones, will receive the monthly benefit for the remainder of the 20 years.

Paper Clips

Annuities are among the most flexible of all financial products when it comes to payouts. Most financial products offer few if any options on how you receive your money, but annuities have a wide range of possible payouts. Later in this chapter, you'll see some of the many possibilities for payouts that may be based on a person's life, the lives of two people, a fixed number of years, a fixed sum of money, and so on. Check with the life insurance company about how they can tailor a payout option to fit your needs.

Monthly Benefit

The owner of this annuity wants a monthly benefit of at least $350. The life insurance agent who sold this annuity worked with the owner to arrive at the funds it would take to generate this benefit in the future. The calculation considered current and future interest rates, time until the owner needed the benefit, amount of money invested, and the age of the owner. The owner may defer the payout for a number of years while the owner continues to deposit money every month.

Benefit Statement–Variable Annuities

Variable annuities offer many of the advantages of regular fixed annuities, with the extra possibility of earning more than a guaranteed rate. Where fixed annuities are very safe and predictable, variable annuities sacrifice some security for a potentially high rate of return. The life insurance company accomplishes this by letting you invest your money in a selection of mutual funds within the annuity. Variable annuities are always deferred annuities because you don't know the value of the account until you decide to begin receiving a monthly benefit.

A Annuity type

B Initial deposit, monthly investment

C Accounts by percentage

D Beginning fund balances

E Combination of contribution & growth

F Ending fund balances

G Payout option

H Target benefit based on payout option

I Annuity owner

Benefit Statement for Variable Deferred Annuity

		D	**E**	**F**
A Type of Annuity:		Variable Deferred Annuity		
B Premium:		$5,000 initial, $300/month		
Subaccounts:		Begin. Balance	Contr. Growth	Ending Balance
C Growth 40%		$23,483.34	$276.56	$23,759.89
Income 40%		$19,176.23	$311.76	$19,487.99
Technology 20%		$13,678.90	$82.79	$13,761.69
G Payout:		Single Life		
H Monthly Benefit:		$550		
I Owner:		Paul Jones, age 60		

Statement Detail

The major difference between variable and fixed annuities is how your money is invested. With fixed annuities, the life insurance company makes all the investment decisions and takes all the investment risk. With the variable annuity, you decide which subaccounts (these are the same as mutual funds) you want to invest your money in and in what proportion. If the funds do well, your annuity will pay a better rate than you could have earned with a fixed annuity. On the other hand, if the funds don't do well, your annuity will stink.

This statement shows how the owner split the money between three accounts. The accounts split the monthly contribution of $350 according to the percentage allocation. That contribution combined with the growth (or loss) each month changes the balance from month to month. Not reflected in the balance numbers are the fees associated with variable annuities. Some companies may show those, although most will only disclose them on the *prospectus* or some other document.

The Payout Option

All payout options are available for variable annuities. For this example, I chose the single life payout. This option pays the highest monthly benefit and continues paying that benefit as long as you live. However, when you die the benefit ends, and nothing passes to your estate or a beneficiary.

Monthly Benefit

Because this is a deferred benefit, any monthly benefit listed on your statement (and many do not list any) is a target, not a guaranteed benefit. As noted previously, the variable is the benefit. You don't know the value of the subaccounts in the future, so it is not possible to know the benefit for sure. When you are ready to begin receiving benefits, you can convert the variable annuity into an immediate annuity, and the value of your subaccounts is converted so you will know your monthly benefit.

> **Financial Speak**
>
> A **prospectus** is a written offer to sell securities that contains all the information including the risks that an investor needs to know before making a decision to buy. In the case of variable annuities, the prospectus would cover the sub-accounts.

> **Form Alarm**
>
> There are high commissions in selling variable annuities, so guess what products get pushed? However, variable annuities are not for everyone. They often have high fees, and they are risky.

Qualifier

Because this is not a book on annuities, I have oversimplified my discussion of these important financial tools. If you are interested in learning more about annuities, I suggest you pick up a copy of *The Pocket Idiot's Guide to Annuities*. It's available from Amazon.com or may be at your favorite bookstore. (Shameless self-promotion.)

Payout Options

As noted several times in this chapter, one of the advantages of annuities is the flexibility of the payout options. You have many choices when it comes to taking your money out of annuities, and that makes them popular for financial-planning purposes. The following is a list of the major payout options for annuities. These options work on any fixed or variable annuity you might own. However, after you pick a payout option and begin receiving benefits, it is usually impossible to change your mind. In the interest of clarity, I assume a husband and wife own the annuity. That is not a requirement. You do not have to have a spouse or name your spouse as your co-annuitant.

- **Single life only, without refund.** You receive payments for your lifetime, but they cease upon your death.

- **Single life with *x* years certain.** You receive payments for your lifetime. However, if you die before the end of *x* years, payments continue to your beneficiary until the end of the *x*-year period. The *x* period is usually in 5-year increments (e.g., 5 years certain or 15 years certain).

- **Single life with installment refund.** You receive payments for your lifetime. However, if you die before receiving an amount equal to the original premium, payments continue to your beneficiary until the total payments made (to you and the beneficiary) equal the original premium (without interest).

- **Single life with cash refund.** You receive payments for your lifetime. However, if you die before receiving an amount equal to the original premium, your beneficiary gets a lump sum payment equal to the difference between the premium and what you have received.

- **Joint & full survivor (100%).** You and your spouse receive a full monthly benefit as long as you both live. If either dies, it does not reduce the benefit to the other.

- **Joint & survivor (100%) with certain period.** If you both die before the end of the specified certain period (5–25 years), your beneficiary gets the full monthly benefit until the end of the certain period.

- **Joint & survivor (100%) with installment refund.** You and your spouse receive a full monthly benefit as long as you both live. However, if you both die before receiving in periodic payments an amount equal to the original premium, the monthly benefit continues to the estate or your beneficiary until the total payments made (to both of you while living and to the beneficiary after your death) equals the original premium (usually, without interest).

- **Joint & survivor (100%) with cash refund.** You and your spouse receive a full monthly benefit as long as you both live. However, if both of you die before receiving in payments an amount equal to the original premium, the difference between the original premium (usually, without interest) and the monthly benefit received during your lifetimes is paid to the estate or your beneficiary in a single lump sum.

- **Joint & survivor (50% to 75%) reducing on *first* or *either* death.** You receive the full monthly benefit as long as you both are alive. Upon the death of either the annuitant or joint annuitant, the monthly benefit is reduced by a percentage (50% to 75%), and payments will continue to the survivor for as long as he/she is alive.

- **Adding a period certain provision to a joint & survivor (50% to 75%) annuity accomplishes the following.** Even if you or the joint annuitant dies before the end of the certain period, payments to the survivor stay the same until after the end of the certain period (5 to 25 years). If both the annuitant and joint annuitant die before the end of the certain period, full monthly benefit continues to your beneficiary until the end of the certain period.

Fill In the Blank

This is not a complete list of payout options, and life insurance companies may have some that are unique to their products.

◆ **Joint & survivor (50% to 75%) reducing only on your death.** You receive the full monthly benefit as long as you both are alive. Payments are never reduced to you. However, payments are reduced to the survivor should you die first.

◆ **X years period certain (without life contingency).** A monthly benefit is paid for *x* years. If you die before the end of the certain period, the monthly benefit goes to your beneficiary. Payments end at the end of the specified period.

Chapter 20

Golden Years–Social Security (or Not)

In This Chapter

- ◆ Social Security benefit statement
- ◆ Earnings record
- ◆ Benefits estimates

The political rhetoric over Social Security is almost deafening at times. Nevertheless, the agency keeps plugging away. The benefits available under Social Security depend on several factors. In this chapter, we look at those factors and how you can make them work for you.

Social Security Benefits

As you get closer to retirement, Social Security benefits become an important ingredient in your planning process. At age 25, you should begin receiving an annual Social Security statement, which arrives several months before your birthday. This individually prepared report lists your estimated benefits as of the report date and your earnings record.

Ⓐ Earliest you can receive benefits

Ⓑ Based on wage history

Ⓒ Full benefits available

Ⓓ Delayed benefits

Ⓔ Approximate disability pay

Ⓕ Expanded family coverage

Ⓖ Benefits for your family

Ⓗ Death benefit

Ⓘ Medicare qualification

Your Estimated Benefits

Retirement

You have earned enough credits to qualify for benefits. At your current earnings rate, if you stop working and start receiving benefits …

Ⓐ At age 62, your payment would be about $1,125 a month

If you continue working until …   Ⓑ

    Ⓒ Your full retirement age (66) $1,515 a month

    Ⓓ Age 70 $2,003 a month

Ⓔ **Disability**

You have earned enough credits to qualify for benefits. If you became disabled right now …

Your payment would be about $1,569 a month

Family

If you get retirement or disability benefits, your spouse and children also may qualify for benefits.

Ⓕ **Survivors**

You have earned enough credits for your family to receive the following benefits if you die this year.

Ⓖ   Your child $1,180 a month

    Your spouse who is caring for a child $1,180 a month

    Your spouse who reaches full retirement $1,574 a month

    Total family benefits cannot be more than $2,755 a month

Ⓗ Your spouse or minor child may be eligible for a special one-time death benefit of $255.

Ⓘ **Medicare**

You have earned enough credits to qualify for Medicare at age 65. Even if you do not retire at age 65, be sure to contact Social Security three months before your sixty-fifth birthday to enroll in Medicare.

Statement Details

Your Social Security statement of benefits describes what you can expect from the agency based on current law and what it knows about you now. The older you are, the more accurate the estimates will be for reasons that I explain in upcoming paragraphs. If you are in your 30s, this is a pretty meaningless report, with one exception. This is extremely important: you should review it every year for errors. Future benefits depend on its accuracy.

Credits

Despite what some people may think, you are not entitled to Social Security benefits—you must earn them. You earn benefits by paying into the system through payroll or self-employment taxes. The Social Security Administration uses a formula that changes over the years to calculate what they call "credits."

In benefit statements sent out in 2005, you could earn one credit for each $900 of wages or self-employment income. Most people need 40 credits earned over their working lifetime to qualify for benefits. There are special cases such as disability and survivor benefits where there may be lower requirements.

You also must earn credits to qualify for Medicare, the insurance program administered by Social Security. If you have enough credits, you can and should apply for Medicare just before your sixty-fifth birthday, even if you don't plan to retire.

Paper Clips

All of the numbers on your statement are in today's dollars, meaning they do not reflect any cost-of-living increases that may apply before you actually retire.

Your Estimated Benefits

Retirement

You have earned enough credits to qualify for benefits. At your current earnings rate, if you stop working and start receiving benefits …

(A) At age 62, your payment would be about $1,125 a month

If you continue working until …   (B)

(C)   Your full retirement age (66) $1,515 a month

(D)   Age 70 $2,003 a month

Disability

(E) You have earned enough credits to qualify for benefits. If you became disabled right now …

Your payment would be about $1,569 a month

(A) Earliest you can receive benefits

(B) Based on wage history

(C) Full benefits available

(D) Delayed benefits

(E) Approximate disability pay

Estimated Benefits

Your benefits statement has estimated benefits at different retirement ages. Social Security calculates these benefits by looking at your earnings over your lifetime. This is why I noted earlier it is important to monitor the earnings statement.

Many pension plans take your last five years, when you should be at your earnings peak, as a basis for your pension, but not Social Security. In addition to looking at all your earnings, if you were in the military, worked on a railroad, or receive a company pension, your benefit may be affected. You can visit www.socialsecurity.gov/mystatment for more information on these and other conditions.

The formula for actually calculating your benefits is structured so that benefits replace about 42% of the earnings of an average salary. Lower-income wage earners receive more benefits, and higher-income wage earners fewer benefits.

Form Alarm

If you find a mistake on your statement, contact the Social Security Administration immediately using the information on the statement. Don't let an error go unreported; otherwise you could lose benefits that rightfully belong to you.

Retirement

My example is for a person in their mid-50s of middle-income wage history. Although you can retire at age 62, Social Security significantly reduces benefits. Given the problems facing the agency, the days of early retirement with any benefits may be numbered.

If you were born in 1937 or earlier, full retirement is at age 65. That retirement age increases based on a sliding scale that adds months to the retirement age for those born between 1938 and 1942. For those born between 1943 and 1954, the retirement age is 66. Some more months are added to the retirement age for those who were born beginning in 1955 up through 1959. For those born in 1960 and after, the current retirement age is 67.

You will notice there is a real incentive to put off drawing benefits until age 70. If this person can wait four years, the monthly benefit goes up almost $500, or about 32%.

Paper Clips

Social Security is a political hot potato and undoubtedly is facing some major changes in the coming years. Watch for how these reforms may affect your benefits.

Disability

Social Security's definition of disability is very strict, by their own admission. The definition says you are disabled if you can't do the work you did before and can't adjust to other work because of your medical condition. The disability has to be expected to last at least a year or you have to die.

The agency says families should have other resources to cover short-term disability problems.

F Expanded family coverage
G Benefits for your family
H Death benefit
I Medicare qualification

Family

If you get retirement or disability benefits, your spouse and children also may qualify for benefits.

F **Survivors**

You have earned enough credits for your family to receive the following benefits if you die this year.

Your child	$1,180 a month
Your spouse who is caring for a child	$1,180 a month
Your spouse who reaches full retirement	$1,574 a month
Total family benefits cannot be more than	$2,755 a month

H Your spouse or minor child may be eligible for a special one-time death benefit of $255.

I **Medicare**

You have earned enough credits to qualify for Medicare at age 65. Even if you do not retire at age 65, be sure to contact Social Security three months before your sixty-fifth birthday to enroll in Medicare.

Family Benefits

If you qualify for Social Security benefits, some of those benefits may extend to your family. These benefits generally come into play only if you die or become disabled.

Disability Benefits for Your Family

If you qualify for disability benefits, family members may also qualify for certain benefits. Your benefits statement does not list these benefits, but you can find them on the website mentioned above. The family members who may qualify include the following:

- Children under age 18
- Disabled children
- Spouse
- Divorced spouse

There is a limit to how much Social Security will pay your family, which varies between 150% and 180% of your total disability benefit.

> **Fill In the Blank**
>
> The Social Security website has a wealth of information to help you sort through the rules and regulations concerning who is eligible for benefits. You can find it at www.socialsecurity.gov/.

Survivors

Social Security keeps paying even after you die. Your family members receive a monthly benefit estimated for you on the benefit statement.

This portion of the statement details how much Social Security will pay each surviving member of the family. Remember, these numbers are for illustration only. Your benefits are different and may be higher or lower. Social Security caps the benefits it pays to families, which changes also with each situation.

The one-time death benefit of $255 seems almost an insult given the cost of funerals. However, it might cover the cost of a nice obituary in the newspaper.

Medicare

As I said earlier, you have to earn access to Medicare insurance with credits, the same as you do for Social Security. Your statement will tell you whether you have met the requirement. The statement encourages you to sign up for Medicare three months before your sixty-fifth birthday even if you do not plan to retire. Medicare eligibility is not tied to receiving other Social Security benefits.

Earning Record

Part of your statement of benefits is an earning record that recaps by year your earnings. Social Security uses these numbers to compute your benefits for retirement, so it is important that they are correct. You and your employer are responsible for the accuracy of these numbers, so check them every year you get a statement to be sure they are accurate. If you have a high income, remember that Social Security only taxes the first $90,000 (in 2005, up from $87,000), whereas Medicare taxes all of your earnings. This means that in some years these two columns may have different numbers.

Special Insert

If you are age 55 or older, your earnings statement contains a special insert that discusses your options for retirement. The insert has two major topics: your retirement options and how to apply for benefits.

Retirement Options

The insert gives you some information about the options and consequences of the following:

Form Alarm

Social Security is very specific (down to the month) about your retirement age, so be sure you get it right when you file for benefits or it could cost you. You don't want it to start a month too early if you wait until the full age of retirement, because you could lose out on several hundreds of dollars a month.

◆ Retiring at full retirement age

◆ Retiring early

◆ Receiving retirement benefits while still working

◆ Delaying retirement

Retiring at Full Retirement Age

Full retirement age depends on when you were born. I noted earlier in the chapter those dates as determined by Social Security. Given the strain the agency's resources face in coming years, expect the definition of full retirement age to rise.

Retiring Early

You can begin receiving retirement benefits at age 62. However, it is clear the Social Security system is set up to discourage this option. If you do choose to begin early retirement, expect reduced benefits. The special insert lists how much Social Security will discount your benefit depending on your full retirement age. For example, if your full retirement age is 66 and you want to begin receiving benefits at 62, expect your check to be about 25% less than if you wait until age 66.

Receiving Benefits While Working

This is a little complicated, but you can receive benefits and still work. The catch is if you receive benefits before reaching full retirement age while working, your benefit can be reduced. The reduction is $1 in benefits for each $2 you earn above the limit ($11,640 in 2004). There are slightly different rules for the year in which you reach full retirement age. After you reach full retirement age, you can earn as much as you want without affecting your benefits. This question is very much subject to change, so before you count on working and receiving Social Security benefits, check with your local office for the latest rules.

Paper Clips

As you approach retirement, it will be worth your time to visit with a Social Security representative to look at all the options and how your estimated benefits work under different scenarios. You have paid into the system all of your life in most cases, so take advantage of the benefits you have earned.

Delaying Retirement

This is the clear favorite of the Social Security Administration, and they put their money behind this option. They will pay you a bonus in benefits if you delay retirement. For example, if you were born in 1943 or later, which for those nearing retirement is all of the Baby Boom generation, Social Security will pay a yearly increase rate of 8% for delaying retirement.

Part 5

Market Mogul

Whether it's some money invested in a couple of mutual funds or an active trading account, managing investments means managing information. You are flooded with documents written in some language that faintly resembles English and are expected to understand it. Never fear, this part of the book will help cut through the jargon of the documents that follow investments.

Chapter 21

Going for Broke

In This Chapter

◆ Details of brokerage statements
◆ Transactions of brokerage statements
◆ Brokerage fees

Your brokerage account will likely generate a monthly statement whether you have trades or not. If you are not getting a monthly statement, count on one coming quarterly. During the month, your investments change in value, so you'll want to track those differences. Don't think that just because you haven't initiated any activity, your account hasn't generated a fee.

In this chapter, we look at your monthly statement and what you can expect to find there. We also discuss the electronic versions that your broker may offer.

Brokerage Statements

Your monthly broker's statement sums up the activity in your account from the last period in a (hopefully) concise and helpful manner. The purpose of the statement is to document any transactions since the last statement and record the growth or loss experienced by each investment and your account as a whole. If your broker is part of a bank or other major financial institution, your statement may be part of a larger financial picture painted on a consolidated statement.

Form Alarm

Check your brokerage statement each month even if you don't have any transactions. You are responsible for notifying the broker if there is an error. The sooner you report an error, the easier it will be to fix.

Ⓐ Statement period

Ⓑ Type of account

Ⓒ Total account value as of this statement

Ⓓ Beginning and ending balances

Ⓔ Stocks owned

Ⓕ Symbols

Ⓖ Share owned

Ⓗ Share price on statement date

Ⓘ Market value on statement date

Ⓙ What you bought/sold

Ⓚ Date of transaction

Ⓛ Type of transaction

Ⓜ Shares bought or sold

Ⓝ Share price on statement date

Investment Account Statement

Ⓐ Statement Period:	02/01/2006 – 03/01/2006	
Ⓑ Account Type:	Cash	
Ⓒ Total Account Value:	$28,049.00	
Account Summary	Ⓓ	

	Beginning Balance	Ending Balance
Common/Preferred Stock	$26,273.00	$28,049.00

Brokerage Positions

Ⓔ Stocks	Ⓕ Symbol	Ⓖ Share Quantity	Ⓗ Share Price	Ⓘ Market Value
Acme Kumquats	AAKUM	400	$35.45	$14,180.00
Baltic Billiards	BLLLL	100	$12.37	$1,237.00
Cal's Catapults	CACCC	250	$23.24	$5,810.00
U.S. Dog Houses	USDHS	200	$34.11	$6,822.00
			Total Account Value:	$28,049.00

Transactions

Ⓙ Security	Ⓚ Date	Ⓛ Action	Ⓜ Share Quantity	Ⓝ Share Price	Market Value
U.S. Dog Houses	02/12	Buy	200	$33.85	$6,770.00
Nat. Frog	02/17	Sell	300	$19.64	$5,892.00

Statement Details

Your brokerage statement may not look anything like this, but it will contain the same basic information. Some brokers do not send you a statement on a monthly basis if there is no activity in the account, whereas others do. Whatever the format or frequency, there are some key points on all statements that you will want to note.

Investment Account Statement

(A) Statement Period:	02/01/2006 – 03/01/2006	
(B) Account Type:	Cash	
(C) Total Account Value:	$28,049.00	

Account Summary

	(D) Beginning Balance	Ending Balance
Common/Preferred Stock	$26,273.00	$28,049.00

- (A) Statement period
- (B) Type of account
- (C) Total account value as of this statement
- (D) Beginning and ending balances

Starting at the Top

The top portion of the sample statement contains the statement period and other summary information. Obviously, your statement will also contain your name and address, account number, and some marketing message from your broker.

The statement identifies this as a cash account, which means you pay for what you buy, as opposed to a margin account where you may borrow some portion of the purchase price. Your broker has special requirements for opening margin accounts, so check with him for the details.

A separate line summarizes the value of the account at the end of the statement period. This is somewhat redundant information that is found elsewhere on the statement (on the next item, in fact), but many brokers include it somewhere close to the top as a quick reference point.

The next item looks at the balance at the beginning of the statement period and at the end to give you a sense of movement. Some statements calculate the percent change for you, whereas others may leave it as shown in the example with just the raw numbers.

Fill In the Blank

By the time you receive your statement, the share prices for your holding will probably be out of date. If you want the latest values, use the stock symbols from the statement and plug them into one of the websites listed in Appendix B.

Brokerage Positions

(E) Stocks	(F) Symbol	(G) Share Quantity	(H) Share Price	(I) Market Value
Acme Kumquats	AAKUM	400	$35.45	$14,180.00
Baltic Billiards	BLLLL	100	$12.37	$1,237.00
Cal's Catapults	CACCC	250	$23.24	$5,810.00
U.S. Dog Houses	USDHS	200	$34.11	$6,822.00
			Total Account Value:	$28,049.00

- (E) Stocks owned
- (F) Symbols
- (G) Share owned
- (H) Share price on statement date
- (I) Market value on statement date

Your Positions

This next section of the statement details your stock positions as of the end of the statement period. It is worth noting that if you have an account with a firm that offers mutual funds and other financial services, they may want to consolidate everything into your brokerage statement so you get only one report per month. If that is the case, this statement would also show mutual funds as well as individual stocks. It is also possible to buy mutual funds through brokers. (That's the only way some are sold.)

The statement lists the stocks by name and symbol. (This is the symbol you use to look up their price on an online service.) How many shares and the price of each stock makes up the other part of this report, which concludes with a market value as of the close date for this statement.

J What you bought/sold

K Date of transaction

L Type of transaction

M Shares bought or sold

N Share price on statement date

Transactions			**M**	**N**	
J Security	**K** Date	**L** Action	**Share Quantity**	**Share Price**	**Market Value**
U.S. Dog Houses	02/12	Buy	200	$33.85	$6,770.00
Nat. Frog	02/17	Sell	300	$19.64	$5,892.00

The Transactions

This portion of the statement lists any transactions that occurred since the last statement. The statement lists the stocks by date and action (buy or sell), the quantity, the share price, and the market value at the time of the transaction. You will note that the share price differs from the report under stock positions, because some time has passed and the stock's price has changed.

Your statement may not show any fees associated with the buying and selling of stocks. Some brokers show the fees on statements, whereas others simply report "net" proceeds.

If your account is inactive for a long period, your broker may charge you a fee. Not every broker has an inactivity fee, but if you are an infrequent trader, check before you open an account to see whether that will be a problem.

Paper Clips

If your broker charges an inactivity fee, ask whether they will waive it for you. The brokerage business is very competitive, and they may not want to lose a client over a fee.

Online Version

Most brokers, and obviously the online brokers, have extensive and robust online services. In addition to offering trading services, many brokers encourage you to opt in to receive your brokerage statements electronically. Online statements tend to have greater depth and more history available than their paper versions. If you are an active trader, the electronic versions may be the only way to keep up with your activity.

Chapter 22

Mutually Yours

In This Chapter

- Deciphering your statement
- Understanding the different transactions
- Understanding how share prices and values work
- Understanding the online version

Mutual funds are a convenient way to invest your money and let professional managers make decisions for you. However, that convenience comes with a price, including your time to wade through the various forms and reports.

The most frequent information you'll receive from the mutual fund company will come in the form of a monthly statement. This statement details transactions in your account for the past month, although some companies may only provide a quarterly accounting.

Some companies give you the choice of receiving the material either via regular snail mail or online. The choice is yours. The information is essentially the same—mainly because industry rules and regulations dictate most of it. So, do you want your mailbox stuffed or your inbox clogged?

Your Mutual Fund Statement

Your monthly statement from the mutual fund company tracks your activity and summarizes your investments. Although formats vary, you should find the same basic information on every statement. Most mutual fund companies let you view your account online, and some will even quit sending you paper statements, except for year-end summaries and those required by law.

(A) The value of the fund at the beginning of the accounting month

(B) Share price calculated at the end of each day the market opens

(C) A withdrawal from the fund

(D) A regular investment into the fund

(E) The value of the fund at the end of the accounting month

(F) A wire transfer from your bank

(G) An investment by check

(H) The reinvestment of a dividend generated by the fund

(I) The total value of the account at the beginning of the month

(J) Total dollars invested this period

(K) Total withdrawals

(L) The total value of the account at the end of the month

Fund Name				Account Number	
ABC Growth Fund				111111111111	

Date	Transaction Description	Number Shares	Share Price	Amount
07/01/04	**(A)** Beginning Value	119.833	**(B)** $28.23	$3,393.67
07/08/04	**(C)** Redemption	(18.348)	$27.25	($500.00)
07/15/04	**(D)** Systematic Investment	1.829	$27.33	$50.00
07/30/04	Systematic Investment	1.883	$26.55	$50.00
07/31/04	**(E)** Ending Value	105.197	$28.33	$2,980.23

Fund Name				Account Number	
ABC Income Fund				5555555555555	

Date	Transaction Description	Number Shares	Share Price	Amount
07/01/04	Beginning Value	127.174	$17.57	$2,234.45
07/15/04	Systematic Investment	5.770	$17.33	$100.00
07/18/04	**(F)** Wire Transfer	58.038	$17.23	$1,000.00
07/30/04	Systematic Investment	5.624	$17.18	$100.00
07/31/04	Ending Value	196.606	$17.09	$3,359.99

Fund Name				Account Number	
ABC Money Market Fund				222222222222	

Date	Transaction Description	Number Shares	Share Price	Amount
07/01/04	Beginning Value	589.140	$1.00	$589.14
07/15/04	**(G)** Investment by Check	65.00	$1.00	$65.00
07/30/04	**(H)** Dividend - reinvest	1.090	$1.00	$1.09
07/31/04	Ending Value	655.80	$1.00	$655.24

Account Summary

(I)	Account Value on 07/01/04	$6,217.26
(J)	Purchases/Reinvestments	$1,366.09
(K)	Redemptions	($500.00)
(L)	Account Value on 07/31.04	$6,995.46

Statement Detail

This example focuses on the information you really need to know. It is certain that your statement will contain an assortment of marketing messages and customer service tips, which may be nice to know, but this is the important stuff.

The first thing you should do is check the statement against your records. Mutual fund companies do make mistakes, and it is your responsibility to call them to the company's attention.

My sample has only three funds: a growth fund, an income fund, and a money market fund. If you own more funds, they would appear on this list, although some mutual fund companies might send you a separate statement for each fund.

I spread the different types of typical transactions over all three funds for two reasons. First, it breaks up the information into more manageable pieces, and second, to illustrate that all of the different transaction types could occur in any of the funds.

Fund Name		Account Number		
ABC Growth Fund		111111111111		
Date	**Transaction Description**	**Number Shares**	**Share Price**	**Amount**
07/01/04 Ⓐ	Beginning Value	119.833 Ⓑ	$28.23	$3,393.67
07/08/04 Ⓒ	Redemption	(18.348)	$27.25	($500.00)
07/15/04 Ⓓ	Systematic Investment	1.829	$27.33	$50.00
07/30/04	Systematic Investment	1.883	$26.55	$50.00
07/31/04 Ⓔ	Ending Value	105.197	$28.33	$2,980.23

Ⓐ The value of the fund at the beginning of the accounting month

Ⓑ Share price calculated at the end of each day the market opens

Ⓒ A withdrawal from the fund

Ⓓ A regular investment into the fund

Ⓔ The value of the fund at the end of the accounting month

ABC Growth Fund—Transaction Description

The register notes the date and type of the transaction along with the number of shares and share price. There are several different types of possible transactions for any fund listed. Two are listed for the growth fund:

- *Redemption* is the withdrawal of funds from your account, which is expressed in the number of shares and a dollar amount.

- Systematic investment is an automatic debit from your bank account for a fixed amount on specified dates. This may also go by names such as automatic investment plan or something similar.

The other types of transactions, which I list for the other funds on this statement, could also apply to this fund.

These same types of transactions apply to all the funds listed on the statement. If you see something strange in this column, call the customer service number on the statement for clarification.

Financial Speak

Redemption is the term used in the mutual fund industry to describe selling shares. Unlike stocks, which you buy and sell on the open market, you buy mutual fund shares from the mutual fund company and sell (or redeem) them back to the company when you want to cash out.

ABC Growth Fund—Beginning, Ending Values

The Transaction column begins with a Beginning Value notation, which if you follow across the columns note the total number of shares owned in this fund, the share price at the beginning of the statement period, and the dollar value in the fund (number of shares × per share value = beginning fund balance).

The Ending Value Dollar Amount is calculated the same way (number of shares × share value = closing balance). The fund calculates the Share Price on the closing day of the statement.

ABC Growth Fund—Number of Shares and Share Prices

You invest whole dollars that the fund converts into shares based on the value of the fund at that time. This means you will own fractional shares of the mutual fund. This is different from owning individual stocks where you can't own a fractional share of stock. Most mutual funds report fractional shares to three decimal places.

You will notice that two investments of $50 result in two different quantities of shares purchased. Because the value of the fund changed, one investment of $50 bought 1.829 shares, whereas the second $50 investment bought 1.883 shares.

ABC Growth Fund–Redemption

The first item after the Beginning Value is a Redemption for $500, which works out to 18.348 shares at the per share price of $27.25 (500.00 / 27.25 = 18.348 shares). This entry indicates you withdrew $500 from the account by redeeming or selling back to the company enough shares to generate $500.

The fund makes this calculation by taking your dollar amount and the current per share price and converting those two numbers into the necessary number of shares:

$ amount of redemption / per share price = number of shares to redeem

ABC Growth Fund–Systematic Investment

Under Redemption are two items labeled Systematic Investment for the same amount ($50) on two different dates. Systematic Investment is an automatic investment program set up through your bank that periodically debits your account for a fixed amount and sends it to the mutual fund.

You can set up a Systematic Investment program to debit as often as you want. Most people do it once a month or on or near a payday (as this statement indicates). As noted previously, the two identical dollar investments result in different numbers of shares purchased because the share price has changed.

Ⓕ A wire transfer from your bank

Fund Name		Account Number		
ABC Income Fund		5555555555555		
Date	Transaction Description	Number Shares	Share Price	Amount
07/01/04	Beginning Value	127.174	$17.57	$2,234.45
07/15/04	Systematic Investment	5.770	$17.33	$100.00
07/18/04 Ⓕ	Wire Transfer	58.038	$17.23	$1,000.00
07/30/04	Systematic Investment	5.624	$17.18	$100.00
07/31/04	Ending Value	196.606	$17.09	$3,359.99

ABC Income Fund–Transaction Description

The transactions and detail for this fund follow the same description as the ABC growth fund. A new element is the wire transfer to the account of $1,000. This illustrates one other method of purchasing shares of a mutual fund.

You can use wire transfers to send money directly from your bank account to the mutual fund on a one-time basis. The money is available almost instantly to the mutual fund if that is your goal.

The fund converts the $1,000 into shares based on the current share value at the time, in this case $17.23, which gives you 58.038 shares for your $1,000 investment. The $17.23 is called the *net asset value* or *NAV* and it is the mutual fund term for market price.

> **Financial Speak**
>
> **Net asset value** is a term some mutual funds use in place of share price. It is calculated at the close of the market every day and is the sum of the fund's assets (the stocks, bonds, and/or cash it owns) minus its liabilities and is quoted on a per-share basis.

Fund Name		Account Number		
ABC Money Market Fund		222222222222		
Date	Transaction Description	Number Shares	Share Price	Amount
07/01/04 Ⓖ Beginning Value		589.140	$1.00	$589.14
07/15/04 Ⓗ Investment by Check		65.00	$1.00	$65.00
07/30/04 Dividend - reinvest		1.090	$1.00	$1.09
07/31/04 Ending Value		655.80	$1.00	$655.24

Ⓖ An investment by check

Ⓗ The reinvestment of a dividend generated by the fund

ABC Money Market Fund–Transaction Description

The same transaction descriptions apply for the money market fund that we previously covered for the other two funds. In this example, there are two new transactions:

- Investment by check
- Dividend Reinvestment

Each of these transaction types could occur in either of the other funds discussed previously.

ABC Money Market Fund–Investment by Check

The first transaction notes a check deposited to the account for $65. The Systematic Investment and simply writing a check are the two most common ways to purchase shares of a mutual fund.

ABC Money Market Fund–Dividend Reinvestment

The second item, Dividend Reinvestment, is your return from the fund. This represents interest earned and reinvested into the account. In a low-interest environment, this number will be small, but so will other interest-earning investments.

ABC Money Market Fund–Beginning, Ending Values

The money market transaction register also follows the same format for reporting beginning and ending values for the fund and the ABC growth fund report with the exception that the share value is a constant $1.

ABC Money Market Fund—Number of Shares and Share Prices

You will notice a big difference between the ABC growth fund and the ABC money market fund when it comes to these columns. The first difference you will notice is that the share price for the money market fund does not vary from $1 per share.

Does that mean something is wrong with the fund? No, money market funds maintain a constant share price of $1. You earn interest on your money, which the fund reinvests into your account or pays out to you. There is no share price appreciation as you will find in regular mutual funds.

Your number of shares reflects the actual dollar value of your account. It is easy to figure your balance if you know how many shares you own. With regular mutual funds, you have to know the price per share and the number of shares owned to calculate the value of your account.

Form Alarm

A money market mutual fund should maintain a share price of $1. If you notice your money market fund is not doing this, it's time to pick up the phone and find out why. Not all money market funds are created equal.

I The total value of the account at the beginning of the month

J Total dollars invested this period

K Total withdrawals

L The total value of the account at the end of the month

Account Summary	
Account Value on 07/01/04	$6,217.26
Purchases/Reinvestments	$1,366.09
Redemptions	($500.00)
Account Value on 07/31.04	$6,995.46

Account Summary

The account summary pulls together all the funds detailed on the statement to give you a single look at the value of your total account. There is nothing sophisticated about this report. It simply details your beginning balance, the sum of all of the deposits, the sum of any redemptions, and the value of your account at the end of the month.

It is important to note that the end-of-the-month account value is not determined by adding and subtracting the purchases and redemptions from the account value at the beginning of the month. The account value at the end of the month is determined by adding the end values of the three mutual funds.

Year-End Statement

Mutual funds will send you a year-end statement that, in most cases, is identical in format to your monthly statement, but covers 12 months instead of just the current one.

If you have many transactions in your account during the year, these statements can get quite lengthy. They are redundant if you have kept up with the monthly statements and verified that all transactions were posted correctly.

Online Version

Most mutual fund companies offer some form of their documents online these days. Some encourage you to sign up to receive your statements online so they don't have to mail you so many pieces of paper.

Usually you have to agree to electronic delivery and hold the mutual fund company harmless if you can't get to your account for some reason (your Internet provider is down, or their server is too busy, for example).

Statement Detail

What are the benefits of viewing your statement online? Other than less paper to shuffle around your desk, there is not much of an advantage to looking at your statement online. The information is identical in most cases and is usually formatted the same way. The main benefit is you can review your account at any time—you don't have to wait until the mail brings the printed statement.

One other benefit is that you are not limited to the current month. You can usually look at your history with the account if you need to for some reason, which a monthly paper statement can't provide except by your digging old statements out of a file cabinet.

Another benefit is that some funds may not send monthly statements, especially if your account is inactive. You may only get a quarterly accounting of activity with a paper statement.

Chapter 23

Telltale Tables

In This Chapter

◆ Reading stock tables

◆ Reading mutual fund tables

◆ Reading bond tables

Want to know how much your fortune increased today? The place to look is the stock and mutual fund tables listed in the newspaper or online. Of course, you need to know how to decipher the odd abbreviations and funky marks, but that's what this chapter is for.

Stock Tables—Newspaper

Before the Internet, newspapers were the primary source of price information on stocks and other investments. Today, they seem almost quaint because the information is so old by the time you read it. With after-hours trading and other market-expanding innovations (including a push for 24-hour trading), the newspaper stock tables may soon be a memory. In the meantime, they are still the record of choice for many people who don't need the most up-to-the-minute quote.

The *Wall Street Journal* (*WSJ*) remains the gold standard for this information. Many newspapers print abbreviated versions of stock tables, so your local paper may not include all the information in my example.

Ⓐ Year-to-date change

Ⓑ 52-week high price

Ⓒ 52-week low price

Ⓓ Company name and symbol

Ⓔ Annual dividend

Ⓕ Dividends as a percentage of price

Ⓖ Price/earnings ratio

Ⓗ Number of shares traded in hundreds

Ⓘ Price at close

Ⓙ Change from opening

Paper Clips

The *Wall Street Journal* is available in an online edition by subscription only. It is the only major publication to successfully charge for its online content.

Paper Clips

Dividends are usually distributed quarterly. This number takes the latest quarterly dividend and annualizes it.

Ⓐ	Ⓑ	Ⓒ	Ⓓ	Ⓔ	Ⓕ	Ⓖ	Ⓗ	Ⓘ	Ⓙ
YTD	52-WEEK				YLD		VOL		NET
% CHG	HI	LO	STOCK (SYM)	DIV	%	PE	100S	CLOSE	CHG
-6.1	49.69	34.95	Gumball GUM	4.00	8.6	17	658	46.40	-0.47

Table Details

The WSJ packs a tremendous amount of information into a line of type. For most people, this is all you need to know about your stocks on a regular basis. If you are an active trader, this information is way too old to be of much use, and you'll be more interested in real-time quotes.

The columns are easy to understand if you know what you are looking at. Here is a column-by-column explanation of the stock listings:

♦ **YTD % CHG.** Year-to-date percentage change. This number is the percentage change for the calendar year. The percentage is adjusted for stock splits and dividends over 10%.

♦ **52-week HI & LO.** These two numbers record the highest and lowest price the stock traded at during the last 52-week period, but do not include the previous trading day. The numbers may be adjusted for stock payouts or large dividends.

♦ **Stock (SYM).** The stock name, often abbreviated, and the stock symbol are listed. The symbol is boldface in the WSJ, but many newspapers either don't include the symbol or don't boldface it.

♦ **DIV.** Dividend/distribution rates. Unless noted in a footnote, this reflects the annual dividend based on the last regular disbursement.

♦ **Yield %.** The yield percentage is the dividends or other disbursements paid to stockholders as a percentage of the stock's price.

♦ **PE.** The price to earnings ratio or PE is the diluted per-share earnings divided by the closing price. A high P/E indicates investors believe the company has good future growth prospects, but the number should be compared to other companies in the same industry.

♦ **VOL 100sv.** Sales volume is expressed with two zeros missing. For example, if the number reported is 1959, that means sales volume for that stock was 195,900 for the day. An *f* indicates four zeros are missing. These results are unofficial.

♦ **CLOSE.** Close is the last price the stock traded at that day. It does not mean that is the price the stock will open at the next day.

♦ **NET CHANGE.** The net change is calculated from the previous day's close, so you are comparing what the stock closed at this day to what it closed at the previous day.

Symbols and Footnotes

You will see a variety of footnotes and odd symbols scattered throughout the listings. These markings alert you to something different about the listing that may be important for you to know. Here are the major symbols, markings, and footnotes (but not a complete list):

- **Underlined listings.** Underlined listings indicate a large change in volume. These stocks may end up on the Most Active list for the day.

- **Boldfaced quotations.** Boldfaced quotations show issues whose prices have changed by 5% or more from their previous close.

- **Up and down arrow.** An up or down arrow in the far-left margin next to the YTD % CHG column indicates a new 52-week high (up arrow) or low (down arrow).

- **a.** Extra dividend has been paid.

- **b.** Annual rate of cash dividend (annual rate), stock dividend paid.

- **e.** A dividend was declared, but there is no regular dividend rate.

- **f.** Annual dividend rate, increased on latest declaration.

- **m.** Annual dividend rate, reduced on latest declaration.

- **n.** Newly issued in the past 52 weeks.

- **pf.** Preferred stock. A class of ownership in a corporation with a stated dividend that must be paid before dividends are paid to common stock holders. Preferred stock does not usually have voting rights.

- **r.** Indicates a cash dividend declared in the past 12 months.

- **s.** Stock split or stock dividend. The 52-week high-low price is adjusted.

- **v.** Trading halted in this issue.

- **x.** Ex-dividend or after the dividend is paid the price is adjusted.

There are other footnotes, but they don't appear that often. If you find one not listed here on your stock, you can usually find a legend explaining the footnote somewhere in the paper.

Online Versions

The online version of a stock table can be as simple or complex as you want the information. Many websites have a simple stock quote box that allows you to enter a symbol and get a quote on the stock. Obviously, if you go to the financial sites, you are going to get much more information.

Fill In the Blank

You will notice in the WSJ a cloverleaf or club design next to some stocks. This indicates you can order an annual report through the paper for this company.

Form Alarm

Be careful when using online quotes from free services to consider trades. The major stock exchanges delay free stock quotes, so the information you have may be up to 20 minutes old. In a fast-moving market, that could be a disaster. Use an online broker that provides real-time quotes or call a broker that can give you that information.

Quote Details

Websites such as CNNMoney (www.money.cnn.com/quote) do a good job of presenting the important information on their first screen so you don't have to flip through several layers to get the top-level news. Their information parallels the *Wall Street Journal*'s newspaper report.

Extra Information

The other obvious difference is the online quote has a tremendous amount of additional information attached to it. The row of buttons across the top gives you an idea of some of the information you can get on IBM (all free). CNNMoney is not alone in providing this depth of information on companies. You can find more websites listed in Appendix B.

Mutual Fund Tables—Newspaper

Mutual funds are a popular way for many investors to participate in the stock and bond markets. Many newspapers, however, don't carry a complete daily listing of mutual funds. You can count on the *Wall Street Journal* and a few other business-oriented publications to provide you with the information, however.

Mutual funds do not have quite the urgency of stocks, because their prices do not change during the trading day. Mutual funds calculate their price or net asset value (NAV as it is called) at the end of each trading day.

Paper Clips

Besides quotes, newspapers such as the *Wall Street Journal* can provide analysis and other articles that are not time-sensitive.

Ⓐ Name of fund family

Ⓑ Net asset value

Ⓒ Change in NAV from previous day

Ⓓ Year-to-day return

Ⓔ Trailing three-year return

Ⓕ Names of individual funds

Mutual Fund Newspaper Quote			Ⓓ	Ⓔ
FUND	Ⓑ NAV	Ⓒ NET CHG	YTD % RET	3-YR % RET
Ⓐ DownTown Funds				
Ⓕ DivBond	11.80	-0.01	-0.3	6.2
IntlStk	13.19	-0.05	-2.6	3.9
LgCapStk	11.38	-0.01	-2.3	1.5
SmCapStk	13.19	-0.11	-5.5	5.7

Quote Detail

Mutual fund companies offer a "family" of funds under their name. Newspapers organize quotes alphabetically by the mutual fund family name. My example would be listed under the *D* section. Each family may have just a few or a large number of individual mutual funds. To find the fund you're interested in, you must know the fund family. Usually, the individual mutual funds are named using the "family name" as the first word(s) in the name. For example, Wells Fargo Advantage High Income Fund is the full name of a fund listed as the High Income Fund under the Wells Fargo Advantage family.

Quote Terms

The most unusual term you will see in a mutual fund quote is *NAV*, which stands for net asset value, or to be technically correct, the net asset value per share. This is the mutual fund equivalent of share price. It does not change during the trading day, but the fund manager computes it at the end of each session, subtracting the fund's liabilities from its assets and dividing by the number of outstanding shares.

The NET % CHG tells you how the fund's NAV compares to the last NAV of the last trading day, and the YTD % RET is the year-to-date return. The 3-YR % RET is a trailing return for the past 36 months. This number moves forward each day.

Under the Family of Fund name, the newspaper lists all the individual funds that are part of the family. Although you can usually move money between these funds under favorable conditions, the funds themselves are separate entities, so there is no consolidation of results.

Footnotes

Mutual funds have their own set of footnotes to supplement the newspaper quotes. Here are the major ones:

- *e.* Ex-distribution.
- *g.* Footnotes *x* and *s* apply.
- *j.* Footnotes *e* and *s* apply.
- *p.* Distribution costs apply.
- *r.* Redemption charge may apply.
- *s.* Stock split or dividend.
- *t.* Footnotes *p* and *r* apply.
- *v.* Footnotes *x* and *e* apply.
- *x.* Ex-dividend or after a dividend adjustment.
- *z.* Footnotes *x*, *e*, and *s* apply.

Paper Clips

Footnotes for mutual funds can be confusing because many of them reference other footnotes.

Online Version

Although the urgency is usually not there for mutual funds as it is for stocks, there is plenty of information on mutual funds available on the Internet. Like many other financial products, information on mutual funds is abundant and for the most part free or available at a reasonable cost.

Online Quote Detail

MorningStar (MorningStar.com) shows how robust the online world of mutual fund information is compared to what you find in newspapers. MorningStar is not the only online source for mutual fund information, but I consider it the premiere site. If you invest in mutual funds, this is a website you need to know.

Paper Clips ⎯⎯⎯⎯⎯⎯⎯⎯⎯⎯⎯⎯

MorningStar.com, which became a publically traded company in 2005, is one of the premiere financial information sites on the Internet. It specializes in mutual funds, but also offers information on stocks. If you are an active mutual fund investor or just want to know more about mutual funds, MorningStar is a site to bookmark. Much of the information is free, but a premium subscription service buys you even more detail. Much of the analysis is proprietary, especially on the premium service.

Paper Clips ⎯⎯⎯⎯⎯⎯

The value of the online experience is that you can access as much or as little information as you want or need.

MorningStar gets the idea that pictures speak volumes, so central to their presentation is a large chart that shows you a five-year look at the fund. The format is interesting in that they show you what a $10,000 investment in the fund five years ago looks like over the period. You can quickly see how the fund has done in the past.

Below the chart, MorningStar lists the fund's returns for five years and compares the fund to its category and the S&P 500. The category is a system that MorningStar uses to define the types of stocks carried by the fund.

Expenses

One of the other offerings you will find online is a disclosure of fees associated with the fund. This is important information because the higher the fees and expenses, the harder it is for you to make money.

Manager

The manager or portfolio manager of the fund is the person who directs the investment activity of the fund. This person and his or her staff make the buy and sell decisions. Many investors follow portfolio managers closely, because some have reputations for making money for the funds they manage. The portfolio manager of an index fund is not quite as important as a regular mutual fund because there are few buy or sell decisions. The fund does what the index does. If the index adds a stock or drops a stock, the fund does the same.

Chapter 24

Annual Report Cards

In This Chapter

- Details of the past year's financial activity
- Full-color accomplishments and footnoted problems
- Key ratios you can use to check a company's health
- Important information available online

Every mutual fund and stock you own should send you an annual report. In addition, any fund or stock you are interested in buying will send you an annual report. Of course, what good is it if you don't know what to look for? This chapter points out the key areas to study.

The Annual Report

The annual report is a financial document required by the Securities and Exchange Commission that has evolved into a marketing opportunity for most companies and mutual funds. The SEC requires a quarterly and annual accounting of the financial condition of the company or mutual fund.

Companies have seized the opportunity and produced slick, full-color documents full of happy workers, satisfied customers, and caring managers, all admiring state-of-the-art whatever. If you want to find out what is really going on, there are a few places to look:

- The narrative
- The balance sheet
- The income statement
- The statement of cash flows
- Notes to financial statements
- Doing some math

The Narrative

Most annual reports are a combination marketing tool, pat on the back, and fulfillment of a legal requirement. You will find a message from the president of the company, usually telling you what a great year it was, no matter the reality. When you see words such as *restructuring*, *challenging*, or *corrective actions*, you know not all is well.

In fairness, some companies are being more forthright with shareholders about problems and what actions they are taking to correct them. However, the letter to shareholders in the annual report is usually not the forum for those types of confessions. There are other places in the annual report to look for information.

Management's Discussion and Analysis

The most important narrative in the annual report is the management's discussion and analysis section. Although the annual report may not label it this way, you will recognize it by the content. The SEC requires the company to present all the important information about operations, capital, market conditions, and economic trends that might affect the business. The company must include any uncertainties that could affect future operations.

This section will sound scary in places because it is required to look at the possibilities of bad things happening and how they may affect the company's future. Here are some of the items you may see discussed:

- Product liabilities
- Environmental issues
- Labor troubles
- Pension shortfalls
- Foreign operations

The news is not all bad (unless of course the company is a disaster). You will also find a discussion of sales, how different product lines performed and changes that produced improvement, and research projects. This report also covers major expansion plans or acquisition projects, how the company handled its debt the past year, and any changes planned.

The Auditor's Report

All publicly traded companies must have their financial statements audited by a certified accounting company. Recent changes in regulations hold accountants and company officers even more responsible for the accuracy of financial statements.

The auditors will issue an opinion about the financial condition of the company. In most cases, their report will be an unqualified audit report, meaning they find nothing out of the ordinary. If the auditors discover something amiss, they may issue a qualified report, which means they have been unable to resolve a difference with management over some accounting practice or item. Look for this in the management discussion.

The auditors can issue several different types of opinion. One is that they doubt the business can survive as a going concern. This is a sign the company is about to go belly-up if radical changes don't happen soon.

Any report other than an unqualified report is worth examining to determine how serious the problem or potential problem facing the company is.

Form Alarm

Unfortunately, some of the biggest corporate scandals in the recent past involved the auditor either not doing his job or looking the other way regarding questionable practices.

The Balance Sheet

The balance sheet is a snapshot in time about a company's financial condition. It looks at the assets and liabilities, and from these numbers you can get an idea about the continued viability of the company. We will go into more detail later.

INTEL CORPORATION
CONSOLIDATED BALANCE SHEETS

December 25, 2004 and December 27, 2003
(In Millions—Except Par Value)

	2004	2003
(A) Assets		
Current assets: **(B)**		
Cash and cash equivalents	$ 8,407	$ 7,971
Short-term investments	5,654	5,568
Trading assets	3,111	2,625
Accounts receivable, net of allowance for doubtful accounts of $43 ($55 in 2003)	2,999	2,960
Inventories	2,621	2,519
Deferred tax assets	979	969
Other current assets	287	270
Total current assets	**24,058**	**22,882**
Property, plant and equipment, net	**15,768**	**16,661**
Marketable strategic equity securities	**656**	**514**
Other long-term investments	**2,563**	**1,866**
(C) Goodwill	**3,719**	**3,705**
Other assets	**1,379**	**1,515**
Total assets	**$48,143**	**$47,143**
(D) Liabilities and stockholders' equity		
Current liabilities: **(E)**		
Short-term debt	$ 201	$ 224
Accounts payable	1,943	1,660
Accrued compensation and benefits	1,858	1,559
Accrued advertising	894	716
Deferred income on shipments to distributors	592	633
Other accrued liabilities	1,355	1,302
Income taxes payable	1,163	785
Total current liabilities	**8,006**	**6,879**
Long-term debt	**703**	**936**
Deferred tax liabilities	**855**	**1,482**
Commitments and contingencies (Notes 17 and 18)		
Stockholders' equity:		
Preferred stock, $0.001 par value, 50 shares authorized; none issued	—	—
Common stock, $0.001 par value, 10,000 shares authorized; 6,253 issued and outstanding (6,487 in 2003) and capital in excess of par value	6,143	6,754
Acquisition-related unearned stock compensation	(4)	(20)
Accumulated other comprehensive income	152	96
Retained earnings	32,288	31,016
(F) Total stockholders' equity	**38,579**	**37,846**
Total liabilities and stockholders' equity	**$48,143**	**$47,143**

(A) Anything the company owns
(B) Quickly convertible to cash
(C) Brand name, etc.
(D) All the company owes
(E) Debts due within one year
(F) Owners' stake

The Details

The balance sheet works on the balance equations, which is as follows:

$$\text{Assets} = \text{Liabilities} + \text{Equity}$$

As a company's assets grow, so do the liabilities and/or the equity.

Most companies operate on a 12-month fiscal year, and many use a calendar year for their fiscal year. So, its year begins on January 1 and ends on December 31. This makes accounting neat and tidy. Other companies choose a different path, so it is important to know what dates a balance sheet covers, especially if you are using it to compare one company to another.

The example I chose has a different fiscal year than most. It ends it fiscal year on the last Saturday of the year. You will note at the top of the balance sheet that the 2004 and 2003 balance sheets ended on different dates. If you had the complete annual report of this company and read the attached notes, you would discover that some years were 52 weeks, whereas others were 53 weeks. That would be important to know if you wanted to compare year to year or measure this company against another.

Current Assets

Current assets include cash, cash equivalents, securities, and other assets that the company can reasonably convert to cash within one year without suffering a loss. This category of assets is important because the company could use them to pay bills if something disrupted ongoing operations.

Remaining Assets

The remaining assets fall into two major categories: plants and equipment, which is furniture and equipment with a useful life of 1+ years; and intangible, which is an asset that can't be touched or seen, such as copyrights, patents, goodwill (the value assigned to a business's managerial skills). Goodwill is an intangible asset of the company's brand name, reputation, and general standing in the community. It's important and worth something to the company, but you can't sell it on the open market in the same manner as a plant or piece of equipment.

Current Liabilities

Current liabilities are the bills the company must pay in the near future, within one year or less. Short-term debt and income taxes due fall into this category. Other immediate business expenses such as advertising and accounts payable fit here, too.

Long-Term Debt

Companies use long-term debt to finance buildings and major expansions. This debt is usually five years or more.

Paper Clips

How a company classifies assets can make a difference in how important financial ratios come out. Auditors look closely at the procedures a company uses to verify that the system follows acceptable guidelines.

Stockholders' Equity

Stockholder' equity is what the owners have in the company. The big piece of this section is retained earnings. When a company makes a profit, it can return some of that money to shareholders in the form of a dividend or retain it in the company to fund future growth. Retained earnings are the cumulative total of those profits that the company retained over the years.

The Income Statement

The income statement may be more familiar to many people than the balance sheet. This is also called the profit and loss statement. This is where you will find the proverbial "bottom line." The income statement tells you what the company took in and what it spent and if there was any left over for profits.

<table>
<tr><td colspan="4" align="center">INTEL CORPORATION
CONSOLIDATED STATEMENTS OF INCOME</td></tr>
<tr><td>Three Years Ended December 25, 2004
(In Millions—Except Per Share Amounts)</td><td>2004</td><td>2003</td><td>2002</td></tr>
<tr><td>(A) Net revenue</td><td>$34,209</td><td>$30,141</td><td>$26,764</td></tr>
<tr><td>Cost of sales (B)</td><td>14,463</td><td>13,047</td><td>13,446</td></tr>
<tr><td>(C) Gross margin</td><td>19,746</td><td>17,094</td><td>13,318</td></tr>
<tr><td>Research and development</td><td>4,778</td><td>4,360</td><td>4,034</td></tr>
<tr><td>Marketing, general and administrative</td><td>4,659</td><td>4,278</td><td>4,334</td></tr>
<tr><td>Impairment of goodwill</td><td>—</td><td>617</td><td>—</td></tr>
<tr><td>Amortization and impairment of acquisition-related intangibles and costs</td><td>179</td><td>301</td><td>548</td></tr>
<tr><td>Purchased in-process research and development</td><td>—</td><td>5</td><td>20</td></tr>
<tr><td>(D) Operating expenses</td><td>9,616</td><td>9,561</td><td>8,936</td></tr>
<tr><td>Operating income (E)</td><td>10,130</td><td>7,533</td><td>4,382</td></tr>
<tr><td>(F) Losses on equity securities, net</td><td>(2)</td><td>(283)</td><td>(372)</td></tr>
<tr><td>Interest and other, net</td><td>289</td><td>192</td><td>194</td></tr>
<tr><td>(G) Income before taxes</td><td>10,417</td><td>7,442</td><td>4,204</td></tr>
<tr><td>Provision for taxes</td><td>2,901</td><td>1,801</td><td>1,087</td></tr>
<tr><td>(H) Net income</td><td>$ 7,516</td><td>$ 5,641</td><td>$ 3,117</td></tr>
<tr><td>Basic earnings per common share</td><td>$ 1.17</td><td>$ 0.86</td><td>$ 0.47</td></tr>
<tr><td>Diluted earnings per common share</td><td>$ 1.16</td><td>$ 0.85</td><td>$ 0.46</td></tr>
<tr><td>Weighted average common shares outstanding</td><td>6,400</td><td>6,527</td><td>6,651</td></tr>
<tr><td>Weighted average common shares outstanding, assuming dilution</td><td>6,494</td><td>6,621</td><td>6,759</td></tr>
</table>

Fill In the Blank

Many companies choose to use profits to fund more growth of the company rather than pay shareholders. This is a typical strategy of younger companies that believe they can get a better return for the shareholders by growing the business.

(A) Sales
(B) What it cost to make sales
(C) Gross profit
(D) Total operating expenses
(E) Income from operations
(F) Passive income/loss
(G) Bottom line
(H) More accurate number

Statement Format

The income statement or statements of income for a consolidated report sets out how much money came in, how much went out, and what profit or loss remained. You may notice there are several income/expense breaks as you go down the report.

The first break is net revenue less cost of sales equals gross margin. This break tells you what it cost the company to make its product or produce its service. This includes raw material, labor, utilities, and so on tied directly to physically producing a product. This is an important measurement because it tells you how efficiently (or not) the company is producing its product when you compare it to a competitor.

Paper Clips

Management often uses gross margin to measure the effectiveness of division or unit managers, because it excludes expenses outside their control, such as corporate administrations and so on.

The next break is operating expenses and operating income. Operating expenses are those costs, such as marketing, that are not directly tied to production but must be accounted for in expenses. When you subtract operating expenses from gross margin, you get operating income. This figure tells you how the business did as a business. It is not the net income, but is a more pure look at strictly business performance.

After adding or subtracting activities of interest or securities, you come to income before taxes. However, despite what many people think, many businesses do pay taxes, so you can't get a true net income (bottom line) without deducting a provision for income tax, whether the bill has actually been paid or not.

Earnings

Companies report earnings on a per share basis. Earnings per share (EPS) is a common measure of company performance. It lets you compare two companies on an equal basis. However, there are two ways to report EPS—the regular way and the fully diluted way.

The fully diluted way, which you can see from my example, is lower because it includes all the options, warrants, and convertible bonds as if they were converted to stock. This increases the number of outstanding shares as you can see a few lines down, which has the effect of reducing EPS. It does, however, give you a more accurate picture.

Statement of Cash Flows

The statement of cash flows follows the cash in and out of a company for the year. This information tells you much about the sources of cash the company generates during the year. Most of the cash should come from operations and not investments or the sale of assets, which would indicate problems.

INTEL CORPORATION
CONSOLIDATED STATEMENTS OF CASH FLOWS

Three Years Ended December 25, 2004
(In Millions)

	2004	2003	2002
(A) Cash and cash equivalents, beginning of year	**$ 7,971**	**$ 7,404**	**$ 7,970**
(B) Cash flows provided by (used for) operating activities:			
Net income	7,516	5,641	3,117
Adjustments to reconcile net income to net cash provided by operating activities:			
Depreciation	4,590	4,651	4,676
Impairment of goodwill	—	617	—
Amortization and impairment of intangibles and other acquisition-related costs	299	419	668
Purchased in-process research and development	—	5	20
Losses on equity securities, net	2	283	372
Net loss on retirements and impairments of property, plant and equipment	91	217	301
Deferred taxes	(207)	391	110
Tax benefit from employee equity incentive plans	344	216	270
Changes in assets and liabilities:			
Trading assets	(468)	(698)	(465)
Accounts receivable	(39)	(430)	30
Inventories	(101)	(245)	(26)
Accounts payable	283	116	(226)
Accrued compensation and benefits	295	276	107
Income taxes payable	378	(361)	175
Other assets and liabilities	136	417	—
(C) Total adjustments	5,603	5,874	6,012
(D) Net cash provided by operating activities	**13,119**	**11,515**	**9,129**
Cash flows provided by (used for) investing activities:			
Additions to property, plant and equipment	(3,843)	(3,656)	(4,703)
Acquisitions, net of cash acquired	(53)	(61)	(57)
Purchases of available-for-sale investments	(16,618)	(11,662)	(6,309)
Maturities and sales of available-for-sale investments	15,633	8,488	5,634
Other investing activities	(151)	(199)	(330)
(E) Net cash used for investing activities	**(5,032)**	**(7,090)**	**(5,765)**
Cash flows provided by (used for) financing activities:			
Increase (decrease) in short-term debt, net	24	(152)	(101)
Additions to long-term debt	—	—	55
Repayments and retirement of debt	(31)	(137)	(18)
Proceeds from sales of shares through employee equity incentive plans	894	967	681
Repurchase and retirement of common stock	(7,516)	(4,012)	(4,014)
Payment of dividends to stockholders	(1,022)	(524)	(533)
(F) Net cash used for financing activities	**(7,651)**	**(3,858)**	**(3,930)**
(G) Net increase (decrease) in cash and cash equivalents	**436**	**567**	**(566)**
(H) Cash and cash equivalents, end of year	**$ 8,407**	**$ 7,971**	**$ 7,404**
Supplemental disclosures of cash flow information:			
Cash paid during the year for:			
(I) Interest	$ 52	$ 59	$ 66
Income taxes, net of refunds	$ 2,392	$ 1,567	$ 475

(A) Cash at the beginning of the year

(B) Cash from operations

(C) Adjustments to cash

(D) Net cash from business

(E) Cash used/generated in investing

(F) Cash used/generated in financing

(G) Change in cash at year end

(H) Cash at year end

(I) Interest and taxes

The Details

The statement of cash flows is a roadmap that lets you track where cash is coming from and going to in the company. This is an important report because cash is the lifeblood of a company. If a company runs short of cash, it must borrow to cover the shortfall.

As you look at this report, notice the source of most of the cash. It should come from operations, and not investments or sale of property (unless that is the focus of the business).

The main numbers for this report come from the balance sheet and income statement. The beginning year cash number ($7,971) is where the company started the year (and the 2003 end of year number). Net income ($7,516) comes off the income statement.

Form Alarm

CAUTION

A company that experiences significant decreases in cash from year to year is probably in deep trouble. There is no substitute for cash. If the company doesn't have enough, it will have to borrow to get it.

Below net income are adjustments to cash, including some noncash items such as *depreciation* and *amortization*. The company must account for these items even though they do not involve any "real money." Adding net income and adjustments gives the total cash provided by operations during the year ($13,119). That is the cash that flowed in to the company.

> **Financial Speak**
>
> **Depreciation** is the distribution of the cost of an asset over its useful life. A computer has a "useful life" of three years, so the price of the computer is distributed over three years with one third of the price taken as a deduction from income each year.
>
> **Amortization** is the write-off of the cost of an intangible asset over time against income.

Next, uses of cash are divided into two major categories: cash flows for investing activities and cash flows for financing activities. In most cases, these will be negative numbers showing an outflow of cash. Those two categories cover the operations of the business.

When you subtract those two subtotals from the cash provided by operations during the year, you get a net increase or decrease in cash ($436). Because it is positive in my example, it is added to the starting balance to give you the cash position at the end of the year ($8,407). This is the first number on the balance sheet.

Notes to the Financial Statements

An important part of the annual report is the notes to the financial statements. They must be important, because the company tries to hide them. That's not true, but compare them to the company president's message and see which looks more appealing—which is designed so that you want to read it?

That doesn't necessarily mean the company is trying to hide anything. Most companies are honest in their dealings and comply with the spirit as well as the letter of the law when it comes to disclosure.

Accounting Practices

This section of notes, usually the first section, explains the accounting policies used by the company for a variety of circumstances. Unless you are an accountant, most of this is hard to digest. However, there are a few areas to study.

The first is how the company deals with its pension program. If there are problems (and many companies struggle with funding their pensions adequately), they should be noted here. Pension liabilities could pose a significant problem.

Also, look at stock-based compensation plans. These incentive plans can be areas for abuse with top executives getting large rewards for mediocre performance.

> **Form Alarm**
>
> A company that frequently changes accounting firms may be signaling that they are in trouble.

Debt

Another area worthy of your attention is the discussion of both the long-term and short-term debt obligations facing the company. You should find a schedule of long-term debt describing the maturity date, amount, and interest rate. The long-term debt will include bank loans, bonds, and other debt instruments due two or more years in the future.

Short-term debt includes bank loans and credit lines due within one year. Terms and conditions of those loans, along with balances as of the statement date, should be included.

Mergers and Acquisitions

If the company has engaged in a merger or acquisition during the year, that transaction and its effect on the company should be discussed in the financial notes. How was (will be) the new entity integrated into the company? Will there be duplication of services or efforts resulting in layoffs?

Noteworthy Events

What happened during the year that had a material impact on the business? Was there a labor strike? A lawsuit(s)? Did a news event change a particular market segment? What about a governmental action or new law? Anything of material significance should find its way to the financial notes for discussion. If the manager's discussion and analysis mentioned the item, it probably had a financial impact.

Online Access

You can gain access to most companies' (those that are publicly traded) annual reports from their websites. The link is often in the Investor Relations area. If you want a printed copy, you can get a free copy directly from many companies or pick up a copy of the *Wall Street Journal* and see whether they offer a free copy of the report you want.

You can also go to the SEC website (www.sec.gov/edgar.shtml), known as EDGAR, where you can find all sorts of information on companies. It is a little awkward to use, but when you get the hang of it, the site is a gold mine of information.

A version of the annual report called the 10-K is your best bet for all the facts and none of the glitter. Some companies post this report on their website, but all companies must file it with the SEC, and you can view it there. There is a quarterly version called the 10-Q that you can also view.

Paper Clips

You can also find websites that will gather annual reports and other information for you, sometimes for a fee. All of this information is available free from the company directly or online from the SEC. Go to the Securities and Exchange Commission Forms site (EDGAR) http://www.sec.gov/edgar.shtml for more information.

The Numbers

Without going into a course on financial analysis, you can do a few tests yourself with the information from the financial documents we've discussed to check on the health of a company.

These numbers involve looking at the relationship of two sets of figures and comparing the results to some accounting norms. The math isn't hard, and I give you the formulas.

Current Ratio

The current ratio is one of the liquidity tests. Liquidity refers to how quickly and easily can the company pay its bills on a short-term basis.

The current ratio equals current assets divided by current liabilities. In my example, that works out to the following:

$$\$24,058 / \$8,006 = 3$$

A current ratio under 1 suggests the company may have trouble paying its ongoing operating expenses (rents, utilities, etc.). A current ratio above 1 may indicate the company is able to pay its bills with some confidence. However, there are several ways the ratio could be high and the company still be in trouble.

If the inventory was very high and the company had a large accounts receivable number, the ratio might be misleading. Neither one of those seems to be the case with my example, so we might initially assume the company's liquidity is in good shape.

Quick Ratio or Acid Test

Another test of liquidity and a way to check your findings of the current ratio is the quick ratio. This test is the same as the current ratio, but excludes the inventory. The formula for the quick ratio is:

Cash + marketable securities + accounts receivable / Accounts payable + short-term debt + accrued liabilities + other current liabilities = Quick ratio

In my example, this is $\$20,171 / \$6,251 = 3.23$.

This confirms the current ratio number. You can look at the assets of this company (this is an actual consolidated balance sheet of a technology company) and see why there are no liquidity problems. The company is sitting on $24 billion—including $8.4 billion in cash—of current assets, which by definition the company should be able to convert to cash within a one-year period. Most companies aren't this flush.

Debt-to-Equity Ratio

This ratio measures how much leverage a company uses to finance growth compared to equity. In this case, we are concerned with loans, which are a fixed cost, and the company must pay them regardless of how the business is doing. If a company uses too much debt to finance growth (assets), paying the additional interest charges can affect earnings.

The formula for this ratio is as follows:

Long-term debt + short-term debt / Stockholders equity = Debt/equity ratio

In my example, this is: $\$904 / \$38,579 = 0.023$.

A manufacturing company should have a debt/equity ratio of 0.5 or less. A company that is less capital-intensive would want an even lower debt/equity ratio. My example's debt/equity ratio is very low—a reflection of the tremendous amount of cash the company is sitting on and the very low amount of debt.

Days' Sales Outstanding

How long does it take the company to collect accounts receivables? Companies need to extend credit, but if they do not manage it correctly, accounts receivables can become a real problem. This ratio looks at that problem. The first step is to compute the average revenue per day, which is:

> Annual revenue / 365 = Average revenue per day

For my example, that is $93.72 million per day.

The second part of the equation is this:

> Accounts receivable / Average revenue per day =
> Days' sales outstanding

For my example, that is $2,999 / $93.72 = 31.98 days.

Assuming that the credit terms for the company are net 30 days, the average collection is not far off company policy. A number significantly over 30 might indicate some tightening of terms may be in order. Be sure to check what other companies in the same industry are experiencing.

Inventory Turnover Ratio

The inventory turnover ratio measures how effectively a company is managing its inventory. This ratio describes the cost of the product sold over a year and the average inventory needed to support those sales.

Here is the formula:

> Cost of goods sold / Average inventory

You figure the average inventory by taking the 2003 and 2004 inventory figures (from the balance sheet) and averaging them. In my example, $2,519 + $2,621 = $5,140 / 2 = $2,570, so the inventory turnover is as follows:

> $14,463 / $2,570 = 5.62 inventory turnover

This means there is approximately two months of inventory on hand, on average. Determining the correct inventory turnover ratio for a company is not so simple. Different industries may historically have different standards. However, you can compare companies in the same industry, and it is fairly easy to find benchmarks online for an industry.

Gross Profit Percentage

This measure looks at how effectively the business of producing the product or service is actually run. Many consider it a measurement of line managers because it looks at the process and does not include any unrelated expenses. Here is the formula:

Gross margin / Revenue = Gross margin percentage

In my example, that $19,746 / $34,209 = 58%.

This is a staggering gross margin percentage by most standards, which indicates a business that has lowered its operating costs and raised its prices.

Return on Assets

This metric measures the profitability of the company based on the total assets invested in the company. The formula is simple:

Net income / Assets = Return on assets

In my example, that is $7,516 / $48,143 = 15.6%.

Service companies that do not carry as much in terms of assets on their books as manufacturing companies will have a different look.

Return on Equity

Return on equity measures how effectively the company uses stockholders' equity as well as borrowed money. The formula is this:

Net income / Stockholders' equity = Return on equity

In my example, that is $7,516 / $38,579 = 19.5%.

Return on Sales

Return on sales measures how well the company operates. The higher the ratio, the more efficiently the company is running. The formula is as follows:

Net income / Revenue = Return on sales

In my example, that is $7,516 / $34,209 = 21.9%.

Part 6

Taxes, My Taxes

Do you gasp every time you see how much comes out of your paycheck for taxes? If you think that's bad, you don't want to know what happens if you "forget" to file your income tax returns for a couple of years or get real creative with hiding income. This part looks at some of the most common tax forms, helps you with some of the jargon, and provides checklists of financial documents you'll need when tax time rolls around.

Chapter 25

Fed Forms Fun

In This Chapter

- Making sense of the W-4
- Verifying W-2s and 1099s
- Getting an extension
- Estimated income taxes

Every year (and often more frequently), you face the daunting task of dealing with the IRS—make one little mistake and the next thing you know, black helicopters are hovering over your house. Okay, that's an exaggeration, but no one wants to make mistakes. In this chapter, we look at the most common federal forms many of you may face.

Forms and More Forms

The IRS and its love of forms has been the butt of countless jokes and the subject of as many outraged editorials. I won't add my voice to that ongoing dialogue, but the fact remains: you have to negotiate a number of forms ranging from simple to not-so-simple every year to meet your tax obligations. This chapter is not about tax advice, but form advice. I'm going to look at the forms you are most likely to face each year, but not the actual income tax forms themselves. That's a different book.

There are a couple of forms that seem very simple on the surface but have a tremendous impact on your life. They are good examples of why it is important to always take anything related to your taxes very seriously. Some decisions have consequences that last a long time.

The W-4

The W-4 form tells your employer how much to withhold from your paycheck for federal income taxes. Each time you start a new job, your employer will ask you to fill out a new W-4. However, you don't have to wait for a new job to

Paper Clips

Don't forget to adjust your withholding allowances if you have changes in your life. A baby arrives or a child leaves home are two examples of why you may want to revise your W-4. The real biggie, however, is if your formerly unemployed spouse goes to work.

(A) A student, for example, still claimed by parents

(B) Options for deductions

(C) Fewer deductions means more withheld

(D) In most cases, children you claim on taxes

(E) Meet requirements for head of household

(F) Child-care expenses

(G) Child tax credits

(H) Total deductions

change the directions on the form. You can fill out a new W-4 with your existing employer anytime you want.

You determine how much your employer withholds and forwards to the IRS by the number of dependents you claim. The more dependents you claim, the less money the IRS withholds from your paycheck.

Filling Out the Form

The W-4 form is a one-page form that comes with a worksheet to help you calculate how many deductions and adjustments you should claim. The bottom half of the first page is what actually goes to your employer, and the rest you keep, although it is a good idea to keep a copy of the completed certificate for your records.

Form W-4 (2005)

Purpose. Complete Form W-4 so that your employer can withhold the correct federal income tax from your pay. Because your tax situation may change, you may want to refigure your withholding each year.

Exemption from withholding. If you are exempt, complete only lines 1, 2, 3, 4, and 7 and sign the form to validate it. Your exemption for 2005 expires February 16, 2006. See Pub. 505, Tax Withholding and Estimated Tax.

Note. You cannot claim exemption from withholding if (a) your income exceeds $800 and includes more than $250 of unearned income (for example, interest and dividends) and (b) another person can claim you as a dependent on their tax return.

Basic instructions. If you are not exempt, complete the **Personal Allowances Worksheet** below. The worksheets on page 2 adjust your withholding allowances based on itemized deductions, certain credits, adjustments to income, or two-

earner/two-job situations. Complete all worksheets that apply. However, you may claim fewer (or zero) allowances.

Head of household. Generally, you may claim head of household filing status on your tax return only if you are unmarried and pay more than 50% of the costs of keeping up a home for yourself and your dependent(s) or other qualifying individuals. See line **E** below.

Tax credits. You can take projected tax credits into account in figuring your allowable number of withholding allowances. Credits for child or dependent care expenses and the child tax credit may be claimed using the **Personal Allowances Worksheet** below. See Pub. 919, How Do I Adjust My Tax Withholding? for information on converting your other credits into withholding allowances.

Nonwage income. If you have a large amount of nonwage income, such as interest or dividends, consider making estimated tax payments using Form 1040-ES, Estimated Tax for Individuals. Otherwise, you may owe additional tax.

Two earners/two jobs. If you have a working spouse or more than one job, figure the total number of allowances you are entitled to claim on all jobs using worksheets from only one Form W-4. Your withholding usually will be most accurate when all allowances are claimed on the Form W-4 for the highest paying job and zero allowances are claimed on the others.

Nonresident alien. If you are a nonresident alien, see the Instructions for Form 8233 before completing this Form W-4.

Check your withholding. After your Form W-4 takes effect, use Pub. 919 to see how the dollar amount you are having withheld compares to your projected total tax for 2005. See Pub. 919, especially if your earnings exceed $125,000 (Single) or $175,000 (Married).

Recent name change? If your name on line 1 differs from that shown on your social security card, call 1-800-772-1213 to initiate a name change and obtain a social security card showing your correct name.

Personal Allowances Worksheet (Keep for your records.)

A   Enter "1" for **yourself** if no one else can claim you as a dependent . . . .   **A** _____

B   Enter "1" if: {
- You are single and have only one job; or
- You are married, have only one job, and your spouse does not work; or
- Your wages from a second job or your spouse's wages (or the total of both) are $1,000 or less. } . .   **B** _____

C   Enter "1" for your **spouse.** But, you may choose to enter "-0-" if you are married and have either a working spouse or more than one job. (Entering "-0-" may help you avoid having too little tax withheld.) . . . .   **C** _____

D   Enter number of **dependents** (other than your spouse or yourself) you will claim on your tax return . . . . . .   **D** _____

E   Enter "1" if you will file as **head of household** on your tax return (see conditions under **Head of household** above) .   **E** _____

F   Enter "1" if you have at least $1,500 of **child or dependent care expenses** for which you plan to claim a credit . .   **F** _____
    (**Note.** Do **not** include child support payments. See Pub. 503, Child and Dependent Care Expenses, for details.)

G   **Child Tax Credit** (including additional child tax credit):
- If your total income will be less than $54,000 ($79,000 if married), enter "2" for each eligible child.
- If your total income will be between $54,000 and $84,000 ($79,000 and $119,000 if married), enter "1" for each eligible child plus "1" **additional** if you have four or more eligible children.   **G** _____

H   Add lines A through G and enter total here. (**Note.** This may be different from the number of exemptions you claim on your tax return.)   ▶   **H** _____

For accuracy, complete all worksheets that apply. {
- If you plan to **itemize or claim adjustments to income** and want to reduce your withholding, see the **Deductions and Adjustments Worksheet** on page 2.
- If you have **more than one job** or are **married and you and your spouse both work** and the combined earnings from all jobs exceed $35,000 ($25,000 if married) see the **Two-Earner/Two-Job Worksheet** on page 2 to avoid having too little tax withheld.
- If **neither** of the above situations applies, **stop here** and enter the number from line H on line 5 of Form W-4 below. }

Form Details

This is the top part of the form where all of the work happens. This is your worksheet. It does not go to your employer or the IRS. Although it has instructions about what to put in the various blanks, you are not obligated to follow these instructions exactly, and I tell you why a little later in this chapter.

The first part of the worksheet is a census of dependents. You can claim yourself, unless someone else is claiming you. The example might be a college student whose parents still claimed him or her as a dependent on their taxes. Line B covers the situations explained on the worksheet.

Line C allows you to enter a deduction for your spouse (sorry, no deduction for live-in partners). This is where things start getting tricky. If your spouse works, you need to coordinate how you are going to handle deductions. You won't be breaking any "rules" if you both claim each other, but you may not have enough withheld and then face a big tax bill on April 15.

Line D is for the dependents you claim on your income tax return besides your spouse and yourself. Remember, this form always ties back to your tax return. Those dependents mean deductions when you file your return—that's why many people claim them on the W-4. You'll have less deducted now because of the deduction you'll get when you file your return. However, there is no rule that says you have to claim the deductions now, and there may be good reasons not to at this point.

Lines E and F let you take deductions for some credits that you will file on your income tax return for certain expenses related to child care and maintaining a household. There are specific tests for these, but remember you don't have to take the deduction.

Line G recognizes the Child Tax Credit that you will take on your income tax return and lets you enter those appropriate deductions.

Line H is the total of Lines A through G. If you and your spouse both work or you plan to itemize and want to make adjustments, however, there is a worksheet on the second page of the form to allow you to calculate those adjustments.

> **Fill In the Blank**
>
> If you have several years' worth of returns behind you without many changes, you can probably estimate what works for you and what doesn't. If you are regularly getting a big refund, you are withholding too much. If you come up short each April 15, you may want to withhold more.

Following the Guidelines or Not

The instructions for filling out the W-4 should probably be labeled suggestions. You don't have to follow IRS instructions at all (within reason). For example, many people find that with a second job or other income, they are better off claiming zero deductions, which gets the maximum withheld from your check.

On the other hand, if you plan to itemize with substantial exemptions and have a high income, you may want to claim nine or more exemptions, even if you don't have anywhere near that many dependents. Your company will send any request for nine exemptions or more to the IRS for review, but there is no law against the claim. People in this situation want little, if anything, withheld because they have substantial deductions to claim with their taxes.

Deductions and Adjustments Worksheet

The Deductions and Adjustments worksheet on page 2 of the W-4 form is not something you can fill out while at work. It requires too much data, unless you just happen to have all that information committed to memory. I've never found it very useful given the amount of work involved.

If your personal situation has changed, you will probably not have any way to know many of the details the worksheet asks for (estimate of medical expenses in excess of 7.5% of your adjusted gross income). You can use the previous year's tax return as a guide and hope your estimates for the new year are correct.

Frankly, this is a lot of work for some adjustments that you should be able to estimate based on your taxes from the previous year. However, if you want to go through the exercise, there is a better way than doing it on paper. The IRS has an online calculator that walks you through the process. You still need the information and still need to make the estimates, but the calculator does the rest. You can find it at www.irs.gov/individuals/article/0,,id=96196,00.html.

Fill In the Blank

The IRS website may be the most helpful part of the agency. If you want to find something, the search function is very robust. For example, if you want to find the W-4 calculator just mentioned and don't want to type in that long URL, go to www.IRS.gov and type in "W-4 calculator" in the search box in the upper-left corner, and it is the first link that pops up.

Two-Earner/Two-Job Worksheet

This worksheet at the bottom of page 2 is much more helpful and one you can use without an armful of supporting documents.

A Use your total deductions here

B Subtract appropriate number

C Calculate whether to go forward

D Gives you multiplier for withholding

E Amount to multiply

F Additional withholding

G Remaining pay periods to withhold this amount

Two-Earner/Two-Job Worksheet (See *Two earners/two jobs* on page 1.)		
Note. Use this worksheet *only* if the instructions under line H on page 1 direct you here.		
A 1 Enter the number from line H, page 1 (or from line 10 above if you used the **Deductions and Adjustments Worksheet**)	1	_____
B 2 Find the number in **Table 1** below that applies to the **LOWEST** paying job and enter it here	2	_____
C 3 If line 1 is **more than or equal to** line 2, subtract line 2 from line 1. Enter the result here (if zero, enter "-0-") and on Form W-4, line 5, page 1. **Do not** use the rest of this worksheet	3	_____
Note. If line 1 is *less than* line 2, enter "-0-" on Form W-4, line 5, page 1. Complete lines 4–9 below to calculate the additional withholding amount necessary to avoid a year-end tax bill.		
4 Enter the number from line 2 of this worksheet	4 _____	
5 Enter the number from line 1 of this worksheet	5 _____	
D 6 **Subtract** line 5 from line 4	6	_____
E 7 Find the amount in **Table 2** below that applies to the **HIGHEST** paying job and enter it here	7 $ _____
F 8 **Multiply** line 7 by line 6 and enter the result here. This is the additional annual withholding needed	8 $ _____
G 9 Divide line 8 by the number of pay periods remaining in 2005. For example, divide by 26 if you are paid every two weeks and you complete this form in December 2004. Enter the result here and on Form W-4, line 6, page 1. This is the additional amount to be withheld from each paycheck	9 $ _____

Table 1: Two-Earner/Two-Job Worksheet

Married Filing Jointly						All Others	
If wages from **HIGHEST** paying job are—	AND, wages from **LOWEST** paying job are—	Enter on line 2 above	If wages from **HIGHEST** paying job are—	AND, wages from **LOWEST** paying job are—	Enter on line 2 above	If wages from **LOWEST** paying job are—	Enter on line 2 above
$0 - $40,000	$0 - $4,000	0	$40,001 and over	30,001 - 36,000	6	$0 - $6,000	0
	4,001 - 8,000	1		36,001 - 45,000	7	6,001 - 12,000	1
	8,001 - 18,000	2		45,001 - 50,000	8	12,001 - 18,000	2
	18,001 and over	3		50,001 - 60,000	9	18,001 - 24,000	3
				60,001 - 65,000	10	24,001 - 31,000	4
$40,001 and over	$0 - $4,000	0		65,001 - 75,000	11	31,001 - 45,000	5
	4,001 - 8,000	1		75,001 - 90,000	12	45,001 - 60,000	6
	8,001 - 18,000	2		90,001 - 100,000	13	60,001 - 75,000	7
	18,001 - 22,000	3		100,001 - 115,000	14	75,001 - 80,000	8
	22,001 - 25,000	4		115,001 and over	15	80,001 - 100,000	9
	25,001 - 30,000	5				100,001 and over	10

Table 2: Two-Earner/Two-Job Worksheet

Married Filing Jointly		All Others	
If wages from **HIGHEST** paying job are—	Enter on line 7 above	If wages from **HIGHEST** paying job are—	Enter on line 7 above
$0 - $60,000	$480	$0 - $30,000	$480
60,001 - 110,000	800	30,001 - 70,000	800
110,001 - 160,000	900	70,001 - 140,000	900
160,001 - 280,000	1,060	140,001 - 320,000	1,060
280,001 and over	1,120	320,001 and over	1,120

The Details

This is the most helpful worksheet on the form because it addresses a reality for many couples today—two incomes that can play havoc with their taxes. If you don't withhold enough, there's that big tax bill in April. If you withhold too much, you're cash-starved for the rest of the year.

This worksheet helps you figure what you need to do to meet your tax obligations and still have a reasonable cash flow. For many couples, it means having extra withholding taken out of one of the paychecks, probably the largest one.

The first three lines are a test to see whether you should even use the worksheet. If your exemptions, either from line H or from the worksheet above this one, are more than the number you find on Table One, you do not need this worksheet. Follow the instructions and enter the result of subtracting line 2 from line 1 on line 3, and then enter this number on Form W-4 line 5.

However, if line 2 is larger than line 1, subtract line 1 and the answer goes on line 6. Use Table 2 to find the appropriate amount and put that on line 7 and multiply lines 6 and 7. The answer goes on line 8 and is the additional annual withholding tax you need.

The final step is to figure out how many more pay periods remain in the year and divide that number into line 8. The answer is how much extra you need taken out of your paycheck. It goes on line 6 of the W-4.

The Form for Your Employer

The W-4 is what you will actually turn in to your employer. Unless you claim nine or more exemptions, it stays with your employer and doesn't go to the IRS.

Form Alarm

If your spouse goes to work or one of you has a big jump in income, put your heads together and redo both of your W-4s. If you don't, you may find an ugly surprise when you do your taxes.

Cut here and give Form W-4 to your employer. Keep the top part for your records.

Form **W-4**	**Employee's Withholding Allowance Certificate**	OMB No. 1545-0010
Department of the Treasury Internal Revenue Service	▶ Whether you are entitled to claim a certain number of allowances or exemption from withholding is subject to review by the IRS. Your employer may be required to send a copy of this form to the IRS.	2005

1 Type or print your first name and middle initial   Last name   **2** Your social security number

Home address (number and street or rural route)

3 ☐ Single ☐ Married ☐ Married, but withhold at higher Single rate.
Note. If married, but legally separated, or spouse is a nonresident alien, check the "Single" box.

City or town, state, and ZIP code

4 If your last name differs from that shown on your social security card, check here. You must call 1-800-772-1213 for a new card. ▶ ☐

5 Total number of allowances you are claiming (from line H above **or** from the applicable worksheet on page 2)   **5**

6 Additional amount, if any, you want withheld from each paycheck   . . . .   **6** $

7 I claim exemption from withholding for 2005, and I certify that I meet **both** of the following conditions for exemption.
? Last year I had a right to a refund of **all** federal income tax withheld because I had **no** tax liability **and**
? This year I expect a refund of **all** federal income tax withheld because I expect to have **no** tax liability.
If you meet both conditions, write "Exempt" here   . . . . ▶   **7**

Under penalties of perjury, I declare that I have examined this certificate and to the best of my knowledge and belief, it is true, correct, and complete.
Employee's signature
(Form is not valid unless you sign it.) ▶   **Date** ▶

8 Employer's name and address (Employer: Complete lines 8 and 10 only if sending to the IRS.)   **9** Office code (optional)   **10** Employer identification number (EIN)

For Privacy Act and Paperwork Reduction Act Notice, see page 2.   Cat. No. 10220Q   Form **W-4** (2005)

A Your identification and address

B If you just married, for example

C Fill in worksheet amounts

D Income of $800 or less

E Skip 8, 9, 10

Filling Out the Form

After you have done the worksheets, filling out the actual W-4 is a piece of cake. Areas 1 through 3 identify you to the IRS and Social Security, so make sure your Social Security number is correct. This is one mistake that can be very time-consuming to fix later. If you don't catch the mistake, you may miss credits to your Social Security account that could cost you later in life.

Area 4 notes that if your name has changed (due to marriage, for example), you need to get a new Social Security card. For the same reasons mentioned previously, this is an important step you don't want to skip.

Areas 5 and 6 come from the worksheets you completed or zeros if they didn't apply to you. Area 7 lets you claim exemption from withholding if you meet the two tests offered on the form. As of this writing, you could be exempt from income tax liability if your annual income is $800 or less. Just because you got a refund last year doesn't mean you're exempt. You got a refund of overpayment, not a refund of all your taxes, in most cases.

Sign and date the form and you're done, but don't forget to turn it in to your employer. Don't worry about the employer information on the bottom.

The W-2

The W-2 is not a form you fill out, but it is a form you should review carefully. Your employer sends you a W-2 by the end of January for the previous year, and it contains some very important information.

A Your Social Security number must be correct!

B Other identifying information

C Income reported

D Taxes reported

E State and local income and taxes

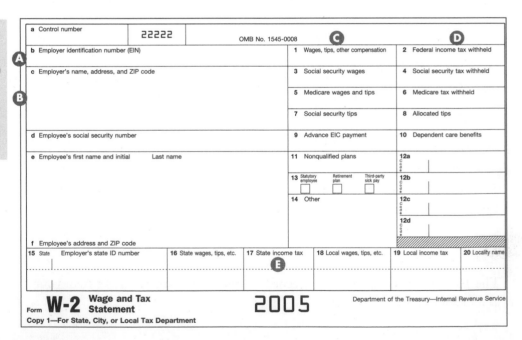

The Details

You are probably familiar with the multiple-copy W-2 that arrives every year. There is a copy for the IRS, a copy for the state, and a copy for any local taxing authority. It is easy to gloss over this form and grab the information for our tax returns, but that's a mistake.

The very first thing you should check is your Social Security number. If that's wrong, and you file your taxes, all sorts of problems arise. The IRS and Social Security can't match your tax withholdings to your tax liabilities, and the next thing you know there's a certified letter from the IRS wanting back taxes you have already paid. Yes, you can fix it, but do you want the hassle? Better to check your number.

If you discover an error in your number or anywhere else on the W-2, notify your employer immediately. Even if you aren't planning on filing your tax return as soon as the W-2 arrives, open it up and review it for errors. Your employer can get you a corrected W-2, but it is much easier to do in February than it is in April.

> **CAUTION** **Form Alarm**
>
> Your W-2 also goes to the Social Security Administration, or at least it is supposed to. It is not unheard of for an employer to deduct withholding, Social Security, and Medicare taxes from employees, but never turn the money in to the agencies. This is why it is important to review your annual Social Security Statement (see Chapter 22). The statement details Social Security earnings by year. If you see a blank year, when you were employed, something is wrong and you need to find out why your wages were not reported to the Social Security Administration.

Check the Numbers

After you have verified your Social Security number, names, and address, look over the numbers for errors. Many companies provide year-to-date sums on their paychecks, so you should have a good idea of what your final income should look like. If you work for tips, make sure all that accounting is in order with your employer.

The other fields on the W-2 relate to special income circumstances. If they apply to you, you will know about it before you get the W-2.

The 1099

The 1099 is a catchall form that records income from sources other than your job, including the following:

- Interest income
- Dividend income
- Miscellaneous income

There are others, but these are the most common and cover the typical situations most of us encounter. The common thread for all 1099s is that they represent a reporting to the IRS of income.

A Your Social Security number

B Interest income

C Income tax withheld

☐ CORRECTED (if checked)		
PAYER'S name, street address, city, state, ZIP code, and telephone no.	Payer's RTN (optional)	OMB No. 1545-0112
		20**05** Interest Income
		Form **1099-INT**
PAYER'S Federal identification number	RECIPIENT'S identification number **A**	1 Interest income not included in box 3 **B** $
RECIPIENT'S name	2 Early withdrawal penalty $	3 Interest on U.S. Savings Bonds and Treas. obligations $
Street address (including apt. no.)	4 Federal income tax withheld **C** $	5 Investment expenses $
City, state, and ZIP code	6 Foreign tax paid	7 Foreign country or U.S. possession
Account number (see instructions)	$	

Copy B
For Recipient

This is important tax information and is being furnished to the Internal Revenue Service. If you are required to file a return, a negligence penalty or other sanction may be imposed on you if this income is taxable and the IRS determines that it has not been reported.

Form **1099-INT**   (keep for your records)   Department of the Treasury - Internal Revenue Service

The 1099 INT

The 1099 INT is the form that reports interest income. Your bank may send you one every year if you have an interest-bearing account. You do not fill out this form, so the only action you need to take is a thorough review of the numbers.

The first number is your Social Security number—make sure it is correct. For most bank accounts, interest is recorded in box 1. If you withdraw money from an account that has an early withdrawal penalty, that number shows up in box 2. A premature withdrawal may also trigger a withholding, which the form lists in box 4. If you are subject to *backup withholding*, because you provided an incorrect Social Security number or another infraction, this is where it will appear.

Financial Speak

Backup withholding is used by the IRS to make sure people without a proper Social Security number or taxpayer identification number still pay taxes. A person who fails to report all interest or dividend income in the past may be subject to backup withholding. The paying company must withhold a certain percentage (28% in 2004) and turn it over to the IRS if you are subject to backup withholding.

Other Information

The other information on the form should be self-explanatory if you understand the investment that triggered the 1099. If you're not sure why you paid a foreign tax, you need to consult with the organization that sold you the investment for some clarification.

The IRS gives you an extra four months to file, but if you owe money, it wants that now. You might well ask, "What's the point of an extension if I have to pay?" There can be several reasons. You may have a complicated return and need additional time to gather all the supporting documentation. You might be out of the country or sick near filing time.

If you don't pay all of what you owe, the IRS will likely charge you a late fee, plus interest from the original due date. If the IRS thinks you could have paid, but just didn't, they might look into more severe penalties.

Paying

You can pay several ways. You can have the IRS draft your bank account, or you can pay by credit card, use a money order, or write a check. You can also file the form via your computer or over the phone or the old-fashioned paper way. However you file, it must be by the original due date or you face a penalty.

Estimated Taxes

Paper Clips

If four months isn't long enough for an extension, the IRS will consider a longer extension, but they are going to need a good reason.

If you are self-employed or do freelance work on the side or get a lot of those 1099s I discussed earlier, you probably need to file estimated taxes on a quarterly basis. In all of these situations, no federal income, Social Security, or Medicare tax is withheld from your compensation. Paying taxes on a quarterly basis is a way to avoid a really awful April 15. Besides, the IRS doesn't want to wait that long for your tax contribution.

Figuring Your Taxes

The process for estimating your taxes is complicated because you have to do it in advance. Many self-employed people find this very difficult because work may not always flow that predictably. The instructions give some guidelines for how you figure your taxes. If you pay too little, however, or in some cases too much, you may face a fine.

Form 1040-ES is used to get you started and includes a worksheet to help you figure your estimated taxes for the year. Plan to spend several hours on this project. The worksheet is too involved for this book, but should be completed in the first quarter of the year because your first estimated payment is due April 15. Although you may be sick of taxes, a good time to fill out the worksheet is when you are doing your taxes for the previous year. You can use much of the same information on your tax return to fill out the estimated tax worksheet.

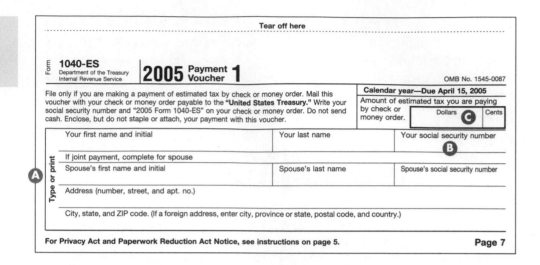

A Identifying information
B Social Security numbers
C How much you're paying

Filling Out the Form

The payment voucher for estimated taxes is simple. Just fill in your identifying information, making sure your Social Security number(s) are correct. After you begin the process, the IRS will send you preprinted vouchers, or you can download from the Internet at www.irs.gov/pub/irs-pdf/f1040es_04.pdf.

If your income changes radically during the year, up or down, you can recalculate your estimated taxes. The IRS wants its taxes, but if your liability drops, don't overpay, because that could get you a penalty, too.

Chapter 26

State Rights

In This Chapter

- State income tax
- Estimated income tax
- Property tax

If you are lucky enough to live in one of the few remaining states that does not have a state income tax, try not to smirk. For the rest of us, state income taxes, for the most part, are the insult added to the injury of federal income taxes. Although they are simple compared to the IRS versions, don't take them too lightly.

Of course, state income taxes may not be the only taxes you pay. There are also state property taxes, plus a bunch of specialty usage and other taxes. This chapter can't deal with taxes in each of the 50 states, so we focus on the two largest taxes in most states: the income tax and property tax.

State Income Tax

The good news (if you can ever use that phrase in connection with income taxes) is that in most cases your state income tax is going to look a lot like your federal income tax. Most of the information comes right off your IRS form 1040.

Your W-2 has a copy to go with your state return, as does any 1099 form. Each state will add some of its own twists that won't be found on the federal form. If you use one of the major tax-preparation software packages, such as Turbo Tax, it will import all of the information from your federal return.

The W-4 Equivalent

Every state that collects income tax should have the equivalent of the IRS W-4 form. This is the form that tells your employer how much to withhold from your paycheck for taxes. The state version accomplishes the same purpose.

A Identifying information including Social Security number

B Total exemptions claimed

C Additional amount withheld

Employee's Wisconsin Withholding Exemption Certificate/New Hire Reporting		WT-4

Employee's Section

Employee's Name (last, first, middle initial)		Social Security Number		Date of Birth
Employee's address (number and street)	City		State	Zip Code
☐ Single ☐ Married ☐ Married, but withhold at higher Single rate. **Note:** *If married, but legally separated, check the Single box.*				Date of Hire

FIGURE YOUR TOTAL WITHHOLDING EXEMPTIONS BELOW
Complete Lines 1 through 3 only if your Wisconsin exemptions are different than your federal allowances.

1. (a) Exemption for yourself – enter 1 ....

    (b) Exemption for your spouse – enter 1 ....

    (c) Exemption(s) for dependent(s) – you are entitled to claim an exemption for each dependent ....

    (d) Total – add lines (a) through (c) ....

2. Additional amount per pay period you want deducted (if your employer agrees) ....

3. I claim complete exemption from withholding (see instructions). Enter "Exempt" ....

I CERTIFY that the number of withholding exemptions claimed on this certificate does not exceed the number to which I am entitled. If claiming complete exemption from withholding, I certify that I incurred no liability for Wisconsin income tax for last year and that I anticipate that I will incur no liability for Wisconsin income tax for this year.

Signature_____   Date Signed_____

The Details

This is an example of the Exemption Certificate from Wisconsin. The form may look different in your state. You may be tempted to just fill in the information from the federal W-4, and in some states that may work just fine. However, read the instructions first (always a good idea when dealing with tax forms).

The instructions for the Wisconsin form say you can claim only actual exemptions, whereas the federal W-4 allows you to claim more than actually exist.

Estimated Taxes

If you are required to pay estimated taxes to the IRS, it's a sure bet the state is going to want you to also. States follow the same basic calendar as the IRS in terms of due dates, although there will be some variation, so check the form for details.

2005 WISCONSIN ESTIMATED TAX VOUCHER

FORM **1-ES**

Make your check payable to and mail your voucher to:
Wisconsin Department of Revenue
Post Office Box 2942
Milwaukee, WI 53201-2942

Calendar year due dates:
Apr 15, 2005   Sep 15, 2005
Jun 15, 2005   Jan 17, 2006

Fiscal year filers:
Enter year ending _____ (month and year)

Your last name | Your first name and initial | Your social security number

Spouse's last name | Spouse's first name and initial | Spouse's social security number

Home address (number and street or rural route) | Telephone number

City or post office | State | Zip code

Check the boxes below which apply to you
☐ Trust (Enter FEIN as "your social security number")
☐ Estate (Enter decedent's social security number)
☐ Individual (or Joint)
☐ Extension Payment

AMOUNT OF PAYMENT $ _____
Please do not staple your payment to this voucher

D-101

Ⓐ Identifying information
Ⓑ Quarter of payment
Ⓒ Amount of payment

The Details

This is a sample voucher from Wisconsin. The voucher from your state will look different, but probably not by much. It looks very much like the federal form and is available from the revenue office or as a download.

Each state will have its own worksheet similar to the IRS model to help you calculate your estimated state taxes. The process will differ somewhat from state to state, but they all roughly follow the federal format.

State Property Taxes

You may never actually see a state property tax bill, depending on the state you live in and whether you own property aside from your primary residence. Many homeowners with mortgages only see the tax bill, but never "pay" it directly, because the mortgage company has an escrow account for that. However, if you live in a state where the state assesses the property tax, you need to know how it works.

The Basics

Each state decides whether and how it is going to tax property. It then defines property, which can be a complicated process and can vary from state to state. For example, in some states personal property means everything from the clothes on your back to the ground under your feet. Other states exempt certain items from property tax roles.

After the state defines property, it is assessed for value, usually at the county level. This assessed value is supposed to be close to the market value (or what the property would sell for in a fair trade).

The state uses the assessed value to figure taxes by applying a tax rate to the property. The state calculates the tax rate by taking the total amount of taxes it needs to raise (the levy) and dividing that by the assessed value of all property. The resulting percentage is the rate at which the state taxes all property. This is also the way all local governments and school districts calculate their tax rates.

Fill In the Blank

Because your state estimated taxes will be much less than your federal taxes, you might be tempted to skip them. Don't do it. Most states impose interest and penalty charges, and there's no point in drawing attention to yourself from taxing authorities.

Paper Clips

Many states struggle with balancing their budgets and putting a heavy tax burden on the citizens. Some have put caps on tax increases at the local level in an attempt to control government spending, all with mixed success.

What You Can Do

If you think your property taxes are too high, you can protest the assessment. In most cases, this process occurs at the county level. You will need to provide evidence that supports your claim that the value placed on your property is too high.

Each taxing authority has its own procedures for appealing assessments, so check locally for the steps to follow. Changing the value placed on your property is about the only real relief you have, and you will need to make a strong case with evidence to change the assessment.

Other Taxes

States usually have many other taxes that cover a variety of usages and other circumstances. Most of these apply to businesses. However, be aware of some instances where you may face a tax bill if you live in one state, but spend a great deal of time in another state on business. (If you live on the border of two states, for example.) States have gone after people for income taxes under these circumstances even if they weren't residents of the state.

Chapter 27

Hometown Handout

In This Chapter

- ◆ Property tax bills
- ◆ Assessed value of property
- ◆ Tax rate
- ◆ Local taxes
- ◆ Income tax

From the school district, to the utility board, it seems like every governmental agency in town wants a piece of you. How do you make sense of all those numbers? In this chapter, we look at taxation on the local level—where it really hurts.

Local Taxes

Local taxes in all 50 states are a hodge-podge of procedures and regulations that, fortunately, you don't have to worry about. All you need concern yourself with is the area where you live. It's a good bet that you pay property taxes in one form or another and, depending on where you live, you may even pay a city income tax.

It's a common misconception that renters don't pay taxes. The correct statement is they don't pay property taxes directly. You can bet the landlord builds property taxes into the rent, and when those taxes go up, so will rents (even properties with rent stabilization will eventually have rent increases because of tax hikes). In this chapter, we look at some of the taxes you might pay on a local level. Because we can't cover all 50 states, we deal with the most common forms of taxes.

Property Taxes

Property taxes are the main source of revenue for most taxing authorities at the local level. These taxing authorities have a legal right to apply a rate or a portion of an overall rate to your property, which in many states includes everything you own, including your bank accounts, cars, and personal possessions.

Paper Clips

The other way taxing authorities raise money is through issuing bonds to pay for one-time projects, such as roads or bridges.

You may not be taxed on everything you own, but many states include vehicles along with real estate when figuring your tax bill. This is how they fund some or most of their activities.

How It Works

If you read the previous chapter on state taxes, you know that governments calculate property taxes using an assessed value and a tax rate. Often a local authority such as a county establishes this assessed value, which other taxing authorities use. There is much more to it in the background, but the bottom line is the assessor assigns a value to your property.

The process works differently from state to state in terms of specifics, but following is a sample apportionment statement where the total tax levy of a county is allotted to each taxing district. I have used round numbers simply for ease of illustration.

A Represents total taxes for county

B How taxes are divided

Apportionment Table for 2006

A Total County Levy:		$1,000
B Apportionment:		
County	18%	$180
City	24%	$240
School	45%	$450
Utility	06%	$60
Fire	05%	$50
Garbage	02%	$20
Total	100%	$1,000

The Details

In this sample apportionment table, each taxing district gets a percentage of the total levy or the amount of taxes raised. This shows you where your tax dollars are going. When you get a tax bill for a piece of property, you will see these same taxing authorities listed. In some cases, bills may just give you a total.

A Statement date

B Date taxes due

C Property on tax rolls

D Tax rate you pay

E Total taxes due

A Tax Statement   01/02/06

B Taxes Due	02/15/06
C Assessed Value of Property	$100,000
D Tax Rate:	4%
E Taxes Due:	$4,000

Your Tax Bill

Your property tax bill may be very simple, or very detailed, depending on where you live. It may list all the taxing districts and how much each is getting or just a lump-sum amount.

The taxing district comes up with a bill for you by taking the assessed value of your property and applying a tax rate. Because I can't cover all 50 states, I will simply explain the process, which will be true everywhere, but may be expanded on in some locations.

The taxing authority determines the tax rate by figuring how much it needs to run the agencies and governmental units. The authority then takes the levy and divides it by the total assessed value of all property. For example, if a county needed $1,000 to run its operations and the property in the county was assessed at $25,000, then the tax rate would be 4% ($1,000 / $25,000 = .04).

In most communities, you receive one tax bill for the tax rate times the assessed value of your property for all taxing authorities.

Of course, it's never quite that simple. Many communities, for example, exempt all or part of a senior citizen's property from taxes. If you meet other conditions or if your house has historic value or is in a certain redevelopment district, all of these conditions might gain you breaks on your tax bill.

Fill In the Blank
Most homeowners never directly pay a tax bill because the mortgage company handles that directly out of the escrow account. The reason mortgage companies do this is to make sure the taxes stay current on the property. Taxing authorities can place a lien on the property for back taxes and, if the taxes aren't paid, sell the house to satisfy the tax obligation.

Fighting City Hall

If you think your property taxes are too high, you can appeal the assessed value of your property. Your community will have an appeal board and process in place. However, whining because your taxes are high won't change anything. Come armed with evidence that the authority assessed comparable property at a substantially lower value.

Income Taxes

For those of you who may find this shocking, yes, there are cities that impose an income tax, and they make you pay even if you don't live in the city, but just work there. As of this writing, I don't know of any major tax-preparation software packages that do city taxes. In general, they are not difficult to do after you have done the federal and state forms.

Glossary

This glossary contains definitions for the terms in this book, plus a few more for good luck.

401(k) plan   A 401(k) plan is a qualified defined contribution plan offered by employers. It allows employees to have a certain percentage of their salary deducted and invested in the plan. The deduction is pretax, so employees experience a reduction in current income tax.

403(b) plan   Similar to the 401(k) plan, the 403(b) is the retirement plan for religious, educational, and other nonprofit groups. This plan is a tax-deferred annuity plan because the investments must be annuities.

account aggregation   This online service enables you to view all of your financial accounts, such as banking, brokerage, credit cards, and so forth on one screen. The service requires you to provide passwords and account information for the information you want aggregated.

adjustable-rate mortgages   Mortgages with an interest rate that adjusts on a predetermined schedule are called adjustable-rate mortgages or ARMs. For example, the rate may adjust once every three years. Because the interest rate is not fixed, ARMs typically start at a lower interest rate than fixed-rate mortgages.

amortization schedule   Your lender will provide a computation of the principal and interest payments over the life of a loan in a chart called an amortization schedule. It shows how the interest decreases and the principal portion increases until the principal is paid off.

annual report   An annual report is a required document all publicly traded companies, including mutual funds, have to produce. It presents the financial results for the past fiscal year, and an accredited accounting firm audits the results.

annuitant   The annuitant is the person the life insurance company uses to determine the annuity payments. In most cases, the owner and the annuitant are the same person; however, this doesn't have to be the case.

annuity   An annuity is a periodic payment of equal amounts over a period in time. Annuity also refers to a contract with a life insurance company guaranteeing a certain payout over a period. It may contain a death benefit that would pay a survivor in the case of death.

asset allocation   Asset allocation is the process of distributing your investment assets in a manner that is consistent with your investment goals among different classes of investments.

backup withholding   The IRS uses backup withholding to make sure people without a proper Social Security number or taxpayer identification number still pay taxes. A person who fails to report all interest or dividend income in the past may be subject to backup withholding. The paying company must withhold a certain percentage (28% in 2004) and turn it over to the IRS if you are subject to backup withholding.

balance sheet   A balance sheet is an accounting for a company's assets, liabilities, equity, and net worth at a certain point in time. It is part of the annual report.

bearer bond   A type of bond that is not registered to any individual, but can be cashed by the person in physical possession of the bond. It is virtually as good as cash.

beneficiary   The person (or organization) you name to receive the proceeds of your life insurance policy or annuity is the beneficiary.

bonds   Bonds are debt instruments. They represent an obligation on the part of the issuer to repay the debt. Governments and private corporations may issue bonds.

capital gain   A capital gain is the profit from the sale of an asset. It is realized when you sell a stock or bond for a profit and when a mutual fund does the same. Any asset sold for a profit and held less than one year is subject to ordinary income tax by the owner. This is a short-term capital gain. An asset held for more than one year and sold for a profit is a long-term capital gain.

cash equivalents   Cash equivalents are financial instruments that represent a deposit of cash. They include certificates of deposits, money market accounts, and savings accounts. They are highly liquid.

certificates of deposit   Banks issue certificates of deposit. They have a maturity ranging, for the most part, from six months to five years and pay a fixed interest rate. There can be penalties for withdrawing the money early.

common stock   Common stock is the primary unit of ownership in a corporation. Holders of common stock are owners of the corporation with certain rights, including voting on major issues concerning the corporation. Shareholders, as they are known, have liability limited to the value of the stock they own.

compounding   Compounding is the mathematical means by which interest earned during one period adds to the principal; then in the next period interest is earned on the resulting principal plus interest in the first period. Another way to say this is "interest earning interest."

condominiums   Individually owned units in a larger complex. Each owner has a nonexclusive interest in certain common areas. A board made up of homeowners manages the complex.

convertible bonds   Convertible bonds carry a feature that allows the owner to convert the bond to common stock instead of paying it off with cash.

co-ops   Cooperative housing units where the residents own and manage the complex. They range from low-cost student housing to exclusive high-rise residences.

corporate bonds   Corporations issue bonds to finance a number of different projects, including the acquisition of other companies. Issuing bonds is often cheaper than commercial loans and better than issuing new stock. One or both of the major services rate corporate bonds.

death benefit   The annuity contract pays the death benefit to the beneficiary upon the death of the annuity contract owner. Several optional death benefits may increase the payout.

deductible   Most insurance policies require you to pay the first dollars for services each year up to the plan limit per individual or family. Some expenses don't apply toward the deductible, so check your policy for details. After at least two members of the family have met the individual deductible, no other members need meet the individual deductible.

defined benefit plan   The defined benefit plan states what the ultimate benefit will be in advance. They are typical company pension plans. The years of service determine the benefit and some average the last three years' salary.

defined contribution plan   Defined contribution plans are plans that specify the contribution, but not the benefit. These plans focus on what goes into the plan and who contributes what. How much the plans will pay on retirement depends on the return earned by the plan.

dilution   When the value of your stock drops because more stock is issued, thus dividing the ownership of the company into even smaller pieces, your stake is diluted.

diversification   Diversification is the calculated spreading of your investments over a number of different asset classes. This cushions your portfolio if one part is down, because different asset classes (stocks, bonds, cash, and so on) seldom move in the same direction.

Dividends   Dividends are portions of a company's profits paid to its owners, the stockholders. Not all companies pay dividends. The board of directors makes that decision. Companies that don't pay dividends reinvest the profits back in the company to finance additional growth. Financial professionals refer to these companies as "growth" stocks and companies that pay regular dividends as "income" stocks.

escrow   Lenders establish a special account whereby the lender deposits a portion of your monthly house payment. From this account, the lender pays property taxes and homeowner's insurance premiums.

equity   Ownership or equity is the difference between what your house is worth and what you owe. For example, if you house is worth $150,000 and your mortgage balance is $70,000, then your equity is $80,000.

health maintenance organizations   HMOs are a form of prepaid medical services, at least that's the way they started. They emphasize preventive care, but have been criticized for not approving more expensive treatments in the past. Patients pay a fixed fee for most services but must use doctors and facilities that belong to the HMO.

inflation   Inflation is too much money chasing too few goods. The result is a sharp rise in prices without any extra value added making money worth less. Inflation leads to rising interest rates and a cooling of the economy. If the economy slows down too quickly and too far, it may slip into a recession or even a depression.

market value   The price at which buyers and sellers agree and a sale occurs.

money market accounts   Money market accounts are special savings accounts usually offered by financial institutions that pay a higher interest rate than regular savings, but require a higher minimum balance. They are not the same as money market mutual funds.

mutual funds   Mutual funds represent a pool of individuals who have pooled their money and hired a professional management company to invest their money. Each mutual fund has specific goals and objectives that drive its buy and sell decisions. Mutual funds may invest in stocks, bonds, or both.

net asset value   The net asset value (NAV) is the mutual fund equivalent of a share price. This is the price you pay when you buy into a mutual fund. Unlike stocks, mutual funds have no problem with fractional shares. However much you deposit gets divided by the NAV to arrive at your shares. The mutual fund calculates the NAV by subtracting the liabilities from the holdings of the fund and then dividing by the outstanding shares.

pro forma   A financial statement that reflects an anticipated change of some sort in the business's condition. The results may or may not work out as projected.

prospectus   A legal document that must accompany any application or sales material for a mutual fund or a new issue of stock. It spells out the terms and conditions of the fund, the risks, the fees, and the identities of the principal money managers.

qualified retirement plans   The Internal Revenue Service authorizes qualified retirement plans, and they must adhere to certain rules and regulations. Participants in the plans, often sponsored by an employer, may accumulate money in their accounts on a tax-deferred basis.

redemption   Financial talk for the term used in the mutual fund industry to describe selling shares. Unlike stocks, which are bought and sold on the open market, mutual fund shares are bought from the mutual fund company and sold or (redeemed) back to the company when you want to cash out.

revolving credit   When you have credit that lets you replenish the line by paying off outstanding balances. A credit card is an example of revolving credit. You have a limit, and your available credit is determined by how much you borrow and pay back.

tax deferred   Tax deferred refers to investment vehicles that allow principal and interest to grow without paying taxes on the earnings until sometime in the future. Qualified retirement accounts allow tax-deferred growth. Annuities, whether qualified or not, also allow tax-deferred growth.

Additional Resources

You can generally find help online for many of the major financial documents mentioned in this book by going to the website of the provider. Some will be better than others.

General Resources

These websites offer resources and information on a variety of topics that cut across more than one financial document.

- ◆ The IRS (www.irs.gov/)

  Maybe the most helpful part of the IRS, the website has a strong search function if you are looking for particular information. The search function divides into a forms area, so you can search just for forms without getting bogged down in results from other areas of the site.

- ◆ Energy Information Administration (www.eia.doe.gov/)

  This government site is full of helpful information and a little propaganda about the state of energy in our economy.

- ◆ Social Security Online (www.ssa.gov/)

  The Social Security site covers many topics, but you can usually find what you're looking for without too much trouble.

- ◆ State websites (www.loc.gov/rr/news/stategov/stategov.html)

  This website is part of the Library of Congress, and it features links to all the websites of all 50 states. Some commercial sites do the same thing, but I can't verify the safety of each one of them.

- ◆ The Securities and Exchange Commission (www.sec.gov/edgar.shtml)

  This link takes you to the search function within the SEC site. If you want to look up information on a company, this is the place to go. The documents are all text and not easy to read, but packed with information.

- ◆ The National Association of Securities Dealers (www.nasd.com/)

  This industry watchdog is the place to go for information on investments and if you have a problem with your broker or mutual fund.

- ◆ The Federal Deposit Insurance Corp. (www.fdic.gov/)

    This is the agency that insures bank deposits up to $100,000 per account from bank default. The site has consumer information on what the agency does and how to get help.

- ◆ Sallie Mae (www.salliemae.com/)

    This group is the largest college loan provider in the nation. Check out their website for information on their programs, but remember, they aren't the only ones who make student loans.

More-Specific Resources

These websites offer information that is more specific to a particular type of financial product or service.

Investment Help

These websites and publications offer education and information on investing and personal finance topics.

- ◆ MorningStar (www.morningstar.com)

    This site has comprehensive information on stocks, but excels on mutual funds reporting.

- ◆ CNN Money (www.money.cnn.com/)

    Go to this site for breaking news on the markets and stock quotes.

- ◆ Stocks at About.com (www.stocks.about.com)

    This site offers tremendous education and information resources on investing in individual stocks.

- ◆ The *Wall Street Journal* (available at newsstands and by subscription)

    This is a pricey publication, but it is packed with information. If you are serious about business and investing, it is considered must reading.

- ◆ The *Wall Street Journal* Online (www.wsj.com)

    The online version of the *Wall Street Journal* offers much of the same information and interactive graphics as the printed paper. You get a discount if you are a subscriber to the print edition.

Index